THE ROYAL LATIN SCHOOL, BUCKINGHAM

Paul K. Poornan

First published 2001

ISBN 0-9539926-0-8

PUBLISHED BY:

Dusty Old Books Ltd, 7 Pear Tree Farm, Marsh Gibbon OX27 0GB

www.dustyoldbooks.com *E-mail: paul@dustyoldbooks.com*

Tel: 01869 278160 *Fax: 01869 278163*

DESIGN BY:

HGM Publications, HGM House, Nether End, Baslow, Bakewell DE45 1SR

Tel: 01246 584002 *Fax: 01246 584006*

www.hgmpubs.com *E-mail: mail@hgmpubs.com*

DEDICATION

The success of this school has depended on and continues to depend on the pupils, parents, teachers, support staff, headteachers, governors, benefactors, County Departments, and even Kings and Queens. Yet there are so many people who have given their support, even their careers and lives, from ages past to recent times, some of whom we may never discover, whose names we may never know. To all the people of the Royal Latin School; past, present, and future; known and unknown, this book is dedicated to you.

It is a shame that over the centuries Buckingham seems to have forgotten its oldest institution, and hopefully this may now be rectified. I suspect that much of its history still lies in cupboards, attics and cellars in Buckingham; please show anything you may discover to the archivist at the school. This book has been written with the children, parents, staff and historians in mind; that is to say, I have tried to make it both informative and educational. The research hours involved in compiling this book do not bear thinking about, and I have many librarians, archivists, rectors, vicars, past pupils and local historians to thank, especially those at Buckingham, Aylesbury, Lincoln, Highclere, Gloucester, Oxford, London, Thornborough and Hereford. I would also like to thank the Mercers and acknowledge the permission to reproduce documents from the Public Records Office, the British Library and the Society of Antiquaries, London.

On a personal note, I would to thank my wife, Cecilia Galloway, the current, and first female head of the Royal Latin School in seven centuries.

AUTHOR'S NOTE

This is the biggest "jig-saw" I have ever attempted. The pieces were scattered through seven centuries, in dusty old books, in dry vellum sheets stitched together in rolls, in fragments of writing dating almost from the Magna Carta, and in the most unexpected stockrooms of lost information. Even the pieces themselves were fragmented. I have tried to record where I obtained information, so that if others wish, they may try to finish parts of the puzzle. If I have quoted verbatim from sources, I apologise; I have tried not to, but often these were the only sources available and when one has been mining for months without success and then uncovers a raw gold nugget of data, one is reluctant to reforge it. Higher definition photographs of the illustrations in this book may be found at www.dustyoldbooks.com.

This jig-saw will never, in my opinion, be completed. The pieces may not be an exact fit, there are holes and patches of assumption, and long-forgotten gems may appear from family treasures or may be archaeologically sieved from national or private archives which may force a future reconstruction of the puzzle. Often, in the search for pieces, sources have been contradictory; and where this has occurred, I have tried to ascertain and present the truth. However, I hope that enough pieces survive for you to enjoy the beauty of the image that still remains. Whilst sorting this puzzle, I have studied Medieval Latin of the 13th to 15th centuries to decipher its coded shorthand, and learned how to unravel the scrawl of 16th century Secretary hand. I have asked others to check my work, but the mistakes that survive are all of my own making.

As we approach the 21st century, History is becoming ever more accessible and tactile: the Internet is just reaching the domestic consumer; libraries are busy scanning documents and going on-line; genealogists are communicating by Newsgroups; a growing army of interested people are publishing their private research on web-sites. As time progresses, more information will come to light, more discoveries made. One could spend a lifetime or more discovering the history of the Royal Latin School, but at some time, one has to draw a line. Today is that day.

CONTENTS

INTRODUCTION

The Chapel of St John the Baptist and St Thomas of Acon is the oldest building in Buckingham. From the outside it looks ordinary, except for its Norman doorway, but on the inside the piscina is ancient, and a minstrel gallery has been constructed from 17th century pew ends. These are the only tangible historical features of a building that first started life as a 12th century medieval hospital. Out of the hospital grew a chantry chapel which housed a school until the 20th century, when the school outgrew its physical confines.

The School has had a series of founders, benefactors & supporters over the centuries, however the original foundation developed from an endowment given by the Archdeacon of Buckingham in 1268, to provide a chantry priest to say masses for his soul. The chantry priests were supplied by an Order of holy knights who served in the Crusades. The school survived the Reformation in the 16th century by using a priest's Reformation pension of £10-8s-0½d to re-endow the school. This annual sum was dutifully paid by the government for 336 years.

There have been endless discussions about the identities of the founders of the school, and in my opinion Matthew Stratton, Robert the hermit, the Knights of St Thomas of Acon, John Ruding, John Barton senior and junior, Isabel Barton, Richard Fowler, John Fortescue, William Abbott, Alexander Denton and Thomas Cockram deserve special recognition (see *Biography*). Overall, the school has a history of some 730 years and encompasses three schools and three Archbishops of Canterbury; and in brief, this is its story.

Alle May God Amende

A MEDIEVAL BUCKINGHAM HOSPITAL

In medieval times (see *Glossary*), the King owned all the land and could offer its use to a tenant-in-chief, if in return the tenant-in-chief provided services such as knights for military service. This was called the tenure of knight service and the tenant had to 'furnish without grievance, one soldier, well armed and fully equipped' (Giles, 1852, i, p484) for 40 days each year. If the tenant-in-chief wanted to alienate (see *Glossary*) this land to a religious house, he had to apply for a Crown licence, and then the Crown usually initiated an enquiry, an 'inquisition ad quod damnum', literally an 'inquisition to what damage'. Security was particularly important to King Edward Ist (Fowler, p20, 1929), and he ensured that a proposed land transfer would not mean a reduction in the supply of knights or in income to the Crown.

The Hospital of St Thomas of Acon in London was providing knights to the Crown, in return for the use of property in Buckingham. In order to pay off its debts to the Hospital of St John of Jerusalem in London, the Master applied for a Crown licence of mortmain to alienate the Buckingham property. On the 10th February 1289/90, King Edward I issued a writ to the Sheriff of Buckingham for an 'Inquisition ad quod damnum' (C143/14/5). The Sheriff of Buckingham, Ralph de St Lucius, replied with the backing of 11 expert witnesses, giving the full history and background to the property of St Thomas of Acon in Buckingham. They stated that the property was originally 'built by William Frethet in the time of John de Braose (see *Biography*) senior, the Lord of Buckingham' and given to the Order of St John of Jerusalem to provide hospitality for the poor, infirm and sick (see Appendix I)[1].

It must be remembered that this inquest was taking place in 1289/90, and that the witnesses were attempting to recall events of at least eighty years before. In 1289/90, their Lord was William Braose, his father was William (1220-c1284), his father was John de Braose (1198-1232) and his father was William de Braose junior (not John senior) who died in 1210. William de Braose junior gained the Manor of Buckingham as dowry when he married Matilda, daughter of Richard de Clare in the late 12th century. So

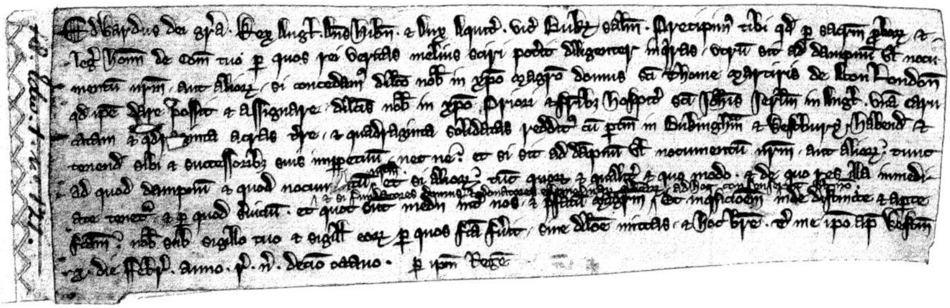

Writ from King Edward I to the Sheriff of Buckingham

Reply from the Sheriff of Buckingham giving the full history of the hospital (C143/14 No 5)

---

[1] The Knights Hospitallers of the military Order of St John of Jerusalem were monks who had taken vows of poverty, chastity and obedience and chose St John the Baptist as their patron Saint. The Order dates from the time of the first Holy Crusade in 1099, when the order ran a hospital in Jerusalem for ill and tired pilgrims. The Hospital was said to have been able to cater for 2000 patients. In the 12th and 13th centuries, the Knights of St John of Jerusalem set up many St John the Baptist hospitals in English towns and at sites of pilgrimage, which catered for the well-being of the soul and the provision of 'hospitality' ie. shelter, comfort and food, rather than medical aid. In the Buckingham locality, there were hospitals in Brackley, Oxford and Northampton.

it seems likely that the hospital was built at some time prior to 1210, probably late 12th century.

The hospital provided hospitality for many years, and then when it fell into disuse, Roger de Wymbervill, steward of the Lord of Buckingham, asked his Lord's permission to take possession of it and sold it to Peter Miller. When Peter Miller died in 1249 (Elvey, Vol ii, 1975, p116) it was inherited by his brother John who sold it to Ernald le Ferur. Ernald sold the building and its 10 acres of land, to Matthew [Stratton], Archdeacon (see *Glossary*) of Buckingham'. Matthew carried out his duty as an archdeacon and restored the hospital, and then gave it to the Master of St Thomas of Acon in London (prior to his death in 1268). The revived hospital was endowed by:

- Matthew Stratton (see *Biography*) who gave 12 acres of land in Bourton[2]
- The Master of St Thomas of Acon who gave 12 acres of land
- William the son of Reginald who gave two acres and three roods of meadow in Morton near Buckingham, from his wife's inheritance
- Various free tenants in Buckingham, Bourton and Moreton gave five cottages and twenty-two and a half acres of land
- James de [unknown, possibly St Lys] who enfeoffed a chaplain called Brother Robert de Wappenham, a hermit, of forty acres of land in Westbury park for celebrating mass for ever, for the souls of his ancestors. Robert subsequently enfeoffed the Master of St Thomas of Acon.

Technically the 'Hospital of St John the Baptist' became the 'Hospital of

---

[2] Matthew Stratton was involved in many land deals, and in 1320 it was confirmed that prior to his death in 1268, he had conveyed all the land in Morton that he had received from five different parties, including 3 acres formerly owned by Arnold Le Ferur, and a messuage and lands from John and Robert de Moreton, and their father William son of Reginald, to the abbot and canons of Osney (Cal.Chart. Rolls, 1300-1326). It would thus appear that William de Moreton gave land to Matthew Stratton to endow the Hospital of St John the Baptist at Buckingham; and in the year of his death (in 1268) Stratton granted that land to the Abbot of Osney (VCH, Bucks, iv, p201). As Matthew Stratton specified that he should be buried at Osney in his will, it is speculation whether this land deal was connected to his subsequent burial.

St John the Baptist and St Thomas of Acon' prior to 1268, however, the title of the Hospital of St John the Baptist 'stuck' for centuries[3]. As the House of St Thomas of Acon fell on hard times, it presumably drained the chantry (see *Glossary*) chapel and hospital of its resources over the next twenty one years, until it once again fell into disuse. By 1289/90 the Master of St Thomas of Acon had removed everything, leaving behind one carucate (see *Glossary*), forty acres and forty shillings worth of rents with appurtenances (see *Glossary*) in Buckingham and Westbury. So the Master of St Thomas of Acon applied for a licence to sell the property and its revenues to the Order of St John of Jerusalem, in order to pay off a debt to them (Forey, 1977, p493). Thus the history of the Hospital from the late 12th century to the late 13th century is remarkably documented. However, this Inquisition document dated 1289/90 also provides us with two very important links with the Reformation, 250 years later, in 1538.

Firstly, the document states that prior to 1289/90, the hermit Brother Robert de Wappenham, enfeoffed (see *Glossary*) 40 acres of Westbury to the Master of St Thomas of Acon, to celebrate mass for the souls of his master's ancestors. In 1538, the Order of St Thomas of Acon surrendered Hermytt's Grove in Westbury. Thus an unknown family had indirectly provided land which remained with the Buckingham Hospital to support the chantry priest (see *Glossary*) for the next 250 years.

Secondly, Matthew Stratton gave the Hospital of St John the Baptist to the Hospital of St Thomas of Acon prior to his death in 1268. At the Reformation Thomas Hawkyns confirmed that he belonged to the Order of St Thomas of Acon in London, and he was the chantry priest of 'Matthew

---

3. The Hospital of St John the Baptist is mentioned in the Hundred Rolls for the year 1279, where it is stated that the master held 1 acre of land in Morton for which he paid 1d (1 *denarius*) yearly (Hundred Rolls, ii, p341). The Hundred Rolls are known not to be comprehensive, though it does seem to reflect reduced land holdings in Moreton due to Matthew Stratton's dealings. The Hundred Rolls were the first attempt at operating local government by Edward I in order to establish the rights to hold courts, markets etc. (Hey, 1997).

Stratton's chantry' in the chapel of St John the Baptist in Buckingham. Thus Matthew Stratton was the original chantry founder for whom a succession of St Thomas of Acon priests prayed for the next 270 years.

As 'the great majority of the schoolmasters in the Middle Ages were chantry priests' (Rashdall, 1951, Vol 3, p350) it is probable that the chantry priest, to augment his living, started a chantry school sometime between 1290 (when there was no mention of a school) and 1423 (when a Buckingham schoolmaster is known to have existed). Thus the first Buckingham schoolmasters were provided by an Order of fighting monks from the Hospital of St Thomas of Acon, funded by various legacies including those of Stratton, possibly St Lys, and the Masters of St Thomas of Acon.

THE ORDER OF ST THOMAS OF ACON

In the late 12th century, the Hospital of St Thomas of Acon was founded for twelve brethren in London, by Thomas Fitz Theobald de Helles whose wife Agnes was the sister of the murdered Thomas à Becket, Archbishop of Canterbury (VCH, London, i, 1974, p491). Their London site was formerly owned by Gilbert à Becket, the father of St Thomas, who was a mercer (see *Biography*) and had a shop near the Cheapside entrance of the present Mercers Hall (Watney, p7-9, 1892).[4]

In 1236, Pope Gregory IX (1227-1241) gave permission for the Order of St Thomas of Acon to change their 'modus operandi' to that of a military order, so that

The seal of St Thomas of Acon

---

4. St Thomas of Acon was also known as St Thomas of Acres, St Thomas à Becket and St Thomas the Martyr. Thomas à Becket was Archbishop of Canterbury when he was murdered by four knights of Henry II in 1170. The Order is often referred to as a College or Hospital. As most hospitals were dependent on a large number of small donations, very few foundation records survive; and thus many hospitals appeared and disappeared without leaving any documentary evidence (Salter, 1917, pv). There are a number of theories about the foundation of the Order (Watney, p1-2, 1892). Matthew Paris the historian (died 1259) wrote that the Order was founded in 1190 when Richard I (1189-1199) was on the Third Crusade (1189-92) to the Holy Land and was miraculously saved from shipwreck by the personal intervention of St Thomas à Becket. When the Crusaders captured Acre in 1191, they founded a hospital there in his name (Watney, 1892, pp14-16, p45). Thus the Order of St Thomas informed Pope Gregory IX (1227-1241) that they had been established by King Richard I, who had died before endowing the foundation to the extent intended (Forey, 1977, p486). It would appear that the main purpose of the Order was to take care of poor and wounded Crusaders and to bury those that died.

they would be both a military and charitable order, and as such should find it easier to raise funds. This strategy was successful, and with the backing of both the pope and king, the Order was able to 'tap' donations from a number of sources, not least King Henry III himself, who gave the Order a gift of 200 marks in 1239 (Forey, 1977). It was not unusual for military orders which undertook charitable work to be granted existing hospitals, and Matthew Stratton, archdeacon of Buckingham, gave St John's hospital at Buckingham to the Order of St Thomas of Acre, probably in return for the establishment of a chantry to say masses for his soul[5, 6].

The maintenance costs of numerous chantries and chantry priests were high, and in 1291 it was assessed that the income of the Order was only £50. Considering the burden of supporting their Crusade outposts in the Holy land, it is not surprising that the Order 'ran down' their Buckingham hospital prior to 1289/90. Their lack of resources led to debts, and the debt of 164 marks that they owed to the Hospital of St John forced them to liquidate some of their assets and may explain why in February 1289/90 they sought 'permission from the King to alienate (see *Glossary*) land at Buckingham to the Hospitallers' (Forey, 1977, p493). It is doubtful if the licence was implemented, because:

a) In 1445 at the Institution of the Vicarage of Buckingham, the Master of

---

5. It is of note that hospitals which existed at Doncaster (St James), Beckhamstead (St John), Kilkenny (St John) and Carrick-on-Suir (St John), were also given to St Thomas of Acon by other parties for similar reasons (Forey, 1977, p489-490).

6. The Hospital and College of St Thomas of Acon was relatively well-known in medieval Buckinghamshire: in 1307 the rectors and brethren of the College of Ashridge (now in Hertfordshire) tried to take control of the Order (Watney, p27-29, 1892); from c1278 to 1538 the Order owned land in Westbury (Hermits Grove) and in Hulcott from 1452 to 1535 (VCH, Bucks, ii, p342). In his will dated 1478, Sir Ralph Verney, knight, mercer and alderman of London, requested the 'Master of the house of St Thomas of Acres to sing placebo, dirige and mass of requiem by note, for him in their own church' (Watney, 1892, p48).

the Hospital of St Thomas of Acon is cited as owner of property in Buckingham;

b) In 1545/6, Thomas Hawkins, formerly clerk of the late College of St Thomas of Acon, London was incumbent (see *Glossary*) at the Chantry of Matthew Stratton;

c) St Thomas of Acon still owned 'Hermytt Grove by the towne of Buckingham' in 1538 (Watney, 1892, p124).

Thus there is little doubt that the Order of St Thomas of Acon had a continued presence at the chapel in Buckingham, for some 270 years from c1268 (when Stratton died) to 1538 (when the Hospital of St Thomas of Acon, London, surrendered to King Henry VIII (E322/139 & C54/411)).

The fall of Acre in The Holy Land in 1291 was the pivotal moment for the Order of St Thomas of Acon; they abandoned their outpost in Acre and evacuated to Cyprus and elsewhere. They lost their 'mission' of 'defending the Holy Land against the enemies of the Christian faith and blasphemers'; lost their reason for fund-raising; their fighting knights had no cause to fight; and their resources and income were drying up quickly. The Order tried to merge with the wealthy Knights Templars (see *Biography*), but failed, as had their previous attempts. In 1379, the Mastership of the order moved back to London from Nicosia (Forey, 1977, p496-499). Once in London, the Order established strong links with the Mercers Company.

The Order recognised the need for education, and were able to influence the Mercers, the 'power brokers' in London. In 1447, John Neell, the Master of the Hospital of St Thomas of Acon, and three other rectors (see *Glossary*) appealed to Parliament for more schools in their five London parishes. They stated that the numbers of Grammar schools had recently declined, and 'for where there is great number of learners and few teachers, and all the learners be compelled to go to the same few teachers, and to none other, the masters wax rich in money and the learners poor in cunning, as experience openly sheweth, against all virtue and order of the public weal' (Watney, 1906, pp14). The brothers of St

Thomas of Acon in London were few, but very influential.[7] Within a few years six Grammar schools were set up in London. The school of St Thomas of Acon in London survived until its dissolution in 1538, when it was re-established in 1542 as a Free Grammar school, the Mercers School, for 25 pupils (Watney, 1896, p3-9).

7. The Order numbered twelve monks in 1248, nine in 1436, twelve in 1444, and six in 1534 (Ditchfield, 1904, pp17-22, Knowles & Hadcock, 1971).

JOHN BARTON (SENIOR)

A brass memorial to John Barton's father, William Barton, in Thornborough church

In the 14th century William Barton, Coroner of Buckinghamshire (see *Biography*) had two sons, both of whom were called John Barton. John Barton (senior) (see *Biography*) was a very successful lawyer and Recorder (see *Glossary*) of London. John Barton (junior) was also a lawyer. The Bartons became wealthy and well connected, and their property deals involved such notables as: Alan Ayete, John Smith the Bailiff (see *Glossary*) and William Purefreye (Willis, 1755, p384). Although their business took them all over England and involved some overseas travel, they retained their homes in Buckingham and Thornton. They both had close links with the Mercers, the Hospital of St Thomas of Acon and Henry Chichele, the Archbishop of Canterbury (see *Biography*).

In 1422, John Barton (senior), gave 200 marks to the master and brethren of the hospital of St Thomas of Acon for their relief, an annual rent of 7 marks from some of his London property, in return for which they had to provide a permanent chantry priest in London to say prayers for his soul and the souls of his parents (Roskell, 1992). Two hundred marks was a considerable fortune, amounting to about £133. Nine years later in 1431, he paid St Thomas of Acon about £16 for a chantry priest to say 4000 masses after his burial in Romwald's aisle in Buckingham church. If Roskell (1992) is correct, these sums are puzzling, and it seems likely that the 200 marks involved more than a chantry priest. Perhaps John Barton (senior) was impressed that the Hospital of St Thomas of Acon was able to provide chantry priests for Stratton for 163 years (1268 to 1431), and/or perhaps familiar with the aims and purpose of the Mercers company, asked their church to provide him with his own exclusive chantry priests. This meant that the Hospital of St Thomas of Acon, London had two priests on 'permanent assignment' in Buckingham, one at Barton's chantry (see *Biography*) in the parish church and one at Matthew Stratton's chantry. Thus it is possible that some of their responsibilities were shared. It is interesting to note that Matthew Stratton's chantry existed for 270 years (1268-1538), and John Barton's for 107 years (1431-1538).

In Michaelmas 1423, John Barton (senior) of Buckingham received a quarterly rental of 40d from the schoolmaster (de magistro scolarum) for his lands in Buckingham, payable at each of the four terms of the year, equivalent to 13s 4d (one mark) (see *Glossary*) a year (BM Lansd.572). Leach (see *Biography*) points out that this was a huge rent in 1423 when the annual salary of a grammar school teacher at this time was about £2 to £3 (Leach, 1969, p226 & p243). How could a schoolmaster afford to pay such a high proportion of his estimated salary in rent ? and what was being rented ? Was the priest involved in farming? letting property ? Or was there some sort of a deal with St Thomas of Acon ? This is the earliest documented evidence for a school in Buckingham, and thus some authorities have stated that the Royal Latin school is the oldest known in Buckinghamshire (VCH, Bucks, ii, p145 & Elliott, 1975, p163). There is unfortunately, no absolute proof that this school is the Royal Latin School. There is however, overwhelming circumstantial evidence:

- John Barton (senior) was collecting the rent from a schoolmaster in Buckingham in 1423;
- Most schoolmasters at this time were chantry priests;
- From c1268 to 1538 Matthew Stratton's chantry was supplied by priests from the Hospital of St Thomas of Acon;
- John Barton (senior) trusted and paid significant sums to the Order of St Thomas of Acon for them to set up two chantry chapels;

- The Bartons were familiar with chantry chapels, eg in 1396 they acted for the subprior of Luffield Priory, in a dispute about chantry elections (Elvey, 1975, xxxii);
- John Barton (senior) was familiar with the founding of Chichele's Higham Ferrers college (see *Biography*);
- John Barton was closely connected with the Mercers, who needed to educate their sons;
- The Order of St Thomas of Acon were very supportive of schools;
- The Free-school or St John's Latin school was housed in Matthew Stratton's chantry (see later);

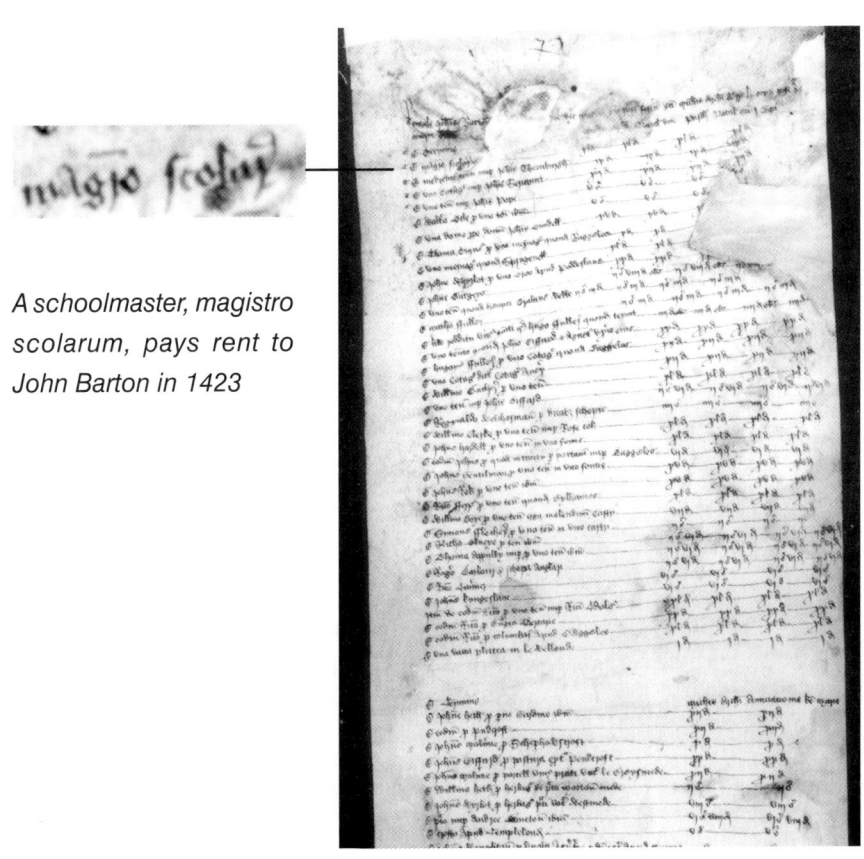

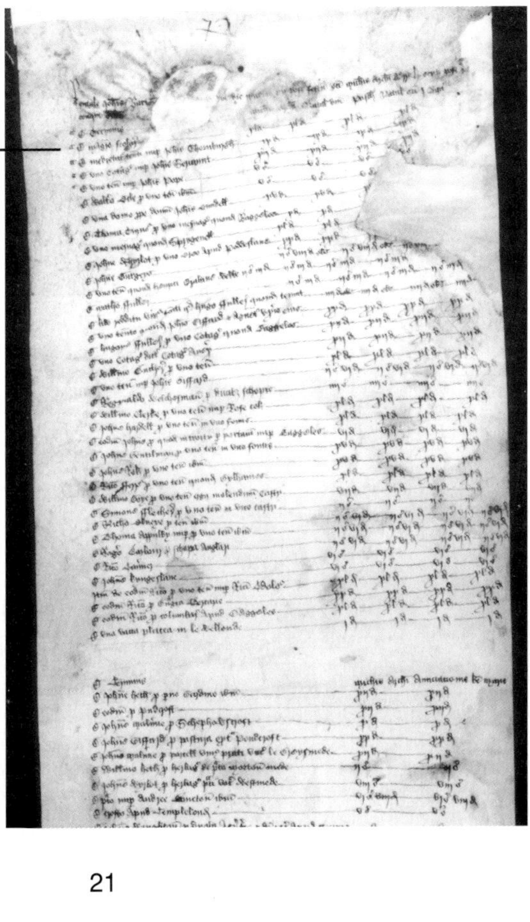

A schoolmaster, magistro scolarum, pays rent to John Barton in 1423

JOHN BARTON (JUNIOR)

John Barton (junior) (see *Biography*) was also a successful lawyer, and although he remained close to his brother it seems he took more career risks than his elder brother.

In 1418, Sir John Chastillon (see *Biography*) transferred the manor of Thornton, and its church containing the Chastillon chantry, to John Barton (junior). The Chastillon chantry was originally founded in 1356 by licence from the Bishop (see *Glossary*) of Lincoln to John le Chastillon, and included two messuages (see *Glossary*) and 100 acres of land in Thornton (VCH, Bucks, iv, p244-248). When John Barton (junior) died in 1434, his will directed that he be buried in Thornton Church, and that a chantry priest be provided there to say mass for him and to look after six poor children - effectively setting up a chantry school. Perhaps it was a combination of his elder brother's example of a chantry fund for six poor people of Buckingham to pray for his soul (Barton Hospital), and Henry Chichele's example of refounding a chantry school (Higham Ferrers); that gave John Barton (junior), the idea of refounding the Chastillon chantry as a school for six poor boys (Willis, 1755, p296).

But his wishes were delayed as his widow Isabel became embroiled in litigation, fighting against Chastillon descendants for possession of her husband's manors (Long Crendon, Stone, Foscott and Moreton). Between

Alabaster effigy of John Barton (junior) at Thornton church

Alabaster effigy of Isabel Barton at Thornton church

1440 and 1442 she managed to grant some of these manors to All Souls College in order to found the first Barton chantry at Thornton (see *Biography*) whose priest was to say masses for herself and the late John Barton (Roskell, 1992). Presumably, Isabel believed that the welfare of their souls could be entrusted to All Souls College, which her husbands friend, Henry Chichele the Archbishop of Canterbury had founded just three years earlier in 1438. In return for the manors, All Souls paid Isabel 200 marks and supplied two chantry priests at All Souls and one at Thornton. The manors were conveyed to the king by the trustees of the Bartons marriage settlement; the king conveyed them to the first warden of All Souls, and thus All Souls was entitled to call itself a Royal foundation (Leach 1896, p49-52). Indirectly, John and Isabel Barton endowed All Souls.

Further litigation was initiated by William Fowler (see *Biography*), the nephew and subsequent heir of John Barton (junior). Isabel was unable to refound the Chastillon chantry, as it seems these lands (at Thornton) were left in trust to her, as well as William Fowler and others (Willis, 1755, p296), and William refused to honour the terms of John Barton's will. Then William died in 1452, followed by Isabel (now married to Sir Robert Shottesbrook) in 1457. It was left to William's son and heir, Richard Fowler, Chancellor of the Duchy of Lancaster, to put right all the wrongs. But now the situation was even more complicated, because, the cofeoffes had sold the manor of Thornton and in 1463 it was held by Robert Ingleton, Chancellor of the Exchequer (see *Glossary*) to Edward

IV, and JP for Buckinghamshire (VCH, Bucks, ii, p245). However it seems that Richard Fowler had prepared well, because on 8th July 1468 Edward IV granted a licence at the request of:

> *'Thomas Littilton, one of the justices of the Common Bench, Thomas Conyers, John Watkyns, William Foweler, were lately enfeoffed together with Robert Conyers, knight and Thomas More, deceased, of certain lands in the county of Buckingham to the use of Dame Isabel Shottesbrook, late the wife of John Barton the younger, late Lord of Thornton, co. Buckingham that they might found a chantry in the parish church of Thornton; the king at their request hereby grants licence to Robert Ingilton, their assign, now lord of the manor of Thornton, or his heirs or assigns to found a perpetual chantry of one chaplain to celebrate divine service daily in the said church for the good estate of the king, his consort Elizabeth, queen of England, George, archbishop of York, and the said Thomas, Thomas, John, William and Robert Ingilton, and for their souls after death and the souls of the said John Barton and Isabel and their relatives, friends and benefactors and Dame Isabel Blaket, Robert Shotesbrook, knight, and John Barton the elder, to be called the chantry of St Mary the Virgin in the said church, and to present a suitable chaplain at each voidance, and for the chaplain to acquire from the said Robert or others, lands and other possessions, not held in chief, to the value of 20l yearly, in mortmain (see* Glossary*), for the sustenance of himself and six poor feeble persons of either sex and the relief of six poor boys by the grant to them of a gown apiece yearly, according to the ordinance of Robert Ingilton in fulfilment of the intention of the said Dame Isabel.*
>
> *By p.s. and for 50l paid in the hanaper* (see *Glossary*).' (Cal.Pat. 1468, p112).

Richard Fowler finally put to rest all the outstanding issues in his will of 1477, where he honoured Bartons will and Isabel's wishes by bequeathing a number of churches including:

> *'Thorneton, Thornebough and Padbury 40s in money in satisfacc[i]on and discharge of my faders soule of such money as was youen and biquethen unto them by Dame Isabel Shotesbroke aforenamed which shulde have been paied by my saide fader and others his cofeoffees' (32 Wattys, 1477).*

Thus there were two Barton (junior) chantries in the same church at Thornton. The first one was set up c1440 by Isabel Barton herself and All Souls College, Oxford. The second Barton chantry, dated 1468, was a refoundation of the Chastillon chantry, whilst Ingleton was Lord of the manor, and the chantry priest was appointed by the lord of the manor. This latter chantry was financially more valuable (see Reformation) as it included the lands and mansion house given by Chastillon and the chantry school (E301/4 No 10). The fact that there were two chantry priests of whom one was also a teacher from 1468 is clear, however, it is not now possible to positively identify the names of the Thornton school teachers from the two positions until c1520.

Thus history has confusingly credited what became known as Barton's chantry to Chastillon, Barton and Ingleton. But the founder of Thornton school, was John Barton (junior); but only because of the persistence of his widow Isabel, and the

A brass memorial of Robert Ingleton in Thornton church

duty of his great nephew Richard Fowler, and the permission of Robert Ingilton.

The importance of the Thornton Chantry school is that it was founded by John Barton (junior), and that it later merged with the Matthew Stratton Chantry school in Buckingham which has been linked to John Barton (senior).

RUDING AND THE CHAPEL OF ST JOHN THE BAPTIST

John Ruding (see *Biography*) like many clerics of his time, had a varied career. It would seem that John Ruding became Archdeacon of Bedfordshire in 1460 and Prebendary (see *Glossary*) of Biggleswade prior to 1467, Archdeacon of Northamptonshire in 1468 (Willis, 1730), and Archdeacon of Lincoln and Prebendary of Sutton-cum-Buckingham in 1471 (Willis, 1755, p57).

The duties of an archdeacon were to ensure that the 'fabric' of church buildings were kept in good order, that priests were kept on the 'straight and narrow' and that poor behaviour was suitably punished. Ruding, as archdeacon, followed in the steps of Matthew Stratton and carried out extensive restoration at the parish church of St Peter and St Paul and at the Chapel of St Thomas of Acon in Buckingham. Ruding's work must have been sorely needed, if no refurbishment had occurred since Stratton's time in 1244 (Papal Letters, x).

Ruding's restoration and redecoration of the parish church and chantry chapel took place between 1471-1481, and must have been thorough, extensive, and enduring, as they lasted well into the 17th century. The designs in both buildings appear to have been identical: scallops, crescents, the head of St John the Baptist on a charger supported by angels, and Ruding's motto 'All may God Amende'. The chantry chapel decorations were sufficiently durable and visible to give offence, and were destroyed in the new religious atmosphere of 1688. Thomas Ford, a former schoolboy at the Royal Latin School drew a sketch in 1733, (in a letter to the famous Buckinghamshire historian, Browne Willis) describing his schoolboy memories of Ruding's decorations of the interior of St John's Chapel:

> *'Over the altar, upon the boards or ceiling, was a painting of holy lamb bleeding, and on each side two angels or monks*

with cups to catch the Blood, under that St John the Baptist's Head in a charger, and Ruding's motto: 'All may God amende'. The rest was al covered with figures of stars, crescents and escalyn. As also the back of the masters seat, and the same was painted on some panes of the glass window. As also in the chancel of Buckingham Church founded by the same Rudyng' (Ford, 1733).

As testimony to the durability of the interior decorations in the Parish Church, a Royalist soldier in the Civil War in 1644 described:

'All may God Amend, is painted on the wall. All the windows are done with crescents and escallops' (Long, 1859, p20).

As the original church of St Peter & St Pauls collapsed in 1776, and as the decorations in the chantry chapel of St Thomas of Acon and St John the Baptist were destroyed in 1688, it was thought that Ruding's image of the 'Head of John the Baptist' was lost. However, before Ruding came to Buckingham, he was based in Biggleswade, and in the chancel

The head of John the Baptist at Biggleswade.

Reproduced with the kind permission of the Society of Antiquaries (Griffin, 1936).

A current photograph of the remaining brass showing scallop shells and crescents decorating Ruding's poetical curriculum vitae

of St Andrew's church there still survives the remains of a monumental brass that Ruding constructed. He apparently built a crypt for himself and its huge covering slab - measuring about 12 feet by 6 feet - is inlaid with an impressive monumental brass. The brass was constructed prior to 1471 and remained in a relatively complete state until c1861; and a drawing of the brass dating from c1796 (Gough, 1796) still survives. A reproduction of St John the Baptist's head is shown here on the left (Griffin, 1936, p285).

The poem is an imaginary conversation between Ruding who extols his achievements to date, and Death who replies that to him, achievements are irrelevant, everyone is the same: 'Dust thou art and unto dust shalt thou return' (Dominey, 1976).

The Ruding Bible

Willis (1755, p 57) was a little ambiguous about whether Ruding left the Bible to the parish church or to the school:

> *'John Ruding also repaired or rebuilt St John Baptist's chapel in the town, as appears by his Arms there. This is also called St Thomas Acon, and the St Thomas Becket's chapel; and is now the Free-School. He gave a folio Latin Bible in Vellum, now in my possession, to this church; in which his arms are painted, and this inscription written in it:*
> *'Hunc librum dedit Magister Johannes Rudyng Archidiaconus Lincolniensis Cathedrae curandum in principali disco infra cancellum Ecclesiae suae prebendalis de Buckyngham, ad usam capellanorum et aliorum ibidem in eodem studere volencium quam diu duraverit'**
> *The Motto of his Arms, as drawn twice in the bible, (folio 11 and the 28th folio from the end) was 'All may God Amende' '.*
> *Master John Rudyng, archdeacon at Lincoln Cathedral, responsible for the great lectern within the chancel, gave this book to the prebendal church of Buckyngham, for the use of the chaplains and others wishing to study there, for as long as it shall endure.

The bible was in Willis's possession prior to 1755 (Willis, 1755, p57), and when Willis died in 1760, the Bible was left in his house, until his entire library was sold at Christies in c1851. The bible was purchased by a Bristol bookseller, Thomas Kerslake, who later advertised it in his catalogue.

The Rev H.Roundell, vicar (see *Glossary*) of Buckingham, and friend of the school, purchased it, and on his death, his widow presented it to the Church of St Peter & St Paul in Buckingham where it now resides (1999).

Ruding died in c1482, having been archdeacon of Lincoln and Prebendary of Sutton-cum-Buckingham for ten years. His will states his request 'to be buried in the chancel of my Prebendal Church of Buckingham under a marble stone heretofore placed there by me'. He left 100 shillings to Lincoln cathedral, and lesser amounts to his brother John, and for the relief of prisoners at Newgate (Gibbons, p196, 1888).

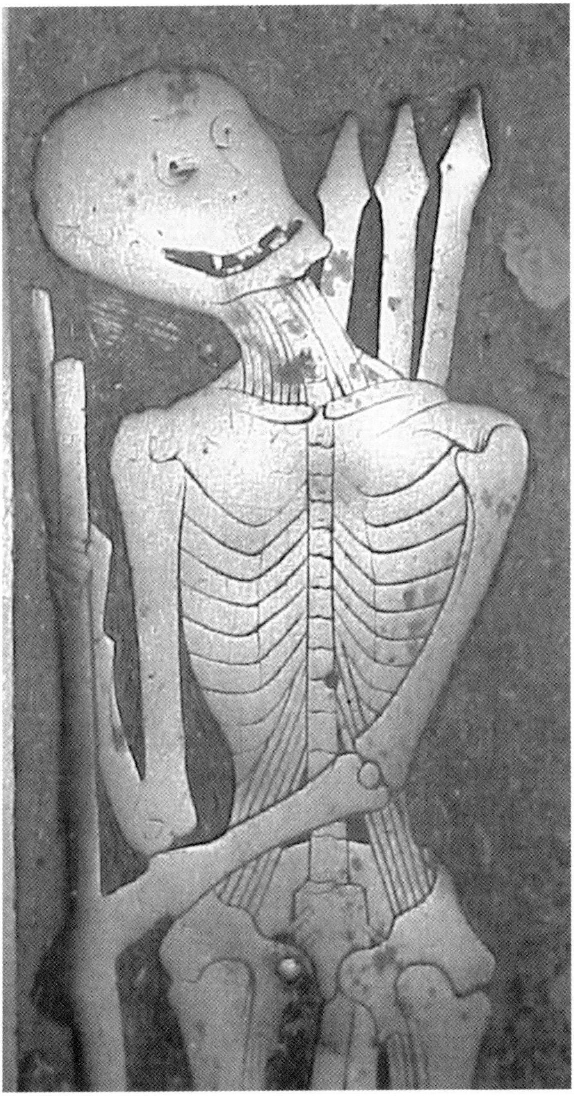

The brass figure of Death on Ruding's monumental brass at Biggleswade

A MEDIEVAL BUCKINGHAM SCHOOL

It has been estimated that in the Middle Ages there were some 400 grammar schools in England and Wales - mainly held in ecclesiastical establishments such as cathedrals, churches, chantry chapels and guilds. These schools were full-time, there were no holidays other than certain feast days. It is fairly certain that religious instruction was given, as well as instruction in English, Latin and Arithmetic which would have been essential for every day life either as a merchant or cleric. Students left school at 14, and if they wanted to and could afford to pay, they could apply for entrance to University. Oxford and Cambridge were the main Universities and had established minimum entry requirements which included a basic knowledge of Latin (Chapman, 1992, p25-27), thus St John's Latin School was well placed to help students to gain entry to Oxford.

The Oxford Admissions Registers (Emden 1959 & Boase 1885) are difficult to search on a place name basis, and they rarely give the origin of the scholars. As a result, only three pre-Reformation Buckingham entrants have been found: Simon Lambert admitted 1499 aged 12; Robert Chalner, Fellow of New College 1507; Thomas Duke, Fellow of New College 1509; William Lambert, Fellow of New College 1558.[8]

---

[8] New College was founded in 1379 by William de Wykeham, Prebendary of Buckingham in 1365 - the same year he purchased Radclive Manor, near Buckingham, possibly for endowment purposes. There is some evidence that Wykeham purchased such lands to aid poor scholars in grammar schools to facilitate their entry into New College (Leach, 1969, p201-210).

THE REFORMATION

There is no doubt that the Reformation was a time of great upheaval: a change in religious authority from the Pope in Rome to Henry VIII King of England; as well as a succession of four Monarchs over 12 years, which meant that a position of ecclesiastical or political authority under one monarch could be rescinded under the next. As a result, many gifts and grants were 're-legalised' to ensure the 'authorisation' of the current monarch:

Henry VIII	1509-1547	Catholic then Protestant
Edward VI	1547-1553	Protestant
Mary	1553-1554	Catholic
Philip & Mary	1554-1558	Catholic
Elizabeth	1558-1603	Protestant

The Reformation comprised three Acts to survey and suppress monasteries, and two Acts to suppress 'Chantries and other superstitious institutions' enacted by Henry VIII and Edward VI in the years 1535 to 1548. Their methods were chillingly efficient.

Dissolution of the Monasteries

In January 1535, Henry VIII passed a Royal Act which appointed 12 commissioners to value all monastic and church property, under the control of the vicar general, Thomas Cromwell, Earl of Essex (see *Biography*). In July, Cromwell appointed the archdeacon of Buckinghamshire, Richard Layton (see *Biography*), as one of four inquisitors of the monastic clergy. The inquisitors made a very rapid tour of most of the religious houses in England and Wales, and are said to have made reports on upto 90 institutions within a two week period (Constant, 1934, p162), and completed a survey of some 900 houses within four months. The inquisitors went armed with questionnaires : seventy five questions for monks, eighty six for nuns - questioning their faith, belief, morals, wealth, age, sexual activities, rules of fasting and abstinence. The commissioners compiled an inventory of religious property now called the *Valor Ecclesiasticus*, where the total revenue was estimated to be £320,280 (Constant, 1934, p140-199). They also issued reports on the 'morality' of each house.

In 1536, an 'Act for the suppression of the Lesser Monasteries' was passed, and the smaller monasteries with an annual income of less than £200 were suppressed. This affected 327 religious houses, of which 52 were allowed to survive in return for an annual payment. So much money was involved that an 'accounts department' known as the Court of Augmentations was created to handle and dispose of all the religious land, property and contents (Belloc, 1934, p140-199). Perversely, the Act of 1536 gave a legal basis for allowing the larger monasteries to continue, although it would appear that this was not the original intention. There was resistance to the dissolution which culminated in a rebellion called the 'Pilgrimage of Grace'. The King quashed the rebellion, and then initiated the suppression of the larger monasteries using coercion. The Royal Commissioners visited the monasteries with ready-made forms, which stated that the monastery had voluntarily surrendered to the King. The abbot or prior was persuaded to face the inevitable, to sign the document voluntarily and receive a decent pension; or to refuse and face charges of treason, for which they could be executed and their lands seized by the King. Not surprisingly, most gave in gracefully, and the majority of the larger monasteries had surrendered by the end of 1538.

The income of the Hospital of St Thomas of Acon in London was valued at over £277 in 1535 (*Valor Ecclesiasticus*) and they 'voluntarily' surrendered on Sunday 20th October 1538 (E322/139, & C54/411) in compensation for which, the master received the enormous pension of £66 13s 4d (100 marks), whilst six other priests received between £5 and £8. On the following Wednesday, Thomas Mildmaye (see *Biography*), audited the 'value of all lands and possessions' owned by the Hospital. The inventory included the woods called 'Hermytt Grove by the towne of Buckingham 5 acres of the age of 7 yeres' (Watney, 1892, p124). As the chantry chapel is not listed, it is supposed that the Order did not own the chantry but used the income from Hermytts Grove at

Westbury to support its Buckingham chantry priest, Thomas Hawkyns.

The Minutes of a Mercers meeting, called the Acts of Court, on the 18th of December 1538 record:

> *'it is ordeyned & Agreed by this worshipfull assemble that sute shalbe made to the kyng[es] grace for the churche lately called Seynte Thomas of Acres & the mancion place therof w[ith] the smale ten[emen]ts adioynynge yf there may Be convenyentely hadde etc'.*

Sir Richard Gresham (see *Biography*), on behalf of the Mercers, made an unsuccessful petition to allow it to continue its 'aid of the poor and sick'. Sheer persistence enabled the Mercers Company to purchase the entire London site on 21st April 1541, from the Court of Augmentations for their own use, with the aid of a loan from Sir Richard Gresham for the sum of £969-17s-6d (Watney, 1892 p125-31).

In 1539, the 'Second suppression Act' was passed in order to retrospectively legalise these dubious practices. Between 1537 to 1540, some 158 large monasteries and 30 nunneries had been dissolved. In 1540, some 43 Commanderies belonging to the Knights of St John of Jerusalem were confiscated. It had taken less than five years for the Commissioners to destroy the network of religious houses. All their valuables were seized and nine tons of gold and silver were sent back to London; all revenues were annexed to the Crown; the rest of the monastic goods including lead, glass, windows, vestments, bells, carving, woodwork, etc were sold locally at auction. Libraries were sold to shopkeepers for wrapping goods or for use as scourers, and ships were filled to supply continental bookbinders (Constant, 1934, p188).

The Chantries Acts

England was at war with France, Scotland and Ireland in 1543 to 1546, and the expense rapidly drained Henry VIII's war-chest. So in order to raise more funds he turned his attention to the Chantries which had been founded to employ priests to say masses for the souls of their founders (Dickens, 1989, p230).

The Chantries Act of 1545 was designed to stop the illegal dissolution of chantries by private individuals for their own benefit, and to reassign the financial income of chantries to the Crown. This Act only affected chantries, hospitals, brotherhoods, guilds free-chapels, colleges, hospitals, fraternities and similar institutions through England and Wales, that were liable to first-fruits (see *Glossary*). This meant that almshouses or hospitals that were run by laymen or by municipal organisations would be exempt. Less than 10 chantries are known to have been dissolved by this Act (Leach, 1896 p61-74). When Henry VIII died in 1547, so did the authority to enforce this Act.

The Chantries Act of 1548 was passed in the first year of the reign of Edward VI. As he was only 10 years old at the time, his councillor Somerset was probably responsible for its enactment. The wording was similar to that of Henry VIII's Chantries Act, but omits any mention of hospitals. It also makes specific provision for Grammar schools, in that if any religious foundation was originally conceived to house or found a Grammar school, then that school should be allowed to continue. The decision to allow a school to continue was made by the 'Commission for the Continuance of schools' which comprised two commissioners: Sir Walter Mildmay (see *Biography*) and Robert Kelway who had total authority over chantry secondary education in 1549. If a school existed within a chantry, but was not specifically mentioned in the foundation deeds, then the school was suppressed - because the only reason for the chantry's foundation was 'superstitious use' (Leach, 1896, p30).

The Chantries Act was different to the dissolution of the monasteries, in that it was actually welcomed by some eminent clergy, as they believed that money left to a priest to say mass for a long dead soul, was a total waste of time, money and manpower. There was also a little jealousy within the clergy that chantry priests had access to their own funds and were not directly responsible to the parish clergy.

Combined effects of the Dissolution and Chantries Acts

The overall scale of devastation is almost incomprehensible: some 2,374 free-chapels and Chantries were seized, sold or converted to secular use (Kelke, 1858, p61) and the redundant chantry priests were then assigned a pension; it has been estimated that 600 foundations, 7000 monks, 2000 nuns, were affected (Aylesbury Library, L000:27) and some 40,000 to 80,000 monastic dependants (the poor, the sick and the employed servants) were deprived of care, support and their employment.

The sale of the religious contents alone is estimated to have raised £1,423,500 for the Treasury (Belloc, 1934, p140-199), and perhaps £2 Million in all. By 1603, it has been estimated that 75 per cent of all the seized property had passed to the landed gentry. Some historians believe that the net result was that the rich got richer as they could buy everything at a 'knock-down' price. Others believe that realistic prices were achieved for the properties and their possessions. However there is little doubt that the poor got poorer as their support systems of food, shelter, medical care, education and employment were wiped out. Staple food items such as eggs and fish - previously farmed by the monasteries - quadrupled in price. The rise in beggars resulted in a new law punishing all beggars with mutilation or worse (Belloc, 1934, p140-199).

The Documents of the Reformation

The Documents of the Reformation include the:

- *Valor Ecclesiasticus* (1535);
- Surrender forms of the monasteries (1536-38);
- Chantry Certificates of Henry VIII (1545-1547) and Edward VI (1548-9);
- abstracts of Edward VI Chantry Certificates for the provision of pensions to the Ex-Religious and continuance (or not) of schools.

With respect to schools, as the intention of the reformation was to raise money from foundations that had superstitious uses, the Commissioners acting under the Acts of Henry VIII had no interest in the fact that a school was attached to a chantry, church or cathedral, and thus schools were rarely recorded. Under Edward VI, only Grammar schools were recorded, but those run by hospitals or municipal organisations were exempted and not recorded (Leach, 1896, p66).

Many of these documents still exist, and provide us with information on Matthew Stratton's chantry at Buckingham, and Barton's Chantry at Thornton.

Right: The Matthew Stratton chantry as described by Henry VIII's commissioners in 1545/6 (see Appendix II).

E301/4. Reproduced with kind permission of the Public Records Office

MATTHEW STRATTON'S CHANTRY - BUCKINGHAM

On the 4th February 1545/6, the commissioners visited 'seynt John the Baptist & Thomas of Acon' chantry chapel also known as 'Mathewe Strattons chauntry'. There they found the incumbent, Thomas Hawkyns, who received an income of 37s 8d from the late house of seynt Thomas of Acon in Westcheppe London' (see Appendix II). As Thomas Hawkins was a chantry priest in Buckingham in 1524 (Lipscombe, 1847, p574) it is likely that he was also the schoolmaster, and that he had been in service at the Chapel of

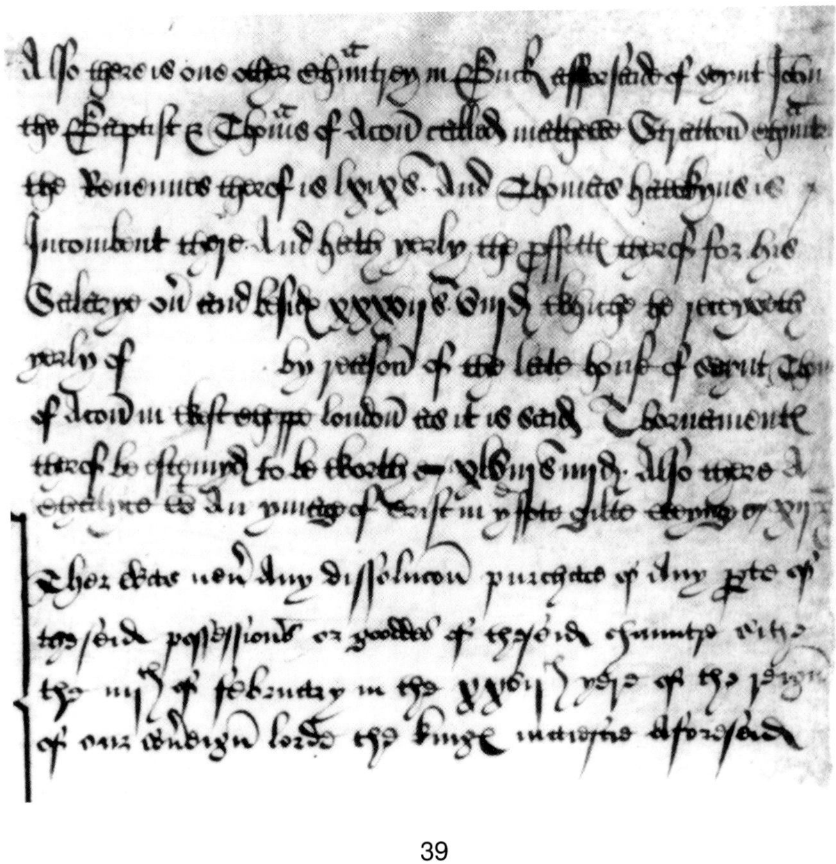

St John the Baptist & St Thomas of Acon for at least 14 years.

In 1554 it was confirmed that Thomas Hawkyns is 'priest of Buckingham, formerly chantry priest in a chapel at Buckingham with a pension of £5-6s-8d' (Hodgett, 1959, p97). His pension, is recorded in the Land Revenue Records from 1548 to 1565 for celebrating divine service in the chapel of St John the Baptist (VCH, Bucks, ii, p208). The average pension of an ordinary monk, regular canon or poor priest with a single chantry was about £5 or £6 per annum, which in the years 1540-1550 represented the wage of an unskilled workman (Dickens, 1989, p172). It would thus appear that Thomas Hawkyns was working in Buckingham for a total of 41 years (1524-1565).

In 1540, King Henry VIII visited Buckingham and held a council in the town (Gibbs, 1878). In the same year, John Josselyn, MP for Buckingham in 1545 (Clarke, 1984, p52) received a grant for life of three properties in Buckingham which had belonged to St Thomas of Acon's chantry chapel. These included two closes of wood called Heremytes Grove/Fields in Westbury comprising 28 acres in Westbury which were occupied by John Lambert (VCH, Bucks, i, p265). It is known that the Hermit associated with this land belonging to the chapel was Robert of Wappenham (C143/14/5).

In 1553/4, a small chapel called 'Seint Jonys Chapple' in the town of Buckingham, and all its houses, lands etc., leased with the same in the parishes of 'Buckingham, Maydes Morton and Burton, co. Bucks in the tenure of Thomas Haukyns, clerk, formerly belonging to the late college of Acon in the city of London' were granted by Queen Mary to Thomas Reve and Giles Isham (with hundreds of other properties). There began a series of transactions over the next 40 years when the property was given to the use of new grantees (VCH, Bucks, iii, p486). Hermits Grove (C143/14/5) in the parish of Westbury 'to the late Colledge of Acon formerly belonging' followed a similar series of transactions (Ussher, p136-137). When the Ordnance survey was initially conducted, field names were recorded and a field in Westbury called Hermitage Ground comprised 11 acres 0 roods and 22 perches; it is believed that this field is now called Lower Park Fields (Ussher, p154).

BARTONS CHANTRIES - THORNTON

The Chantry Commissioners visited Thornton on the 4th February 1545/6, the same day that they visited Buckingham (see Appendix III). They found two chantries called 'Bartons Chantry' which they ascribed as being founded by Roberte Ingleton and John Barton respectively. The commissioners recorded that the Ingleton chantry provided 6d a week for 'six poore folkes' and a clothing allowance of 4s a year to 'six poore children' and that the chantry priest, William Abbotte, should 'teache the children' (Chantry Certificate, No.4, 10). Thus the first teacher that can be identified with certainty at Thornton school is William Abbott.

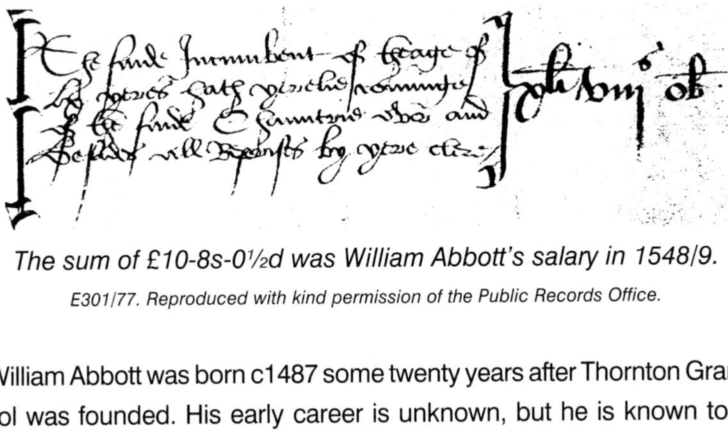

The sum of £10-8s-0½d was William Abbott's salary in 1548/9.

E301/77. Reproduced with kind permission of the Public Records Office.

William Abbott was born c1487 some twenty years after Thornton Grammar school was founded. His early career is unknown, but he is known to have been appointed to be the Thornton chantry priest and teacher from c1520, when he was appointed by his 'cousin', Humphrey Tyrell who had (in 1519) married Jane Ingleton (Tricker, 1996), the daughter and heir of Robert Ingleton (Lipscombe, iii, p119). Abbott is mentioned as being a chantry priest in 1526 (Salter, 1909, p242), and was poorly treated by his patrons and was deprived of the profits of the chantry income for some 15 years. The final straw was when, four days before Christmas 1530, William Abbott was thrown out of his chantry house and so 'hampered' his teaching duties. In 1535 he brought an action against his patron and wrote a letter to the Bishop of Lincoln explaining and complaining about his rough treatment. His letter to the Bishop still survives in Lincoln archives (Chantries 3).

Ten years later, in 1545, William Abbott was accused of a similar crime in a case that was heard in the Court of Requests. This court was linked to the Kings council and designed to give poor people access to Royal justice. Apparently, Abbott had rented out 36 acres of Thornton for some 18 years at '9s 2d yerlie' to Richard Leche, a farmer. Abbott then supplanted this farmer with another, a Lawrens Bee. Richard Leche complained to the court that as he had just ploughed the land he was reluctant to leave, and that Bee had 'plukkyd (him) owte of his said hous by vyolens and felle upon him & beate hym'. The court ruled that the 'seid bill of complaint is insufficyent in the law to be answered' (REQ2/Bundle4/128).

In 1547/8 the first Barton chantry supported by All Souls at Thornton was forcibly closed 'for the chantry lately come to the king's hands', and the college had to pay for 'sweeping up and cleaning the choir after the last deportation of images' (Leach 1896, p52). However the school which was part of the second Barton's chantry, the refounded Chastillon chantry, was allowed to continue. In 1548/9, the commissioners confirmed that William Abbott is a chantry priest 'of the age of 60 yeres ... and yett doth teach a free schole of grammer" (see Appendix III & IV). He was the incumbent as well as school teacher and received a pension of **£10-8s-0½d**. In the margin of this document, presumably written by officers of the Court of Augmentations, are the words ***'Continuatur the Schola quousque'*** (see Appendix V), meaning 'the School is continued until further orders' (Leach,

'Let the school be continued'.

E301/77. Reproduced with kind permission of the Public Records Office.

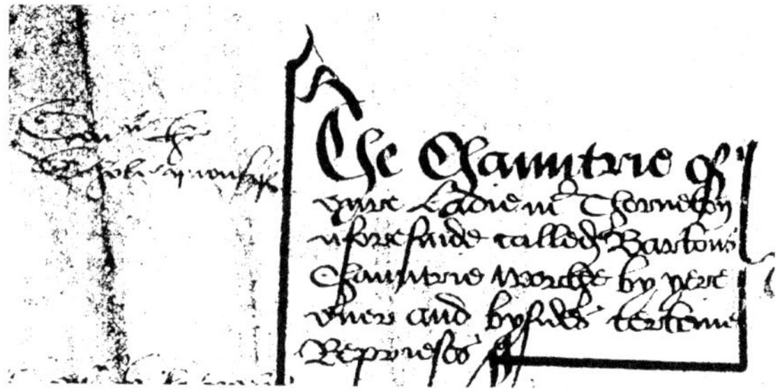

1896, p86). This instruction was put into action by a continuance warrant dated 20th July 1548/9 assigning the master his salary:

> *"A grammer schole hath been contynuallie kept in Thorneton ... with the revenues of the late chauntery of our ladye there, called Bartons Chaunterye ... Wee therefore ... haue assigned and appoynted that the saide grammer schole shall contynewe, and that William Abbot, scholemaster there, shall haue and enjoye the rome of scholemaster there, and shall have for his wages yerelie £10 8s 0 ½d" (Leach, 1896, p19).*

It was commonplace for chantry grammar schools teachers to be given the same salaries as they had previously enjoyed (Dickens, 1989, p235). This pension was used to sustain schools for the next 336 years (1548/9 to 1884).

In 1550 Edward VI bestowed the Barton's chantry in Thornton and its lands in Thornborough - 'including the messuage and land in the tenure of John Joslyn' - to Edward Chamberlain of Fulwell, Oxfordshire (VCH, Oxon, iv, p241).[9] Chamberlain sold the Bartons chantries and lands of Thornton and Thornborough in c1556, which passed through several hands until they came to John Temple of Stowe in c1561 or c1601 (VCH, Bucks, iv, p241 & Willis, 1755, p290).[10]

The accounts of the Augmentation office record the payments of £10-

---

9. John Joslyn co-incidently was the owner of three properties in Buckingham in 1540/1 which had belonged to St Thomas of Acon's chantry chapel, including Heremytes Close in Westbury, and was tenant of lands in Thornborough and Thornton belonging to Barton's chantry in Thornton in 1550 (L&P Hen VIII, Vol XVI, p716).

10. It has not been ascertained whether this Edward Chamberlain was the same person as the High Steward of the borough of Buckingham by charter of Queen Mary in 1553 (Elliott, 1975, p246). He may also have been the son of Richard Chamberlain and Sibyl Fowler and therefore Richard Fowler's son-in-law.

8s-0d (the halfpenny was omitted) to William Abbott describing him as the schoolmaster of the school of letters *(ludimagistro ludi litterarii)*, a Grammar school *(palestra litteraria)* from 1550 until 1574, when he presumably died aged about 86 years (VCH, Bucks, ii, p146).

Why did the Barton-founded Thornton school survive through the Reformation, and the Stratton-founded Buckingham school remain invisible ?

The Commissioners visited both Buckingham and Thornton in February 1545/6, and noted the chantries but not the school at Buckingham. On their second visit to Thornton in 1548/9, they did not visit Buckingham. The answer to this puzzle is probably that Matthew Stratton's foundation in Buckingham was that of a hospital, run by a hospitaller, Thomas Hawkins. Hospital schools were usually ignored by Henry VIII's Commissioners, and were exempted from Edward VI Chantries Act (Leach, 1896, p25). As Henry VIII's Commissioners had already closed the other Buckingham Chantries, there was no need for Edward VI's Commissioners to visit a hospital school in Buckingham whose headquarters in London had already been dissolved. Thus the silence on the issue, is simply because the school was left to continue without interference. Even the Bishop of Lincoln was not sure of the situation, and in 1549/50 listed Stratton's chantry as a 'doubtful chantry' - 'chantries about which it is doubtful whether they be in the hands of the Lord King or no'; although he knew that the two other Buckingham chantries (John Barton (senior) and the Fraternity of the Holy Trinity) were 'before the Auditor [of the court of Augmentations]' (Foster & Thompson, p272-4, 1927). The chantry school in Buckingham only became 'visible' after 1553, when Queen Mary came to the throne and changed the political climate.

THORNTON AND BUCKINGHAM SCHOOLS MERGE

To recap, with the exception of the Fraternity of the Trinity, there were chantry priests in:

Location	*Founder*	*Priest supplied by*
St John the Baptist & St Thomas of Acon	Matthew Stratton	St Thomas of Acon (c1268)
Buckingham Church	John Barton (senior)	St Thomas of Acon (1431)
Thornton Church	John Barton (junior) (Isabel Barton)	All Souls College (c1440)
Thornton Church	Chastillon, Ingleton & John Barton (junior) (Richard Fowler)	Lord of the Manor (1356 & 1468)

The Dissolution of St Thomas of Acon in London in 1538 stopped the flow of funds to St John's chantry chapel school in Buckingham, except for the pension paid to Thomas Hawkins. When Thomas retired as schoolmaster prior to 1553, it is presumed that the cash requirements were high; St John's Chapel was now in private hands so that rent as well as the new schoolmaster had to be paid.[11]

At Thornton church the situation was similar; the Reformation had only

---

11. The Buckingham chantry was privately owned from 1553. In 1590, the owners were William Tipper and Thomas Dawe (Willis, 1755, p48), who seemed to have specialised in purchasing the fishing rights to various manors including: Marsh Gibbon; Westbury; Aston Clinton; Buckland. At the time of the merger, 1592-1597, the Sergeant family owned the chantry chapel at Thornton, and they sold it to John Temple in 1601.

allowed a priest sufficient funds for himself, with no means of maintaining the fabric of a chantry school on his pension. By 1584/5 Thornton church was in a neglected state, there was no surplice (see *Glossary*) for the priest to wear, nor even a cloth for the communion table (VCH, Bucks, i, p318). That the interior and exterior of the church was left to decay is in little doubt, and in 1637 it was even reported that an elder tree was growing on its roof (VCH, Bucks, i, p324-325).

In c1574, William Abbott was succeeded by 'John Kinge' as the 'schoolmaster of Our Lady the Queen at Thorneton'.[12] King was paid the endowment (see *Glossary*) for 5 years until 1587 when Anthony Gate succeeded him as schoolmaster of the grammar school. Then for one year, 1592, the Thornton endowment was switched to James Smith, 'schoolmaster of the grammar school of the town of Buckingham'. For the next 5 years, payment is again made to Anthony Gate, 'master at Thornton', but in 1597, payment is permanently switched to Buckingham. This payment is made to James Smith, and then his successor, Robert Tomlyns, under a warrant indicating that an order had been made to transfer the school or its endowment, from Thornton to Buckingham (VCH, Bucks, ii, p146-7).

The endowment of £10-8s-0½d

Headteacher	***Thornton***	***Buckingham***
Abbott	1548-1574	
King	1582	
Gate	1587	
Smith		1592
Gate	1593-1596	
Smith		1597-1603
Tomlyns		1603-1609

---

12. The title referring to the Ingleton/Barton chantry chapel origins of the Blessed Virgin Mary in Thornton church.

It was entirely logical that a merger, or transfers should occur. The new Bailiff and Burgesses (see *Glossary*) at Buckingham (1553/4) probably wanted the best possible education for their sons[13]. Tranfers had been instigated by chantry commissioners in other locations eg. Cornwall: 'the school of ... is in decay by reason it standeth in a desolate place, and far from the market, for the provision of scholars' and recommended its 'removal' to a town seven miles away (Leach, 1896, p117), but in this case, the merger takes place much later.

So two chantry schools, both of which had been founded or refounded by two brothers called John Barton were merged. Thus the school now known as the Royal Latin School has two origins: Thornton provided the 'Royal' title courtesy of Edward VI, and the sum of £10-8s-0½d from William Abbott's pension, and the requirement for six 'foundation boys'; and Buckingham provided the premises, master and pupils. So William Abbott's pension of £10-8s-0½d fixed in 1548/9 was paid annually to the Latin school in Buckingham from 1597 to 1884. [Over the years the ½d was sometimes omitted and sometimes appears as ¾d].

One question remains: who had the authority to merge the two schools, fifty years after the Reformation? The 1603 payment to Smith, the schoolmaster of Buckingham, was authorised by a warrant of Thomas, Lord Buckhurst and John Fortescue (see *Biography*) (Elliott, 1975, p172). Baron Buckhurst was also known as Sir Thomas Sackville (see *Biography*) - a powerful figure and Lord Treasurer from 1599 to 1608. Sir John Fortescue was MP of Buckingham from 1586 and Chancellor of the Exchequer from 1589 to 1603. Thus it is likely that John Fortescue was the influential authority who merged the two schools.

---

13. The year 1553 is the first in which Willis finds a named schoolmaster at Buckingham.

THE ISABEL DENTON MYTH

Browne Willis is probably Buckinghamshire's greatest historian. Without his efforts, much of the county's history would have been lost, including that of the Royal Latin School. According to Willis books 'History of Mitred Parliamentary Abbeys' (1719, p39), and 'History and Antiquities of Buckingham' (1755, p81) the Return made into the Exchequer of Colleges and Chantries at their Dissolution in 1547, says that:

> *'Dame Isabel Denton gave by her will about the year 1540, 4 marks yearly to a priest to teach children in this town [Buckingham], in augmentation of his means of living for 20 years; of which 8 years were then said to have expired, Anno 2 Edward VI' [1548-9] (Willis, 1755, p81).*

Although this statement has been repeated by historians over the centuries, no documentary evidence has ever been found. Despite much research on Isabel Denton née Brome (see *Biography*), it would now seem likely that Browne Willis made an error. In his 1755 book, in the Shalston section he states:

> *'Dame Isabel Denton gave to a priest here eight marks yearly, for 20 years' (Willis, 1755, p266).*

In his hand-written manuscript of this same book (lodged at the Bodleian Library) the 'Shallston' section states:

> *'Out of the Augmentations Office this memorandum that here is 4 marks given for 20 years whereof 8 are past by Dame Isobel Denton to a priest there to teach children for the augmentation of his living'.*

In the Buckingham section of his manuscript there is no mention of Dame Isabel Denton (Willis, MS22, p120).

A Chantry Pension certificate dated 1548/9 from the Court of Augmentations (see E301/77 overleaf) has been found which lists the chantries under the Act of Edward VI. The Buckingham Hundred lists only three towns and starts with Thorneton (the two Barton chantries), then Buckingham (the Trinity Fraternity and Barton) followed by Shalston. The Shalston entry states:

> *'there is iiii mark[es] yerelie geven for the terme of xx yeres wherof viii yeres be past by Dame Isabell Denton to a prieste there to teache Children for theaugmentat[i]on of his lyvinge'.*

Thus it seems conclusive that Isabel Denton was involved with the school at Shalston in Buckingham Hundred, and not Buckingham town.

In defence of Willis, his manuscripts show that he was involved in a massive collection 'hunt' of history. Not only did he examine vast numbers of historical documents himself, and appears to have been an expert in reading old wills, but he entered into written correspondence with people all over the country who accessed historical repositories on his behalf or who were able to recall stories or legends. Thus it is not surprising that some errors were made.

However, it would be wrong to conclude that there was no link between the school and the Denton family (see *Biography*) at this time. In 1547, the Manor of the Prebend End of Sutton-cum-Buckingham was surrendered by Richard Cox (see *Biography*) the Prebendary to King Edward VI, who converted it into a lay fee (see *Glossary*). In 1613, the lay fee of the Prebend End of Buckingham cum Gawcott was purchased by Sir Thomas Denton of Hillesden for £4,500 (Bucks, District Councils, 1554-1974 (AR 29/73/3/1 354-359)). So the Dentons became the new lay lords of the manor. A second link occurs through Giles Isham, to whom Queen Mary granted 'Seint Jonys Chapple', Buckingham in 1553/4. Giles Isham and Thomas Denton were

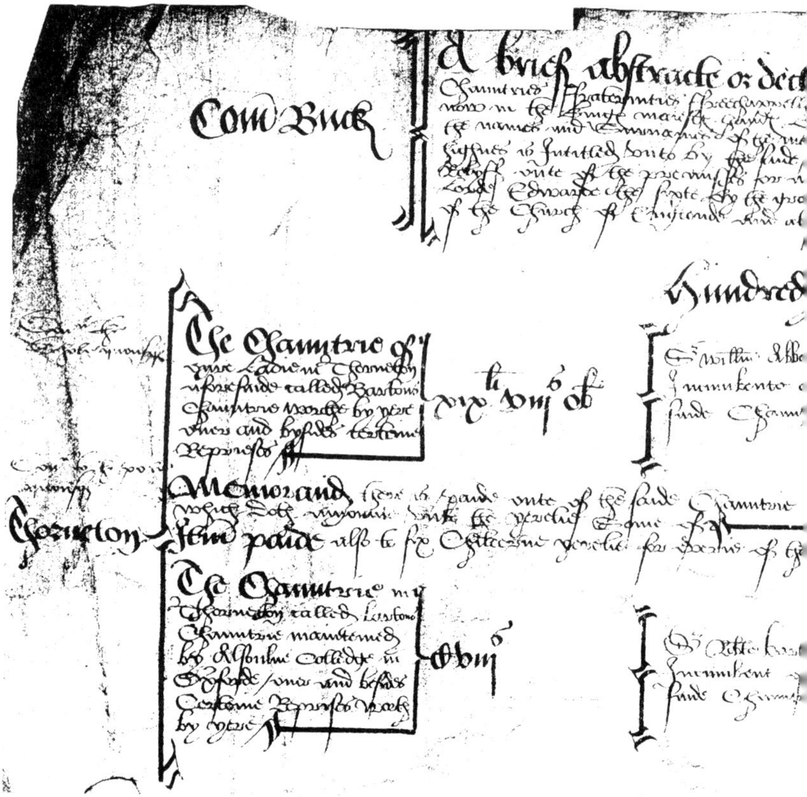

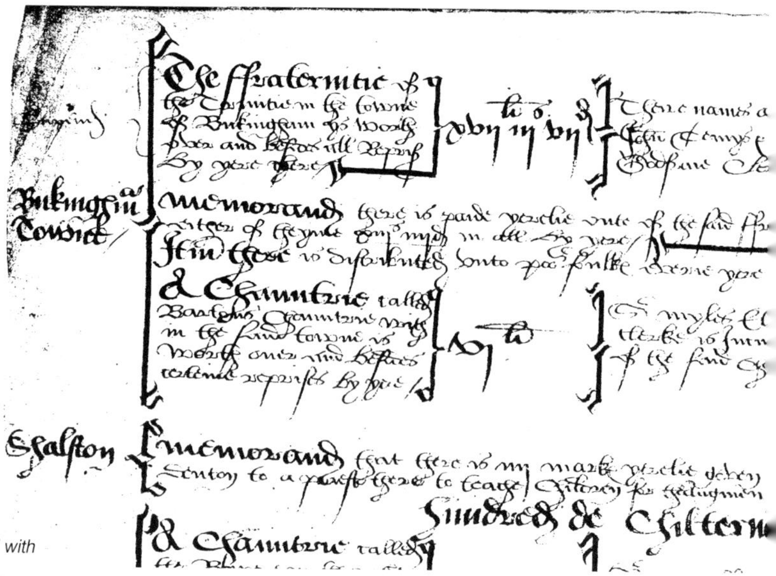

E301/77. Reproduced with kind permission of the Public Records Office

...ticularly of the names of all the late Colledges

...Chauntryes, Stipendaries and such others within the said Countie of Buck ... of the late Acte of Parliament ... and provided for the same ... [illegible] ... incumbent ... [illegible] ... scoles ... [illegible] ... in the seconde yere of the reigne of oure soveraigne ... of Englonde Fraunce and Irelonde defender of the faith and ... [illegible] ... that is to saye

...uck

The said Incumbent of the age of ... yeres hath yerelie commyng of the said Chauntrie ... all reprises by yere clere	xl s viij d ob	The said Incumbent doth teach a ... Scole ... and ... other lyvyng but the said Chauntrie
... to ... of them by ...	vij li ...	
... which hath ... to the yerelie some	xl s ... xxvj s	
The said Incumbent of the age of ... yeres hath ... commyng ... the said Chauntrie ... the said ... Colledge ... by yere clere	xxvj s	The said Incumbent hath no other lyvyng but the said ... that is presented
The said Incumbent of the age of ... the above ... yerelie commyng of the said ... by yere clere	vj li	The said Incumbent hath no other lyvyng but this
... clere ... for the ...	xxvj s viij d	
...	xxvj s viij d	
The said Incumbent of the age of ... yeres hath yerelie commyng of the said Chauntrie ... Gabriell ... by yere ...	vj li	And the said Incumbent hath no other lyvyng ... and is ...

... of xx yeres ... yeres ... past ... Isabell ... his name is not presented

The said Incumbent of the age ... | And what other lyvyng

both attorneys to Francis, the Earl of Bedford in 1555, and thus may have been colleagues for some time. One of Giles Isham's brothers was the warden of the Mercers, another was the chaplain to Queen Mary (Ramsey, 1962, pxii). Thus Giles Isham through his close links to Thomas Denton, the Mercers, the Church, and the Queen, purchased the Buckingham (St Thomas of Acon) chantry in 1553/4.

THE MASTERS AT BUCKINGHAM

The schoolmasters biographies are listed chronologically, incorporating the history of the school within their period of service.

1524-1553 Thomas Hawkins (?)	1764-1785 James Eyre
1553-1569 Henry Webster (?)	1785-1830 William Eyre (see *Biography*)
1574-1580 Alexander Sheppard	1830-1855 Edward Brittin
1580-1592 Thomas Potter	1855-1858 Thomas Robert John Laugharne
1592-1603 James Smith	1858-1861 Vacant post
1603-1609 Robert Tomlyns	1861-1869 Thomas Owain Jones
1609-1609 John Nichols	1869-1871 Louis Borissow
1609-1625 Richard Earle	1871-1891 Thomas Cockram
1625-1632 Richard Horne	1891-1895 Robert C. MacCulloch
1633-1638 Thomas Dutton	1895-1896 Thomas Cockram
1638-1660 Edward Ummant	1896-1908 Walter Matthew Cox
1660-1664 Thomas Stephens	1908-1931 William Fuller
1664-1665 William Warters	1931-1935 Maurice Walton Thomas
1665-1682 Roger Griffiths	1936-1939 Stanley Arthur Dyment
1682-1684 Thomas Dalby	1939-1941 Henry Bert Toft
1685-1690 Thomas Yeomans	1941-1941 Donald E. Morgan
1690-1691 Mark Noble	1942-1945 Charles Foster
1691-1696 Robert Styles	1945-1948 Henry Bert Toft
1709-1715 Samuel Foster	1948-1979 George K.Embleton
1715-1723 Richard Cardwell	1979-1992 Peter Luff
1723-1763 William Halstead	1992-date Cecilia Galloway

1524-1553 (?)

Thomas Hawkins first appears as a chantry priest in Buckingham in 1524 (Lipscombe, 1847, p574), and then in 1548 he received a pension 'by reason of the late house of St Thomas of Acon'. The Land Revenue records the payment of his pension from 1550 to 1565 for celebrating divine service in the chapel of St John the Baptist (VCH, Bucks, ii, p208). Thus it is likely that Thomas was a schoolmaster at Buckingham before the Reformation, though whether he continued to teach after the dissolution of the College of Acon in 1538 can only be speculation.

1553-1569 (?)

Henry Webster was master of the school, and later became a curate (see *Glossary*) of Buckingham when he probably resigned the mastership (Roundell, 1857, p34). His burial is recorded as Henry Webster, priest on 29 June 1569 (Willis, 1755, p71).

Roundell (1857, p34) states that Joseph Williams became master of the school after Webster resigned and was buried at Buckingham on 5th December 1563. However it has not been possible to find any mention of him as a schoolmaster.

1574-1580

Alexander Sheppard is known to have become schoolmaster by 1574. Prior to this post he had been appointed clergyman of Tusmore on 18th April 1562 under his patron Thomas Piggott (Kennet, 1818, Vol II, p240).[14]

Alexander Sheppard became vicar of Whitchurch in 1580 and of Buckingham in 1599. In the Borough Minute Book he appears as an LLB (Bachelor of Law) and acted as a 'commissary or official of the peculiar and exempt jurisdiction of King's Sutton', and was able to prove wills. He achieved a doctorate in Law from Jesus College, Oxford, in 1609 (VCH, Bucks, ii, p209).

---

14. Tusmore had a church in 1274, but the Black Death wiped out the village in 1348-1349. In 1354 complete relief from taxation was given, and in 1358 the village was enclosed as a private park as all the labour-force had died (Allison et al). There were only some six rectors of Tusmore after Sheppard. By 1718 the church had disappeared, and today there is no visible trace of the old hamlet, which is located on Tusmore estate (Rayner-Smith, 1972, p12).

1580-1592

Thomas Potter MA succeeded Sheppard in 1580. On 13th June 1591, his son William was admitted to Gonville and Caius College, Cambridge, at the age of 14, having been born in Buckingham and educated 'under Mr Herl'. Thus Mr Earle or Herl, (presumably the man who became master in 1609) must have been an assistant teacher (VCH, Bucks, ii, p209). Potter left in about 1592.

In 1599, the Archbishop of Canterbury, John Whitgift (see *Biography*) issued an inhibition against Potter forbidding him to preach or teach school in the town of Buckingham (VCH, Bucks, ii, p209). It is possible that Potter might have had Catholic tendencies (Elliott, 1975, p171), and so he may have been removed from this post (Willis, 1755, p81).

1592-1603

James Smith succeeded as master of Buckingham school in 1592, when the Exchequer payment of £10-8s-0½d to Thornton school was first transferred to him. James Smith, *Ludimagistri*, (Schoolmaster), had a daughter, Mary, on the 1st December 1594; and a son Francis, on 15th May 1599 (Willis, 1755, p70).

It is likely that funding became a major issue, which is probably why in 1597, the Free school at Thornton with its annual income (pension) of £10-8s-0½d was permanently transferred to the Free school at Buckingham. At this point, the school in Buckingham inherited the 'Royal' status, the requirement to teach six boys and a fixed annual income.

1603-1609

Robert Tomlyns became master for six years (VCH, Bucks, ii, p209).

1609-1609

John Nichols was schoolmaster for perhaps six months; this was probably a temporary post until a new master was appointed. Nichols was Deputy High-Steward of Buckingham, and had been Bailiff in 1597,

1604 & 1639 (Elliott, p172,1975).[15]

1609-1625

Richard Earle appears to have been teaching at the school in 1591, before he was appointed master in 1609. He was 'discharged by the Corporation on Lady Day 1625, for neglecting the school' (Ford, 1733); it has been conjectured that this was the result of living some distance away from the school (VCH, Bucks, ii, p209) because he was also a vicar of Stowe where he eventually died in 1635 (Willis, 1755, p82).[16]

In 1610 John Speed published a street map of Buckingham, and highlighted the site of the 'chappell'.

1625-1632

Richard Horne (1595-1677) matriculated at Hart Hall, took his BA degree in 1621, MA in 1624, and began his duties as schoolmaster on Lady Day 1625. He had a daughter, Mary in 1630, and a son Richard in 1632 (Willis, 1755, p70),

He left the school in 1632 to become rector of Finmere (VCH, Bucks, ii, p209 & Blomfield, Finmere, 1887, p47), and had a daughter Anna in about 1640, and sons Gustavus in 1642, Charles in 1651, and Richard in 1655. In

---

15. When, in 1613, Thomas Denton purchased the manor and parsonage of Buckingham, commonly called the Prebend and Parsonage of Buckingham, the rights to the tithes of those lands in the occupation of Simon Lambert and John Nicholls were specifically excluded (Bucks, District Councils, 1554-1974 [AR 29/73/3/1 p354-359]). On 22nd June 1622 John Nichols married a daughter of Simon Lambert, then bailiff of the borough, and he died in 1646 (Willis, 1755, p69 & 72).

16. It would appear that 60-80 years after William Abbott's salary was fixed as a pension and subsequently endowed to the school, that £10-8s-0½d was insufficient to maintain a clergyman in the early 17th century. So Richard Earle took on extra responsibilities to augment his income, to the detriment of the school. This problem was not addressed for 300 years, until in 1904 it was first specified that the Master should not hold a benefice.

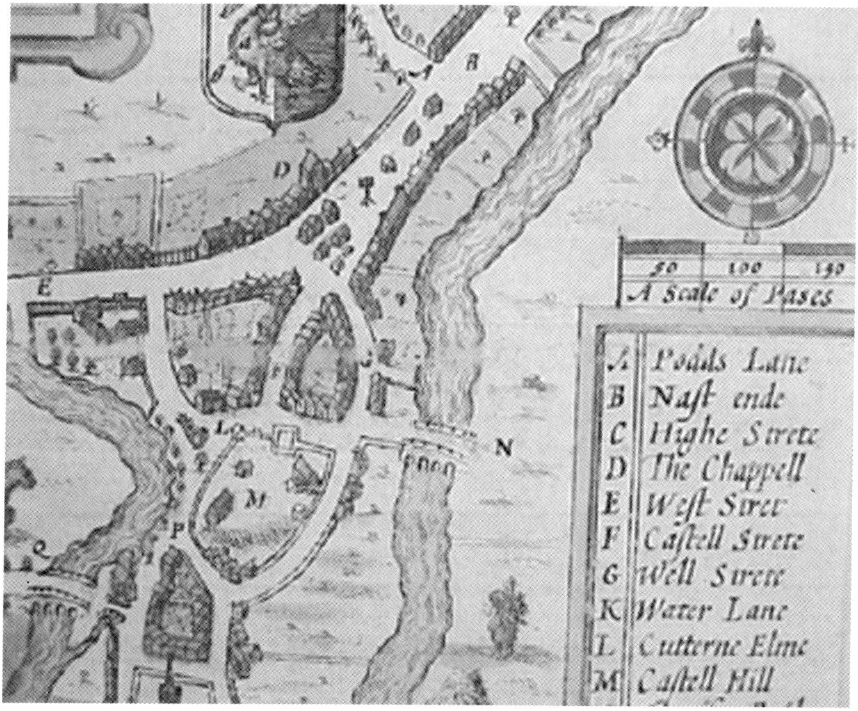

Buckingham by John Speed, 1610

the parish registers at Finmere he noted events that he thought of importance, including in 1642, the start of the Civil War: 'War, more than belongs to citizens, through the fields of England; and a legality is now given to wickedness'. His politics led to his ejection from Finmere in 1647 and he noted: 'I have fared badly, having been driven from home by force and arms ... and become almost destitute through all kinds of misfortunes'. He regained his post during the period 1658-1662. In 1658 he noted: 'Oliver Cromwell, Tyrant, ... who conspired against our most Serene King, Charles the Martyr, died Sept. 20, 1658'. The parish register, records Horne's burial on September 30th 1677, aged 82 years (Blomfield, Finmere, 1887, p46-49 & Genealogist, n.s.ii, 48-49, 103-106).

1633-1638

Thomas Dutton, born circa 1607, eldest son of Thomas Dutton the Rector of Eversholt, Bedfordshire (Longden, 1939 & Elliott, p172, 1975), graduated at Merton College, with a BA in 1628 and an MA in 1632 (VCH, Bucks, ii, p209) and was elected schoolmaster on May 27th 1635 (Halstead, 1734). He may be the Mr Dutton in Buckingham who had a daughter, Mary, in 1639 (Willis, 1755, p70).

The year after he graduated, aged 26, he became the headmaster of the school and at 31 left Buckingham to become the schoolmaster of the Free school at Somerton, Oxfordshire. He remained in post there for 52 years until he died and was buried on January 30th 1691, aged 83 (Blomfield, Bicester, 1887, p153,).

1638-1660

Edward Ummant MA was elected as master on 18th May 1638 by the Corporation. The following year his wife, Anna, died and was buried on 20th August 1639 when her name is given as Ummans, *'Uxor Magistri'* (Willis, 1755, p71, 81). In 1645 he obtained the vicarage of Padbury, which he held along with the school. Ummant employed three assistant teachers: Paine; Thompson; and Stephens (Willis, 1755, p82).

In July 1643, Prince Rupert arrived in Buckingham with a strong detachment of horse to protect the Queen and her entourage from the North to Oxford. He skirmished with Essex's forces and left Buckingham on the 6th July for Oxford (Roy, 1975, p444).

In mid January 1643/4, Parliamentary forces entered Hillesden House the home of Sir Alexander Denton and stayed there for almost a month. Royalist forces recaptured the house in late February. Orders were sent to Colonel Oliver Cromwell who was in the vicinity of Hillesden 'to be as active to the prejudice of the enemy as with your safety you may' (VCH, Bucks, iv, p173). On 4th March, Cromwell was Commander in Chief of a force of 2000 men and destroyed the house causing £16,000 damage (Johnson, 1962-63, p201).

A Royalist soldier, Richard Symonds, kept a diary of the marches of the royal army, and wrote: 'From [Bisseter] parish wee marched that night (Friday 21st June 1644) with the whole army and ten pieces of battery to Buckingham'. He had time to visit the church of St Peter & St Paul and noted:

'All may God Amend, is painted on the wall. All the windows are done with crescents and escallops. Never were any windows more broken, in May 1644 by the rebels of Northampton. North yle were many coates, but all broken. Fowler built this yle. A poore towne, one church, Sir Alexander Denton is lord of it, who lives at Hilsdon, two myles off. The Bayliffe and the Aldermen mett the King at the townes end, and the bayliffe made a speech to his majestie. And on Sunday morning went before the King to church' (Long, 1859, p20).

King Charles I entered Buckingham on Saturday 22nd June 1644 (Roundell, 1864, p29), and resided at Castle House for four nights (Elliott, 1975, p118).

On 1st February 1658, the Committee for Maintenance of Ministers and Schoolmasters ordered that:

'the yearly summe of £10 be graunted to and for increase of the maintenance of the schoolemaster of the freeschoole att Buckingham ... and that the same bee from time to time paid unto such godly and able schoolemaster as shall bee from time to time settled there'. (VCH, Bucks, ii, p209).

Then on the 10th February, 1658:

'the Trustees for maintenance have thought fit to allow the augmentacions herafter mencioned and have certified the same

for the approbacion of his Highnesse and the Councell ... His Highnesse and the Councell doe approve the said augmentacions and order that the same be paid accordingly ... To the schoolemaster of Buckinghame Towne £10' (VCH, Bucks, ii, p209).

1660-1664

Thomas Stephens, possibly the assistant teacher under Ummant, was licensed by the Bishop as master on 19th March 1660. The historian, Browne Willis, said that 'the great William Lowndes (see *Biography*) of Winslow spoke much to me in his praise .. and that he bred up several good scholars ... and that he quitted this for a greater school' (Willis, 1755, p82).

Thomas Ford, a schoolboy at the school under the Master, Mr Griffith (1665-1682), recalled that Thomas Stephens nickname was 'Whipping Tom'. 'Whipping Tom was very well remembered by the old men who had felt his rod, which none ever escaped' (Ford, 1733). Thomas Ford later became master himself (1696-1709).

1664-1665

William Warters took over the vacancy at the church of Ambrosden in 1661 as his predecessor [Edward Bagshaw] having been 'a turbulent non-conformist, was ejected'. In 1663 Warters, on 'defect of title, or other incapacity was by the authority of Bishop Skinner obliged to remove to the Cure of Buckingham' (Kennet, 1695, p675). In addition to his duties as vicar of Buckingham, Warters was appointed master of the school on 1st October 1664 (Halstead, 1734).

In March 1665, he became rector of Foxcote (Willis, MS22, p66), and presumably relinquished his post at the school to attend to his parishioners in Buckingham and Foxcote. In 1668 his son, William, matriculated from Balliol. Thus it may be inferred that William Warters junior had been educated in the school. Warters died and was buried at Foxcote on 8 May 1672 (Willis, 1755, p80).

1665-1682

Roger Griffiths, a Welshman, matriculated from Balliol in 1660 and achieved his BA in 1664 (VCH, Bucks, ii, p209) licensed on 20th February 1665 (Roundell, 1857, p34) and was elected master on 1st October 1665 (Halstead, 1735). He and his wife taught Thomas Ford (Ford,1733).

On Monday 8th June 1668, Samuel Pepys the diarist visited Buckingham. His diary states: " So to Buckingham a good old town. Here I to see the church which very good and the leads and a school in it. Did give the sexton's boy 1 shilling" (Lathan & Matthews, 1976).

Griffiths became vicar of Padbury at the same time as being master of the school. In 1669, Archbishop Sheldon questioned the clergy about non-conformists, and on July 20th 'Roger Griffyth, vicar de Padbury', confirmed that no unlawful assemblies had taken place, 'neither have I any person in my parish that refuseth to come to church at the tyme of divine service' (Broad, 1993, p37). On the same day, the previous master, William Warters at Buckingham "certifye that about twelve weekes since there were two conventicles upon two Sundayes immediately succeeding each other att an house which was formerly the signe of the Bell. I am informed that there were about twenty inconsiderable persons at each meeting. But since that tyme that they were forbidden by our Bailiffe I am confident that there have been noe such unlawful meetings" (Broad, 1993, p36). Griffiths died in post in 1682 (VCH, Bucks, ii, p209).

1682-1684

Thomas Dalby, MA was elected master on 16th January 1682 (Willis, 1755, p82). Dalby did not live in the school house, which was occupied by Mrs. Griffiths and Miss Mary Griffiths, the widow and daughter of his predecessor. Miss Mary Griffith became the famous Mrs Pix (see *Biography*) - the Poet (Ford, 1733). Apparently, Mr Dalby was an admirer of Miss Mary Griffith and was paying 'an unreasonable visit about midnight before the 24th February 1683', (Ford, 1733) 'when, from some negligence, the premises caught fire; and the young people, most likely occupied with other thoughts, did not perceive that the house was burning, till too late to estinguish the flames' (Roundell, 1857, p8). Thus the master's house was burned down.

In 1647 Buckingham was taxed in order to provide funds to alleviate the Plague. The Plague came again in 1665, and then Small-Pox in 1684. The Mayor and Aldermen of Buckingham wrote to Sir Richard Temple (see *Biography*) in London, so that he could assure the Assize Judges that the town was safe to visit. In their letter dated June 5th 1684, they wrote that only eight families were afflicted, of which "two in ye Streete where ye Judges used to lodge and but one petty Alehouse by the Free Schoole" (Elliott, 1975, p168).

In 1684, Buckingham was granted a new Charter from Charles II by which the bailiff and principal burgesses were given the new titles of mayor and aldermen (Bucks District Council, 1554-1974).

In the same year, Dalby resigned to avoid the smallpox, and became Curate of Marsh Gibbon and 'thence the zealous vicar of Wendover where he discovered his Fanatical Principles' (Ford,1733). He was afterwards Rector of Church-Lawford in Warwickshire where he died in 1728 (Willis, 1755, p82).

1685-1690

Thomas Yeomans was the son of Thomas Yeomans of Charlton in the parish of Newbottle. He matriculated in 1674 aged 17 (Longden, 1939), took his BA degree from Brasenose College, Oxford in 1678 (VCH, Bucks, ii, p209) and became a priest on the 19th September 1680 when he became vicar of Evenley (Longden, 1939). He was appointed master of the Free School at Buckingham in 1685 (VCH, Bucks, ii, p209).

Thomas Ford, a later master of the school, also a student under Yeomans, describes the destruction, in 1688, of the religious decorations and Ruding's Arms in the school by the schoolboys 'as a relic of Popery' (Ford,1733). The reason for this destruction has been attributed to 'the strong wave of Protestantism which had been aroused by James II's attack on the seven Bishops and on Magdalen College' (Verney, Bucks.Advert. & N.Bucks Free Press Oct 19, 1907). In 1688, the Charter of Mary I was reinstated and the mayor and aldermen resumed their older titles of bailiff and principal burgesses (Bucks District Council, 1554-1974).

'Yeomans (a lame man), in consequence of the decrease of the school, resigned at the request of the Corporation' (Ford, 1733). In 1690 Yeomans went on to Brackley Grammar School, one of the Magdalen College Schools (VCH, Bucks, ii, p209). In 1691 he was the Perpetual curate of Radstone as well as vicar of Evenley, and held both until his death in 1715. His will is dated 2nd August 1715, and proved on 20th October 1715 by Elizabeth his widow. He describes himself 'of Brackley, clerk' and left his lands in Evenley in trust for his wife and children. An inventory taken in October 1715 showed that he his worldly goods were worth £76-12s-0d, including £5 worth of books in his study (Longden, 1939).

1690-1691

Mark Noble took his degree from St Alban Hall in 1686 and was curate of Maid's Moreton (VCH, Bucks, ii, p209). It has been inferred that Noble filled the vacant post of master to conduct the school for a brief time until a permanent master was found, as he was never actually elected (Ford, 1733).

There is some doubt as to the date the masters house was rebuilt following its destruction in 1683. One source states it was rebuilt in 1690 by Alexander Denton Esq whose coat of arms, bearing the date 1690, could still be seen over the doorway in 1857 (Roundell, 1857, p8, p34). However Willis's observations are a hundred years earlier, and his date of 1696 is probably correct.

Unfortunately the coat of arms has now been lost. Willis also asserts that the Master's house was formerly used by the Chantry priest of St John the Baptist (Willis, 1755, p81).

1691-1696

Robert Styles was educated at Queen's College, Cambridge, obtained his BA in 1687, and his MA in 1690. He married Jane Danser of Syresham and had 9 sons and 5 daughters; his first child Dorothy was christened in Buckingham on the 1st August 1695 (Longden, 1939).

Styles was elected schoolmaster on the recommendation of Sir Richard Temple (see *Biography*) of Stowe, and his learned chaplain Mr Dell (Ford, 1733). He seems to have been an excellent teacher and is described by Ford as his worthy master (Ford, 1733). In 1696, Alexander Denton rebuilt the schoolmaster's house that had been destroyed by fire some 13 years earlier. This was at his own expense, perhaps as a reward for the success in educating his son at the school.

Styles, 'who having raised a very good school here, to the great loss of the Town quitted it for Northampton school' (VCH, Bucks, ii, p209) where he was master from 1698 to 1719 (Longden, 1939). After his retirement from Northampton he received the benefices (see *Glossary*) of Tyringham and Preston Bisset from past scholars at Buckingham by Mr Backwell in 1699 and Mr Justice Denton in 1724 respectively (Willis, 1755, p82 & Elliott, p174,1975). He died at Preston Bisset on 22nd March 1736, aged 74, and was buried five days later at Syresham, Northants (Longden, 1939).

1696-1709

Thomas Ford BA was born on 30th August 1672 (Willis, 1755, p71), the son of an Alderman of Buckingham. He was taught at the school by Roger Griffiths, married, and had a son, Thomas on 30th August 1672 (Willis, 1755, p71). From 1692 to 1699 he was a Burgess of Buckingham (Willis, 1755, p82) and on 1st September 1696 'was elected school master of the Free school in Buckingham aforesaid in the rooms and stead of Mr Robert Styles MA who voluntarily resigned the same' (Buckingham Corporation Memoranda & Register Book, 1696). It is interesting to note that as usual, this entry is signed by the Bailiffs and Burgesses, but not by Thomas, who had signed the previous entry as one of the two principal burgesses. At this time, Ford had known the previous five masters.

In 1697 the Sir Richard Temple charity was founded, which was land or money payable out of land (amounting to some £10 per annum in 1838) for the apprenticing of poor boys. In 1902 this charity was merged with the Royal Latin School.

On 7th February 1698/9 (Lipscombe, 1847, p577) the tall wooden spire of the old church of St Peter and St Paul was blown down in a gale. A subscription list was opened to rebuild the Spire to its original proportions and Sir Edmund Denton and Sir Richard Temple each gave £100; there were three other donations of about £22, and £5 from Mr Lowndes (Roundell, 1857, p44). The sums collected proved insufficient to complete the restoration, so the shattered tower was patched up (Elliott, 1975, p126).

In 1733, Ford replied to a letter from Browne Willis outlining his recollections of past schoolmasters (Willis, MS22). Without this letter, which now resides at the Bodleian, it is unlikely that the history of the previous 40 years would be known.

Ford was vicar of Buckingham in 1735 (Willis, 1755, p82) and later became Chaplain of Christ's Church, Oxford, a minor Canon of Bristol and Prebendary of Wells Cathedral (Roundell, 1857, p34). He died as Prebendary vicar of Wells and vicar of Barwell and Wokey in Somerset, on August 29th 1746 (Gentlemans Magazine, 1746, p496).

1709-1715

Samuel Foster MA, vicar of Little Horwood, became master on 17th May 1709. He resigned when he was presented to the vicarage of Swanbourne (Willis, 1755, p82). In Bishop Wake's summary of the Responses to his visitation questionnaires from Buckingham Archdeaconry 1706-1712, it was stated that a free school existed, 'the endowment whereof is £10 per annum. Mr Samuel Foster, master, above 20 scholars' (Broad, 1993, p77). This is the first indication that the school comprised a greater number of boys than the six endowed places.

1715-1723

Richard Cardwell MA of Hart Hall, Oxford, became master in 1715 aged 23 years, was ordained a priest in 1716 by the Bishop of Norwich and became vicar of Thornborough in the same year (VCH, Bucks, ii, p209 & Elliott, p175, 1975). He was not instituted at Thornborough until January 18th 1718 (Willis, 1755, p293). He resigned both posts on being made Vicar of Raundes in Northamptonshire in 1723 (Willis, 1755, p82) and died a year later. The inventory of his belongings at his death were valued at £74-3s-7d and included books valued at £6-10s and two flutes valued at 4s (Elliott, p175, 1975).

1723-1763

William Halstead MA of Brasenose College was elected as master of the Free School on 29th July 1723 by the Bailiff and Burgesses of Buckingham, and not only took Cardwell's position at the school but also the post he had vacated as vicar of Thornborough (VCH, Bucks, ii, p209).

A fire on 15th March 1724/5 destroyed almost half of Buckingham town (Harrison, 1909, p37), some 138 houses were destroyed (Elliott, 1975, p48). Two days later, on 17th March 1724/5 a representative from the London-based Sun Fire Office visited Buckingham (SFO, 11,936/19, p567, 1725), presumably to assess the damages on behalf of its policy holders, and to collect new policies. Twenty policy holders in Buckingham delivered their policies to the Insurance 'Riding Officer', including the Rev William Halstead whose policy covered damages to his 'Dwelling House, School, Brewhouse, Stable and other outhouses:'

For the Goods in the Dwelling house	£ 250
Goods in the School	£ 10
Goods in the Brewhouse	£ 30
Goods in the other Outhouses	£ 10
Total	**£ 300**

Thus William Halstead had three simultaneous occupations: Vicar,

Schoolmaster and brewer ! Beer was known to be a much safer drink than water, and brewing was a normal occupation for a vicar so that 'Marriage Ales' could be offered at weddings etc. It is not known when the brewhouse was built, nor how many schoolmasters of the Royal Latin school had taken up the pursuit. It is noteworthy that the contents of the Brewhouse were three times more valuable than the contents of the school; perhaps indicating that many of his teaching aids were kept in his own house. After this disaster, Halstead probably welcomed his additional appointment as vicar of Padbury on 5th February 1729 (Elliott, 1975, p175).

Halstead was acquainted with the antiquarian, Browne Willis and wrote to him in 1734 providing the results of his inspection of the Corporation Records regarding the history of the school, by determining the dates of appointment of previous masters (Halstead, 1734).

In 1753, Browne Willis coerced his friends to fund the restoration of the church tower of St Peter and St Paul (which had fallen in 1698). He even donated the income from his book 'The History of Buckingham' which was published in 1755 (Elliott, 1975, p126). Due to the extravagance of Browne Willis, the tower was raised another twenty-four feet (Roundell, 1857, p44).

In 1755, the Free-school was commonly known by a number of titles: St John the Baptist's Chapel; St Thomas Acon and St Thomas Becket's; and even St John the Baptist's and St Thomas Acon alias Becket (Willis, 1755, p57). It is likely that Robert Hill, the 'learned Tailor of Buckingham' was known to Halstead (see Appendix VI).[17]

Halstead died and was buried at Thornborough on 29th December 1763 (Elliott, p175, 1975).

---

17. In 1760 the Green Coat School at Buckingham was founded by Alderman Gabriel Newton (see *Biography*) for 'the clothing, schooling and educating of 25 boys of Buckingham of indigent or nececitous parents of the Established Church of England' (Charity Trustees, 1838), and was endowed with £26 per annum.

1764-1785

James Eyre entered Merton College in 1753, and gained his BA in 1757, and his MA in 1759. On the 24th February 1764, 'The Rev James Eyre, MA, by and with the assent and consent of the worshipful William Butcher, esquire, Bailiff of the borough and parish and the major part of the burgesses ... was elected and chosen a Schoolmaster of the Free School in Buckingham aforesaid in the place and stead of the Rev William Halstead deceased' (Buckingham Corporation Memoranda & Register Book, 1764). He held office for 21 years.

The new tower of the parish church of Buckingham collapsed again on the evening of 26th March 1776, because the foundations could not take the additional load (see 1698 & 1753). The church was a write-off, and all the materials and debris were sold; some eight or nine pew ends were purchased by James Eyre for use in the schoolroom (Kelke, 1858, p68). Other materials were purchased to restore the roof of the school. 'In the lapse of years, the chapel (of St John) became ... dilapidated, and, the roof falling in, the ground floor was dug up, and occupied by one of the neighbours as a garden. But in 1776, a new roof, constructed principally from the timbers of the old church, was placed upon the building by Earl Temple of Stowe' (Roundell, 1857,p8). The newly restored chapel was used for parish services from 1776 to 1780 (Sheahan, 1862,p236) whilst a new church was built at its new location on Castle Hill (Roundell, 1857,p8). As the chapel was being used for parish services, the school had to relocate to a private house. Elliott (1975, p175) states that the school did not return to the St John's chapel until 1830, 'when the boys returned with a new master, Mr Edward Brittin'. Why this delay occurred is not clear, but it may be because the chapel was used to house a Sunday School from 1781 which later merged with the National School (Sheahan, 1862, p239).[18]

---

18. It is interesting to note that the first Sunday school in Bicester was established by a Mr Eyre who from 1779 to 1797 imparted elementary religious education on Sundays (Blomfield, Bicester, p45, 1887). It may be more than co-incidence that two Sunday schools were established by men of the same name in neighbouring towns.

The old church at Buckingham (RLS Archives)

In 1784, the year before he died, the Rev James Eyre voted for the Right Honourable William W. Grenville, rather than the Right Honourable Ralph Earl Verney or John Aubrey, to be elected Knight of the shire. At this time, Eyre apparently had a residence at Padbury, as well as in Buckingham (Nicholls, 1785).

1785-1830

William Eyre (see *Biography*) was the brother of James Eyre, and entered Lincoln College in 1770, his BA in 1773, and his MA in 1776 (VCH, Bucks, ii, p210). He was Curate of Buckingham during the non-residence of the Incumbent from 1775-1796 (Roundell, 1857, p34). He was appointed on 17th August 1785 as:

> *'schoolmaster of the Free School ... in the room of his brother the Reverend James Eyre MA deceased for teaching and instructing such 6 boys, inhabitants of the said parish, in Latin, Writing and Arithmetic Gratis, as the Bailiff and Burgesses, or any two or more of them for the time being, shall for that purpose nominate and appoint' (Buckingham Corporation Memoranda & Register Book, 1785).*

In 1791, he was Vicar of Padbury, Curate of Buckingham and Master of the Free-school (Stalker, 1791, p393). At this date, there were four incorporated companies in Buckingham: the Mercers; Tanners; Butchers; and Merchant Tailors. All persons admitted to the freedom of the town had to be members of one of these corporations (Pigot, 1823). At this time, Buckingham appears to have been a thriving town, and apart from all the standard trades, its tradesmen include: brandy merchant; watch & clockmaker; collar maker; breeches maker; gilder; hemp-dresser; hair-dresser; gaoler and carpenter; excise man; carman; music-maker; mat-maker; coach-master; brick and tile maker; basket maker; chinaman and agents to the Sun Fire Office and Royal Exchange Fire Office (Stalker, 1791).

There is a detailed and contemporary description of communications in a commercial guide of Buckingham:

> *'The post office opens at 8 and shuts at 6. The mail coach till lately came through Buckingham to Banbury; but the proprietors*

found it did not answer; so that the bags are now carried to and from Stoney Stratford where the postman meets the Liverpool coach. A coach sets out from the Cobham Arms Inn every morning, except Sunday, at 8 o'clock, and arrives at the Bell and Crown, Holborn, London every evening at 6; from whence it sets out every morning at 6 and arrives at Buckingham at 4 in the afternoon. The fare is 16s. A coach from Birmingham calls at The Swan every day, except Sunday, on its way to the Saracens Head, Snow Hill, London' (Stalker, 1791).

The guide notes that there were 540 families in the town and that there were a number of schools in Buckingham apart from the 'Free school': the Rev Thomas Burkitt, Dissenting Minister was master of an academy; Thomas Bason was master of the Green Coat school; Solomon Holloway was a dancing master; and there was a Ladies Boarding school (Stalker, 1791).

The original endowment of £10-8s-0½d was a sufficient annual salary for a cleric in the 1550, but this sum was paltry in the 1800's and thus the schoolmaster had to have access to the additional income provided by being vicar of at least one church (VCH, Bucks, ii, p210). In 1816 Eyre became vicar of Hillesden.

The Posse Comitatus (Beckett, 1985) records that in 1798 the Reverend Mr Eyre was the Minister, and that there were two schoolmasters: Samuel Sheen, and J B Upleby. It is possible that Sheen may be the same that voted in the 1784 election for knights of the shire (Nicholls, 1785). Familiar Buckingham names such as Philip Box the Banker and Thomas Hearn the Attorney are also listed.

In 1818, Nicholas Carlisle did not think much of the Grammar School at Buckingham and stated that: 'It is of little note in any respect, none but the children of the Lower Classes having been educated here, for time immemorial' (Carlisle, 1818, i, p47). 'Although this statement of the status and history of the Royal Latin School is untrue, it must be admitted

The Grammar School c1815 (RLS Archives)

that the good folk of Buckingham have done their best to discredit the school and to destroy its history, by destroying or losing their municipal records' (VCH, Bucks, ii, p207). Carlisle also gave the information that the school had:

> *'six boys, as settled by the Trustees who are the Bailiff and Burgesses, and who nominate the scholars. They are admitted at eight years of age, and are taught English, writing and arithmetic. The present master is the Reverend William Eyre, MA Vicar of Padbury and Hillesden in the county of Buckingham'.*

On the decease of the Rev William Eyre on 18th May 1830 (Charity Commissioners, 1819-1837 p345-7), a sum upwards of £70 was provided for the repair of the chapel (Harrison, 1909, p60). William's son, also called William Eyre (see *Biography*) was resident in Butchers market in 1830 and Vicar of Padbury in 1842 (Pigot, 1830 & 1842). There was considerable public concern at this time that if William could succeed his father as Vicar of Padbury then he might also claim mastership of the school and make it 'a hereditary possession'.

1830-1855

Edward Brittin was baptised in February 1790 at Leckhampstead (Census, 1851), and little is known of his early career, nor his qualifications. However, in 1823, seven years prior to his appointment of master at the school, Brittin was already teaching in Buckingham, and is listed in a Directory under 'Academies' as: 'Britton Edward, Castle St.' (Pigot, 1823-24). As William Eyre is not listed in 1823-24, it is possible that Eyre had been failing, and that Britton was already teaching at the school. Eight years later, after he was officially appointed, he is still in Castle Street (Pigot, 1831-32), and by 1842 he had returned to Butcher's Row (Pigot, 1942).

Aged 40, he became the first master of the Royal Latin School who was not in Holy Orders. On March 25th 1830, an agreement in the form of an indenture combining his appointment with a lease for the dwelling house, was made between him and the Corporation (the Bailiff and the twelve Burgesses). Brittin agreed to keep the premises in good repair at his own expense and to teach a maximum of six boys (inhabitants of Buckingham) between the ages of eight and fourteen, chosen by the Bailiff and Burgesses, Latin, English, Reading, Writing and Arithmetic, and to provide at his own expense: paper, pens, ink, inkstands, slates, pencils, etc, in return for the annual stipend of £10-8s-0¾d paid by the Exchequer and the free use of the house and school. It is interesting to note that the indenture appoints Brittin to the imaginative 'Office of the Master of the Free school, formerly called Archdeacon Stratton's, Dame Denton's, & King Edward the Sixth Free school'. After 1836 Brittin was compelled to take insurance cover for the school for £300 (Charity Commissioners, 1819-1837, p345-347). In 1849 it is recorded that Brittin paid his rent of one peppercorn for the schoolhouse and premises (Charity Trustees, 1849-1851).

As early as 1809 there had been criticism of the education in grammar schools, particularly of the curriculum which favoured Greek and Latin, but excluded such subjects as English, writing, accounts, history, modern languages, geography, science, and mathematics. The ethos and culture embodied by extreme discipline and bullying were also criticised (Curtis, 1968, p140), as were the misuse of (wealthy) educational charities. The arguments became political, and in 1818 a Royal Commission was set up to investigate education (Curtis & Boultwood, 1970, p54). Educational reforms were set in motion with the Factory Act of 1833, which stipulated that: children under 13 who worked in factories had to receive two hours compulsory education every day (Douglas, 1956, p831). The Act also specified that children under the age of 9 years should not work in textile mills; those aged 9 to 13 were restricted to working a 48 hour week (no night shifts); those aged 13 to 18 were restricted to a 69 hour week (Kohn, 1991).

The Select Committee on Charities to inquire into Endowed schools was set up in 1835 (Douglas, 1956, p850). It appears that this may have initiated a change in the management of the Royal Latin school. From the Reformation to 1836, the school had been supervised by the Bailiff and Burgesses of the 'Old Corporation'; however under an Act of the High Court of Chancery dated 1835, charitable estates and funds had to be managed by trustees appointed by the Lord High Chancellor, commencing on 1st August 1836. The Latin or Free school and a number of other charities were amalgamated under the Buckingham General Charities, which were managed by 15 trustees comprising the local curate, the Rev Thomas Sylvester, a clerk, and 13 tradesmen of the town (Charity Trustees, 1838). From 1836, the trustees selected and appointed headteachers to the school, and the bailiff and burgesses temporarily continued to select the six foundationers. Brittin was allowed to increase pupil numbers up to a maximum of 94, excluding the six foundationers, thus a maximum of 100 pupils, although there were only 36 boys in 1833 (Charity Commission 1835).

He was not allowed to request any extra payments, for whatever reason from the parents of the six foundationers, but he was given absolute discretion to charge whatever he liked for the other pupils. The boys could be no younger than 8 years old, and no older than 14 years. The leasehold property comprised the master's dwelling house, the school room (the former chantry), outbuildings, a garden and yard, for which he paid a peppercorn rent. The Bailiff reserved the right to inspect the school on a monthly basis to 'examine the proficiency and to inquire into any irregularities, misconduct or neglect of the master or in the conduct of the six foundationers' (Charity Commissioners, p345-347, 1819-1837). Remarkably, this has overtones of the current (1999) Ofsted inspections which attempts to determine the quality of 'teaching and learning'.

In order for boys to be elected for admission to the Royal Latin School, they had to live in Buckingham and they had to be the sons of tradesmen. If either of these conditions were broken, the boy was removed from the school, as he had 'become ineligible to continue a scholar' (Charity Trustees, 1853 & 1857). This had probably been the 'rule' since 1553, if not before. In 1839 the trustees initiated new rules including:

> *'no boy be allowed to absent himself from the school, without a good and sufficient reason being given to the master and that every boy be required to attend school well clothed and clean. Also that the master keep a register of the daily attendance of the Boys and submit the same to the trustees at the Quarterly meeting' (Charity Trustees, 1838). School holidays were 4 weeks at Midsummer and 4 weeks at Christmas.*

In 1845, Edward Brittin reported to the trustees that the owner of the neighbouring property, Mr Town, had encroached upon school property by building an oven on it. This oven became a running battle for at least the next ten years (Charity Trustees, 1838). Mr Town was a confectioner, biscuit baker and dealer in British wines at Butchers market (Musson & Craven,

The Old Grammar School at Buckingham

1853), so no doubt the oven in question baked biscuits. The smell of biscuits and sweets must have been torture for the schoolboys.

In the period that Brittin was in post, there are an abundant number of references to the school, particularly in newspapers and trade directories. It is apparent that the school had no single title, indeed, during this period it was referred to as: the 'Free School', the 'Latin School', the 'Free Grammar', 'St John's Chapel' and 'formerly called Archdeacon Strattons, Dame Dentons, & King Edward the Sixth Free school'. In Kellys Directory (1847) Brittin is at 'Butcher's Row' (Kelly, 1847), and in the 1850 edition as 'master of the Grammar school'. Another commercial directory lists him as an 'endowed schoolmaster of the Free Grammar School, Butchers Market' with 30 scholars (Musson et al, 1853). In 1853, there were nine schools listed in Buckingham.

The 1851 census shows that Edward Britten was married to Sarah, and their son, Manasseh, aged 20, was an assistant schoolmaster. The same census also shows that a Mr Edward Eyre, aged 56, lodged with them, and received an annuity; presumably he was a relative of the former schoolmasters, William or James Eyre. Their household enjoyed an unusual visitor on the 30th March 1851, from the daughter of a Missionary, Eliza Darling who had been born in Tahiti.

Brittin died on 25th March 1855 (Laugharne Indenture, 1855). The trustees advertised the vacancy and shortlisted ten applicants. In May, the Rev H.Roundell offered a £40 Curacy per annum to any clergyman that was appointed to the post, and accordingly the shortlist was reduced to the nine clergymen (Charity Trustees, 1855). In June, the trustees inspected the school house and decided that repairs were necessary (Harrison, 1909, p61). They also considered that Mr Town's oven was too close to the house and was potentially hazardous (Charity Trustees, 1855).

In September 1855, an article was published in the Buckingham Advertiser entitled 'So much for Buckingham' written by Brother Reverend TA Buckley. He describes the:

> *'ruin of St John's Chapel, the east end or chancel of which abuts upon West Street, close to the shambles (once a wool-hall, in the days of Buckingham's wool prosperity). The door of this venerable chapel is a beautiful specimen of early Saxon architecture; and the beautiful walls, despite many a layer of obtrusive whitewash, tell a melancholy tale of ages when prayer was heard within them; and when churches were not converted into wood cellars. For, sad it is to say so, but such is the fate of the lower portion of St John's chapel. The altar has disappeared, a blacking-bottle occupies the ancient piscina (see* Glossary*), and faggots and logs, with a half-staved tub and an old rusty spade, now people the church. A modern flooring divides the chapel midway, the upper part being used as the schoolroom. The schoolroom contains some handsome old oak filials,*

belonging to the seats of the ancient chapel, but which the Gothic taste for painting everything has ruthlessly daubed a dirty green. The slender income of the master, and the lamentable dilapidation of the whole place, made us think nervously of commissions of enquiry which, unhappily, seem to form a necessary part of the history of every cathedral collegiate (see Glossary*) establishment in this country' (Bucks Advert & Winslow & Brackley Record, Sep 22-29 1855).*

1855-1858

Thomas Robert John Laugharne gained his BA at Jesus College Oxford in 1843, and his MA in 1845. He became domestic Chaplain to the Earl of Pomfret and later Curate of Buckingham, of Aston Turville, of St John's in

St John's Chapel c1855 (RLS Archives)

Gloucester, of Whitnash in Warwickshire, and was elected master on 31st July 1855 by Trustees (Roundell 1857,p34), apparently on the same terms as Edward Brittin (Laugharne Indenture, 1855). He accepted the post on condition that the oven encroachment was removed and that certain repairs would be made to the school (Charity Trustees 1855).

The school was closed from March 1855 and reopened on Monday 8th October, for the start of the Autumn term. Just three days before the start of term the charity trustees received 13 applications from parents of prospective pupils and the six foundation places were filled by election. In late September, Laugharne had not yet moved to his new post and was resident at Whitnash Glebe, Leamington (Bucks.Advert, Sep 29, 1855).

At Spring term 1856, which commenced at noon on 26th January the fees were: 2 Guineas per Quarter; a reduced rate of 1½ Guineas for brothers; and a limited number of boys had the option of not learning Latin were charged the reduced rate of 1½ Guineas per Quarter. Mrs Roberts of Castle Hill advertised that with the permission of the Headmaster, she was prepared to receive, as Boarders, a limited number of boys for which she charged £5 per Quarter for Board and Lodging. On March 1st, the Headmaster himself also offered accommodation at his own house, commencing at Easter at the rate of £30 per annum (Bucks Advert, Dec/Jan 1855/6).

ST. JOHN'S LATIN SCHOOL,
BUCKINGHAM.

Head Master.—The Rev. T. R. J. LAUGHARNE, M.A.

THE next Quarter will commence on Monday, 21st January. School will open at Two o'clock, p.m.

Terms.—Two Guineas per Quarter. Brothers, One Guinea-and-a-half each.

Also, a limited number of Boys, whose Parents may not wish them to learn Latin, will be received at 1½ Guineas per Quarter.

11th Jan., 1856.

The Examiner for the foundationers of St John's Latin School was the Rev Roundell, who expressed himself 'much gratified by the answers and demeanour of the boys'. The Headmaster announced that 'the chief annual examination would henceforth be at Mid Summer, and that the first prize for industry and good conduct given to a boy not on the foundation, would carry with it the additional privilege that his schooling for the last Quarter preceding should be entirely free of cost' (Bucks Advert, Dec/Jan 1855/6). On 24th June 1856, St John the Baptist's Day, the annual midsummer examinations were held. The progress of the elder pupils at St John's School in Latin and mental arithmetic was notable. Boarders were wanting, even though accommodation was available, and a resident matron in place. Laugharne expressed his admiration for the pupils that had been taught at the Middle School at Gawcott (Bucks.Advert. June 28, 1856).

In 1857, the Trustees appealed for subscriptions to put the buildings in repair and a circular was issued (Harrison,1909, p60). In February, the proceeds of two Lectures were given in aid of the Repair Fund. The first lecture, at the schoolroom of St John's Royal Latin School was given by the Headmaster on the subject of 'Monumental Brasses'. The subject of the second lecture was a 'Memoir of Browne Willis, the Historian of Buckingham' (Bucks. Advert. Feb 28, 1857). In July, The Rev Roundell announced that the trustees of the Buckingham Charities had requested the London Board of Charity Commissioners to launch an investigation into the state of the charities, perhaps to raise more funding for the school repairs (Bucks.Advert. July 4, 1857). Later in the year, the school was restored by locally raised subscriptions amounting to £60; the floor dividing the school-room into 'upper and lower compartments' was removed so that the roof timbers were visible and the doorway was restored and a window unblocked (probably sealed during Ruding's renovations) (Roundell, 1857,p32). The increased ventilation obviously reduced the heat in the building to a more bearable level (Bucks Advert, June 27, 1857). Rev Roundell, Vicar of Buckingham, gave a lecture in January 1856 to the Buckingham Literary and Scientific Institution to raise funds: 'you have replaced the ancient Latin School upon a basis more worthy of its Royal Founder' (Roundell, 1857, p32).

In October 1858, Laugharne resigned, to become vicar of Calverton 1858-1866, and of Burton-in-Wirral, near Chester in 1866 (Crockford, 1854 & 1870), and in 1870 he moved to Laugharne in Carmarthenshire (Elliott, 1975, p178).

1858-1861

In November 1858, only one application for the mastership was received, and in April 1859 it was decided to readvertise. It is not known whether a temporary master was put in charge, but the master's premises were not required. The garden and premises were put into the care of the trustees clerk. It seems no progress was made in finding a suitable master, and the school master's house remained empty until Richard Chandler made an application to rent the house. He paid the rent of £1-10s-0d per calendar month with 'one month's notice to quit or of quitting'.

It would appear the trustees decided to poach the head from the Buckingham National Society school. So in June 1861, they placed an advert in the National Society's Monthly Register and within a month made their new appointment.

1861-1869

Thomas Owain Jones, the former certificated master of the Buckingham National School was the new head of the Latin school in July 1861. Jones had no degree. In September the school advertised vacancies for six pupils, and there were 17 applicants.

In February 1862, a Mr Archer was commissioned to make a pair of gates for the school for the sum of £7-10s. Jones was also paid £4-15s-3d by cheque for half his year's salary (£9-10s-6d), equivalent to the standard endowment less deductions (Charity Trustees, 1862).

In 1863, the school was described as the 'Free Grammar school, now known as St John's Royal Latin School', which has 'extensive grounds attached' and makes it a 'very desirable residence for scholars, who are prepared principally for commercial pursuits'. Mr Town was still running his confectionery business next door (Dutton, 1863).

In 1867 the Latin Grammar School received £10-8s-0d annually for the purposes of Education, paid by the Commissioners of Woods and Forests (Charity Commission, 1867). There were 28 boys in all, two of whom were boarders. The non-foundationers paid £4-4s. a year, and all were professedly learning Latin, but in fact only received the necessary English education. The average age of the oldest boys was only 12½ (VCH, Bucks, ii, p210).

In 1869, Henry Coates the butcher took Tom Owain Jones to Buckingham County Court for failure to pay £21-14s-8d for meat. Mr Small, solicitor, appeared for the plaintiff and applied for immediate payment with costs, which was granted (Bucks Advertiser, Jan 23, 1869). Mr Jones tendered his resignation in the same week, and the trustees advertised the vacancy (Charity Trustees, 1869). Early in March 1869 it was reported to the trustees that there had been 32 applications for the mastership. The Rev L.Borissow of Buckingham and Mr Cockram from Gawcott were short-listed (Charity Trustees, 1869).

1869-1871

Louis Borissow was a scholar of St Catherine's College, Cambridge, and gained his BA in 1865, and his MA in 1869. He was curate of Wheathampstead 1866-68. In 1868 he was curate of Buckingham and was closely involved with the National schools where he helped to run a Christmas party for the children in the Town Hall where three Christmas trees were 'decorated with pretty toys, neck-ties and sweetmeats' (Bucks Advert. Jan 23, 1869). He was elected as master of the Royal Latin School on 11th March 1869 (Charity Trustees, 1869).

It also became apparent to the trustees that the school again needed major repairs, and in March 1869 an application for any 'surplus funds not exceeding £200' was made by the trustees to the Charity Commissioners for 'the upkeep of the Royal Latin School ... the only fixed income being a sum of £10-8s-0¾d ... paid out of the Exchequer, the school and residence attached now being in a dilapidated state'. In May 1869, a public appeal was launched to raise £100 towards the repairs, and a proposal to use £200 of surplus funds from the Robert Higgins, Katherine Agar & Dorothy Dayrell's charities (Bucks Advert. Aug 7, 1869). A public protest objecting to the transfer of funds from other charities was launched and a petition was sent to the Charity Commissioners. After much discussions and debate, the Charity Commissioners approved the £200 expenditure. In March of the next year, Borissow was allowed to rent a house for £25 per year, presumably until the repairs, quoted at £296-0s-0d, had been completed.

Life was tough for children at this time, as many children as young as 13 were expected to go to work. In September 1869, a Buckingham youth aged 13 was sentenced to 14 days imprisonment with hard labour for stealing a key and 30 shillings in money from his employer, to be followed by 4 years in a Reformatory school (Bucks Advert. Sep 11, 1869).

The Endowed Schools Act of 1869 forced Grammar schools to broaden their curricula from Latin, English and the three R's, and this seems to be reflected in the advertisement extolling Borissow's curriculum of: 'English and Latin languages, Mathematics, History, Geography, Writing and Book-keeping and the other details of a sound practical education'. The school fees were 6 guineas per annum (Bucks Advert Sep 11, 1869). He is listed in a trade directory as headmaster in 1871 (Mercer & Crocker, 1871). There were some 27 boys at the school (Charity Trustees, 1872). The Education Act of 1870 which was intended to set up new elementary board schools, had little or no effect on the Latin school.

Borissow had more than a passing interest in music and singing, and founded the Buckingham Amateur Musical Society [which became the Buckingham and & District Music Society, and today is called the Buckingham Choral Society] (Grimsdale, 1999). On 9th February 1871, just two years after he was appointed, he resigned stating that 'in consequence of my having been this day appointed to the Precentorship (see *Glossary*) of Trinity College in the University of Cambridge, I herewith beg to tender my resignation of the Mastership of the Royal Latin School'. His resignation was received 'with much regret that the school and town should lose his excellent and efficient services as a master' (Charity Trustees, 1871). His new post of Precentor (Director of Singing and Music) obviously reflected his passion for music.

George Watson French was a pupil who thought so much of Borissow, that he paid him a very fine tribute some 60 years later in December 1939 on the occasion of receiving his Freedom of Buckingham: 'Louis Borissow ... had most to do with the formation of my character and in encouraging me to take a wider view of life' (RLSM, Dec 1939, p162).

Within a week of Borissow's resignation, the trustees had received two applications for his post, including one from Thomas Cockram of Guildford House school in Gawcott. Guildford House offered pupils English composition, Book-keeping, Arithmetic, Penmanship and practical Land-surveying to all pupils, and Latin, French and Instrumental Music on request (Bucks. Advert. June 18, 1864).

1871-1891

Thomas Cockram was born in Great Marlow in 1842 (Census, 1881) and was a graduate of the University of London (Crockford 1882 & 1891). He became Principal of Guildford House Middle School in Gawcott c1864, which prepared some 25 children for the University Local Examination (Bucks Advertiser, Jun 18 1864, Jan 2, & Jun 26, 1869). On 23rd February 1871, aged 29, he was, at his second attempt (see 1869) formally elected as master of St John's Royal Latin School. Cockram studied for the Church during his time at the school and was Deacon at the Trinity Ordination, Cuddesdon in 1881; licensed curate of Adstock in 1881; admitted to Priest Orders, Trinity in 1883; BA Honours in 1882, and MA in 1885.

In March 1871, Cockram met the trustees and suggested modifications to the school buildings, including a boarding house, that he wished to make at his own expense. The alterations and additions were substantial, said to be about £600, and necessitated the temporary removal of the school to Gawcott until the end of the midsummer holidays (Charity Trustees, 1871). He is also credited with paying more than the whole endowments £10 a year, 'for the removal of a nuisance close to the school' (VCH, Bucks, ii, p210) which was presumably the neighbours oven that had been built 26 years before.

By August 1871 the building work was complete and in September the trustees took out an insurance policy for loss or damage by risk fire. The policy describes the school house, and the dwelling and boarding houses which were connected by a covered passage. The school had a heating system comprising a stove and underfloor cast iron pipes; the floor was 'of wood worked in small pieces laid on concrete' (Charity Trustees, 1872). The stove was located in a cellar which was accessed by lifting an iron grating in the floor and descending an iron ladder. On occasion, unpopular boys were temporarily imprisoned under the grating whilst the master was absent (RLSM, 1931-1932, p98). The school and master's house were valued at £500, and the new boarding house at £500; the premium was £1. The trustees at this time were the Rev William Foxley Norris, Rev Joseph Dunne, Samuel Mail Allen, George Nelson, Richard Chandler, Edward Parrott, Richard Warr. Two of the trustees, Allen (a draper) and Chandler (a stationer) had been trustees since the initial foundation of the Charities commission in 1836, 35 years previously. The number of boys at the school doubled to 54 within six months (Charity Trustees, 1872).

Within eight months of reopening the newly refurbished and extended school, the number of boys had risen to 65, of which 25 were boarders.

The RLS at Gawcott? c1871

The RLS in 1874, donated by T. Holton a pupil between 1871-1877

The RLS c1885 including a pupil from Siam

The RLS c1887

RLS Archives

The school comprised four classes, and Cockram was assisted by three resident masters, all working in the one schoolroom. In April 1872, Cockram requested help for extending the buildings by acquiring extra land and an appeal was made to the Endowed School Commissioners, but in the absence of local support, nothing could be done (Charity Trustees, 1872). Cockram had an average of 60 pupils during his mastership, (Bucks. Advert.& N.Bucks Free Press, Oct 19, 1907).

By 1876, Cockram had been unsuccessful in getting help, even for 'pointing and whitening the building, and for varnish for the windows'. So in October he wrote again to the trustees, saying that 'Sir Gilbert Scott R.A. had very kindly given new designs for the renovation of the Royal Latin Schoolroom, and that he would attempt to raise £70 for their implementation. The trustees gave their approval (Charity Trustees, 1838). A new stone bell-cot was erected, the large window in the south-eastern gable filled with suitable mullions and tracery, and two new windows inserted in the south wall. The cost was defrayed by a grant from the Trustees of £30, public subscriptions amounting to £140, and a sum of £30 which were the proceeds of concerts and entertainment given by the masters and pupils (Kelly, 1920, pp55). By 1879, the schoolroom had been restored and the bell re-cast (Harrison, 1909, p62).

An Act of 1876 stipulated that children under 10 should not be employed; and that children aged 10 to 14 should attend fifty percent of classes at a school, unless their parents applied for exemption. Later, the Education Act of 1880 stipulated that all children should receive compulsory education until 10 years of age. At about this time a motto hung in the school 'Remember what you read, and with all thy getting get understanding' (RLSM, 1934, p354).

In 1881, the Ordnance Survey produced a very detailed map of Buckingham town. 'St John's Chapel Grammar school' is clearly shown with extensive buildings and grounds. Formal gardens screened the school from the playground and its swings, and behind the playground was the croquet ground. In the same year the Census refers to the school

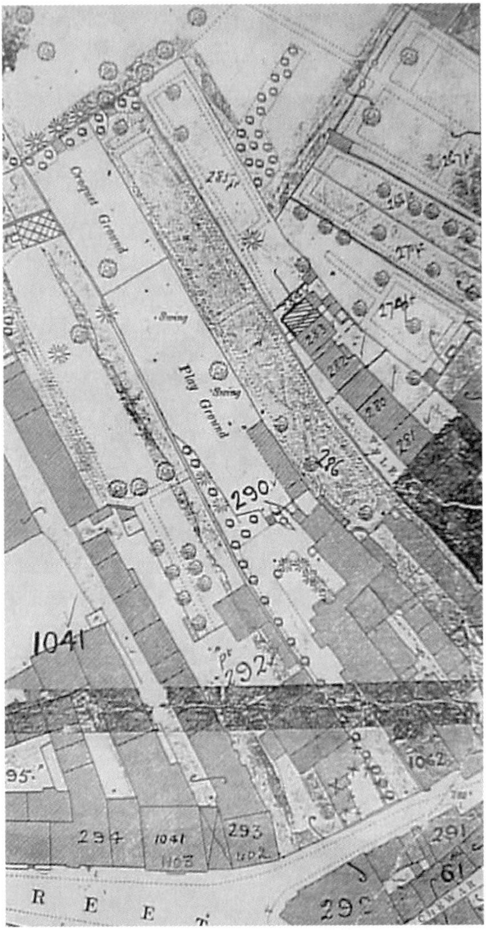

Reproduced with kind permission of Ordnance Survey; surveyed 1879, published 1881

as 'St John's Royal Latin School' where Cockram then aged 39, was married to Anne, employed two teachers, and housed 12 boarders and two domestic servants (Census, 1881). Academic mortar boards were part of school uniform at this time, but fifteen years later were only worn on formal occasions (RLSM, 1932, p48 & 97).

In 1884 the annual payment of £10-8s-0½d which commenced in 1548, some 336 years before, was capitalised into a lump sum of £317-10s with three percent annuities being paid to the Buckingham General charities in trust for the school. This had no effect on the running of the school: the head-master in consideration of the endowment had to educate six boys free of cost; their curriculum was much broader than advertised; fees were charged by the head-master for boys not on the Foundation (Bucks.Advert & N.Bucks Free Press, Oct 19, 1907).

In 1885 Cockram wrote a letter, from his position as master of the Royal Latin school, to the Buckingham Express, in which he correctly and concisely concluded an argument as to the derivation of the name 'Chewar', - an alley in front of the school (Harrison, 1909, p85).

In 1887 there was space for some 65 boys with an average attendance of 63 (Kellys, 1887). The remains of one writing lesson from 1888 still survives. A letter from John Egerton Thorpe, a pupil at the school, obviously drafted under strict supervision, states:

> *'My Dear Parents, I am pleased to tell you that the Christmas Holidays commence on Wednesday the 19th inst. The Term Examinations will begin on Monday next and I hope that my results therein may commend themselves to you, Your dutiful son'.*

In 1890, prizes were awarded for: Mathematics, Arithmetic and Book-

The RLS c1891, with pupils, teachers, vicars and trustees. Probably of Thomas Cockram's retirement with a clock and silver teapot

keeping, Latin, French, German, English grammar and elocution, Geography, English, History, Natural Philosophy, Physiography, Hygiene, Agriculture, English composition, Art, Music, Shorthand and Swimming (RLS Archives).

In 1890, the approach to the school was greatly improved (Kellys, 1895) and in the same year, Cockram became Rector of Adstock, his patron being P Hart Esq., at which time he relinquished his post at the school. In 1891 his gross annual income from 290 acres of glebe (see *Glossary*) was £320, netting £187 and the house. In 1895 the net income had risen to £263 (Crockford, 1891 & 1895).

1891-1895

Robert C. MacCulloch BA was appointed headmaster (Harrison, 1909, p62). He had three assistant masters in 1892 (Elliott, 1975, p179) and died in 1895 (Harrison, 1909, p62).

1895-1896

Thomas Cockram was recalled for a year, as a temporary arrangement to keep the school open (Harrison, 1909, p62) and he was assisted by the Rev J Chevallier, Rector of Great Horwood and Mr Edwin Stowe of Brasenose College, Oxford. In 1901, Stowe presented the school with an engraving of Edward VI (Buck.Advert.& N.Bucks Free Press, Oct 19, 1907).

At about this date, WH Smith the stationers produced a 'Borough Guide to Buckingham', which states:

> *'The Royal Latin school on Market Hill (formerly the Grammar school). A sound business training is given nowadays to day-boys and boarders; increased accommodation having been provided within recent years. The Norman doorway and fine carved seats are very beautiful. The buildings were restored in 1875 from designs by Sir Gilbert Scott and the approach to the school was greatly improved in 1890'.*

1896-1908

Walter Matthew Cox, educated at St John's College, Hurstpierpoint, and BA (1903) and MA (1906) of Trinity College, Dublin, with experience of teaching in Vaud, Switzerland and in Scotland, was appointed master in Easter 1896. He had been teaching at Bletchley School and was 26 years old (RLS, Staff Register).

At the time of his appointment there were 11 scholars including 5 foundationers. He brought some 30 boarders with him, and day scholars and boarders increased steadily to 75-80 boys, which made it necessary to hire additional rooms contiguous to the school buildings for use as classrooms. Within a few years of his appointment, HM Inspectors pointed out to the trustees that the old buildings were totally inadequate and unsuitable for modern educational requirements, and considerable pressure was put upon them to provide better accommodation.

In 1898 there was a large influx of boys (RLSM, 1931-1932, p53-54 & Kellys, 1899). A prefect system was in force at this time, and they were responsible for much of the discipline and customs in the school; one of their annual perks was the Prefects' Supper with the Head and his wife (RLSM 1931-1932, p98). In 1899, Cox presented 'one of the most successful years which the Royal Latin School ... can boast of' (Bucks. Advert. & N.Bucks Free Press, July 29th 1899) where 40 out of 48 candidates had passed the external examinations of the College of Preceptors. The total number of boys at the school was approximately 70 pupils. The school advertised that it offered 'Practical Commercial training, including modern languages, shorthand, typewriting and book-keeping' (Bucks Advert. Jan 7, 1899). Presumably the large number of boys made it necessary to lay a new concrete floor in 1902 (Harrison, 1909, p104).

The Education Act 1902

The Education Act of 1902 reorganised British education by replacing the existing school boards with Local Education Authorities (LEA). The LEA became responsible for administering elementary and secondary education and for providing grant-aid to endowed grammar schools. Buckinghamshire

County Council made an agreement with the Charity Trustees to transfer the School to a new site (Harrison, 1909, p442).

A bold and comprehensive Scheme was drawn up by the Board of Education on 4th July 1904, annexing three charities to a new governing body of the Royal Latin School (BRO AR40/69). The charities were all largely of an educational nature: the Alderman Newton funds (formerly payable to the Green Coat School); the Sir Richard Temple annuity (for apprenticing); and the John Hart rentcharge (for apprenticing). The Schedule of Property gives their combined assets as:

	£ s d	Responsible persons	Yearly Income £ s d
The Latin School			
New Consols	£317 10 0	Official Trustees	£7 18 8
The Green Coat School			
New Consols		Leicester Charity Trustees	£26 0 0
Cash in Bank	£171 17 0	Trustees of Newton's Charity	£0 0 0
Sir Richard Temple's charity for apprenticing			
Annuity issuing out of 'The Old Wharf' Buckingham.	£112 16 8	James Wilson Thorpe	£10 0 0
John Hart's charity for apprenticing			
Rent charge issuing out of Easington, Oxfordshire	£0 0 0	John W. Greenwood (owner)	£9 0 0

The Latin School 'trust fund' of £317-10s-0d invested in consols (see *Glossary*), derived from the pension / endowment of £10-8s-0½d first paid in 1548, formed the largest contribution to the new scheme.

The new Governing Body comprised 18 people, of which:

4 came from the Trustees of the General Charities,

4 came from Buckingham County Council

4 came from Buckingham Town Council

3 came from Buckingham Rural District Council

1 came from the Hebdominal Council of Oxford University

2 came from Cooptative Governors.

The scheme defined the authority of the new Governors, and the Head, and sanctioned the assignment of all property from the Charity Commissioners to be held by the Official Trustee of Charity Lands in trust for the Royal Latin School. The school had to be 'a Public Secondary school for Boys and Girls' and have 'not less than 100 scholars'. The minimum age of admission was set at 8, and children usually had to leave at the closest end of term to their seventeenth birthday.

The scheme also addressed financial matters: annual tuition fees were set at a minimum of £6 and a maximum of £10; the annual fee for boarding accommodation was set at a maximum of £50; the Head's salary was reviewed, for the first time since 1538 and set at 'not less than £100'. The Head Master was not allowed to 'hold any benefice having the cure of souls, nor during a school term perform any ecclesiastical duty outside the School'. The principle of foundation scholarships was continued, reflecting the history of the school and the Newton (see *Biography*) endowment.[19]

The broad curriculum had to provide:

- Religious Instruction,
- Reading, Writing and Arithmetic,
- English Grammar, Composition and Literature,
- Mathematics,
- Latin,

- One Modern Foreign European Language
- Natural Science with experimental teaching (including agriculture & local trades)
- Drawing,
- Vocal Music,
- Drill or other physical exercises.

And for girls:

- Domestic Economy,
- Needlework,
- Laws of Health.

On the 20th September 1904, the Governors assembled for their first meeting: the Minutes show that The Baroness Kinloss (see *Biography*), Lady Verney, the Hon. Cecil Hubbard, Mr Rogers, Reverend AEJ Newman, Messrs J Cheesman (see *Biography*), G Harrison, GW French, FW Denchfield, J Osborne, EH Lawrence, J Hawes, IJ Oxley, J Harper, H Small (Clerk to the Charity Trustees), & CG Watkins (Education Secretary for Buckinghamshire) were present. Dr Cheesman was elected as Chairman of Governors. Ten days later they met again to discuss the costs of building and equipping the new school and appointed Finance and Site Committees. The plans became more complex as the school would teach girls as well as boys, would have a small boarding facility, and would also train pupil teachers on 2 or 3 year contracts. Two weeks later, two acres of a green field site adjoining Chandos Road had been measured (Harrison, 1909, p104) and an agreement made to purchase it from Baroness Kinloss. An advertisement was placed, inviting architects to submit competitive designs. By early January 1905, some 46 sets of designs had been received, which were

---

19. It is poignant to note that on the final page of the Scheme is printed the name of the Administrative Examiner of the Board of Education, Mr AF Leach - an authority on the history of grammar schools whose publications have been used extensively in this book.

The RLS at Chandos Road

(RLS Archives)

Royal Latin School, Buckingham

THE GOVERNORS invite applications from Firms of Contractors desirous of tendering for the ERECTION of the NEW ROYAL LATIN SCHOOL, proposed to be erected at Buckingham, in accordance with Plans prepared by and under the superintendence of the Architect, Mr. W. G. Wilson, F.R.I.B.A., 5, Bloomsbury Mansions, Hart Street, London.

A charge of £1 1s. will be made for each set of quantities issued to applicants, which will be returned on receipt of a bonâ-fide tender.

The firm whose tender is successful will, if the work be proceeded with, be required to enter into a Contract and Bond with two approved sureties for the due performance of such Contract.

The Governors do not bind themselves to accept the lowest or any tender for the work.

Plans and Specifications can be seen at the Office of the Architect, or at the Town Hall, Buckingham.

Applications, endorsed "Royal Latin School," to be addressed to the undersigned, and made on or before the 1st day of July, 1905. Sealed Tenders similarly endorsed and addressed to be delivered on or before the 1st August, 1905.

HENRY SMALL,
Clerk to the Governors,
Town Hall,
Buckingham.

shortlisted by HW Wills - an assessor nominated by the President of the Royal Society of British Architects. The new Governors worked tirelessly to build and fund the new school.[20]

In June 1905 advertisements were placed in the local press for tenders to build the new school, which were assessed by WG Wilson FRIBA of 5 Bloomsbury Mansions, Hart Street, London. In August 1905, tenders had been received for the erection of the building. It then became apparent that more funds were needed to finance the building of the

[20] Dr Cheesman (Physician) and H Small (Coroner) were both veteran governors of schools; in December 1877, they both tied in third place with 450 votes in the School Board Elections; lots were drawn, and Cheesman was elected (Harrison, 1909, p100). As school boards were 'dissolved' by the Education Act, Cheesman (who had been linked with the Alderman Newton endowment) and Small obviously felt compelled to offer their services to the new educational system.

The school on Chandos Road, now the Grenville Combined School

new school, and the sale of the Headmaster's house was put on the agenda.

The new building was brick-built 'in late Jacobean style' (VCH, Bucks, ii, p210) by Messrs G Tombs and Sons of Buckingham, and was fitted with electric lighting, central heating and separate main entrances for boys and girls (Bucks.Advert & N.Bucks Free Press, Oct 19, 1907). It comprised a central hall, class rooms, lecture rooms, woodwork, cookery, laundry and first-aid rooms and laboratory (Kellys, 1920, p55). In 1907, the Royal Latin School (RLS) wrought iron gates 'with wings' were commissioned at a cost of £72-0s-0d.

The new school was advertised as: 'a secondary school for boys and girls, qualified to receive grants from the Board of Education and from the Bucks County Education Committee'. The tuition fees were set at £6-6s-0d per annum. The aims of the school were: 'to provide, on moderate terms, a

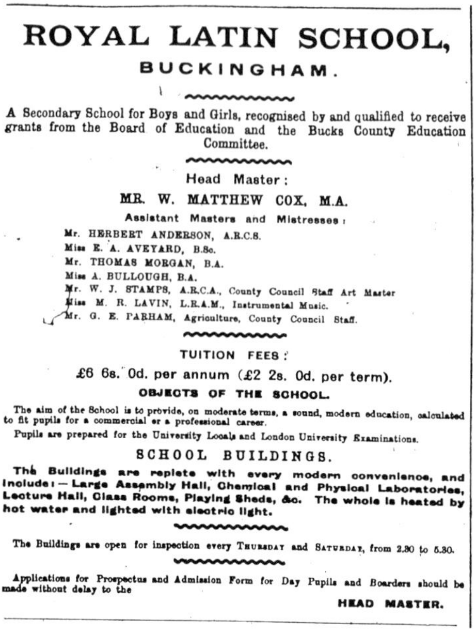

ROYAL LATIN SCHOOL,

BUCKINGHAM.

A Secondary School for Boys and Girls, recognised by and qualified to receive grants from the Board of Education and the Bucks County Education Committee.

Head Master:

MR. W. MATTHEW COX, M.A.

Assistant Masters and Mistresses:

Mr. HERBERT ANDERSON, A.R.C.S.
Miss E. A. AVEYARD, B.Sc.
Mr. THOMAS MORGAN, B.A.
Miss A. BULLOUGH, B.A.
Mr. W. J. STAMPS, A.R.C.A., County Council Staff Art Master
Miss M. R. LAVIN, L.R.A.M., Instrumental Music.
Mr. G. E. PARHAM, Agriculture, County Council Staff.

TUITION FEES:

£6 6s. 0d. per annum (£2 2s. 0d. per term).

OBJECTS OF THE SCHOOL.

The aim of the School is to provide, on moderate terms, a sound, modern education, calculated to fit pupils for a commercial or a professional career.

Pupils are prepared for the University Locals and London University Examinations.

SCHOOL BUILDINGS.

The Buildings are replete with every modern convenience, and include:—Large Assembly Hall, Chemical and Physical Laboratories, Lecture Hall, Class Rooms, Playing Sheds, &c. The whole is heated by hot water and lighted with electric light.

The Buildings are open for inspection every THURSDAY and SATURDAY, from 2.30 to 5.30.

Applications for Prospectus and Admission Form for Day Pupils and Boarders should be made without delay to the

HEAD MASTER.

sound modern education, calculated to fit pupils for a commercial or professional career' (Bucks Advert. & N.Bucks Free Press, Oct 19&26, 1907).

On 1st August 1907, the school was legally transferred, under arrangement with the Trustees (Scheme No 152, Board of Education, 1907) to the newly erected school premises on the Chandos Road (Harrison, 1909, p62). Seven masters were needed and 65 boys of whom 35 were boarders transferred to the new buildings. There were six entrance scholarships, and the school was a centre for the Oxford University Local Examinations. It is remarkable that the six places for boys that had started in Thornton in 1468 had survived in a similar format, some 439 years later.

On 15th October 1907, a revised scheme (No 487) for the administration of the RLS was issued by the Board of Education (BRO AR40/69), and the main changes were that :

- the new Governing Body should comprise 21 Governors (previously 18), the additional 3 to be appointed from Buckingham County Council raising their representation from four to seven.
- some authority was removed from the Head to the Governors, and from the Governors to the Board.
- the leaving age of pupils was raised from 17 to 18
- provision was made by the Board to ensure that the RLS would train children who intended to become Elementary teachers (student teachers).

Three years had passed from the 1904 document and the schedule of property of the foundation had changed substantially as elements of the endowments of the foundation had been used to pay for the new school:

	£ s d	Responsible persons	Yearly Income £ s d
The Latin School			
New School site & buildings, Chandos Road, Buckingham.	£2 0 0	In hand	£0 0 0
Schoolhouse, with Masters house & site & garden & yard	£0 1 15	In hand	£0 0 0
The Green Coat School			
Annuity or yearly sum paid under the will of Trustees Alderman Gabriel Newton	£0 0 0	Leicester Charity	£26 0 0
Sir Richard Temple			
Annuity issuing out of 'The Old Wharf' Buckingham.	£0 0 0	James Wilson Thorpe	£10 0 0
Consols	£112 16 8	Trustees of Charitable Funds	£2 16 4
John Hart			
Rent charge issuing out of Easington, Oxfordshire.	£0 0 0	John Wakeman Greenwood (owner)	£9 0 0

The day after the revisions to the new County school had been issued, the school was formally opened by Alderman Tonman Mosley, Chairman of the Bucks County Council on the afternoon of. This was a 'grand occasion' and speeches were given by: Dr John Cheesman, Chairman of Governors; Henry Small, Clerk to the Governors; Tonman Mosley, Chairman of Bucks County Council; Lady Verney, Governor; Mr Denchfield, Governor and member of Bucks Education Committee; Mr Verney, MP Buckingham; Daniel Clarke, Chairman of Bucks Education Committee and Vice-Chairman of Bucks County Council; Mr Adcock, Mayor of Buckingham; The Honourable Freemantle; and Matthew Cox, Headmaster. The total outlay for the new school was announced to be £6,200 including about £5000 for the building. Some £4350 was received in grants from Bucks County Council, £500 from Buckingham Town Council, and £130-5s from voluntary contributions, and other sums have been provided by the realisation of portions of the endowment of the foundation. The new school was built to accommodate 100 pupils and yet there were already 70. There were some 150 eminent personalities from the locality who attended the ceremony, most of whom were named in the local newspaper who covered the event (Bucks.Advert & N.Bucks Free Press, Oct 19, 1907). Henry Small gave a speech in which he said:

> *'One would think that it must be almost a unique case that a school started over three and a half centuries ago, should have been carried on continuously in the same small building from the time of its foundation by King Edward VI in 1548 down to the present year 1907, in the reign of Edward VII; and that successive headmasters during the whole of that period have received the same amount of remuneration from the Exchequer'.*

Thus the school had undergone huge changes over the recent years: for the first time in its history girls had been admitted, female teachers had been admitted, and now the Headmaster had to live off-site. In 1908, Cox resigned to accept the appointment of Headmaster at the Blue Coat school for boys, in Wells, Somerset (RLS, Staff Register).

1908-1931

William Fuller was a Cambridge Cricket Blue (Morton, 1988) and was Assistant to the Professor of Physics at the Cavendish Laboratory at Cambridge (1889-1897) before graduating in the Natural Sciences (Chemistry, Physics, Botany & Physiology) in 1897. He became Science Master at Worcester Royal Grammar (1897-1898), Senior Assistant Master at Banbury Municipal School (1989-1908) and was appointed Head Master of the Royal Latin School in Michaelmas Term in 1908, then being 38 years of age. He achieved his MA(Cambs) in 1909 (RLS, Staff Register).

Fuller taught science and chemistry, and was also a noted cricket coach. As the school did not have its own playing grounds, it made use of Buckingham Town Cricket club at Bourtonville for cricket, soccer and hockey (Morton, 1988). Perhaps the change in headmaster and change to co-educational status led to a reduction in pupil numbers as the boys outnumbered the girls by thirty-five to eighteen when Fuller joined the school (RLSM Summer 1931, p21). Numbers grew steadily, and by the time he submitted his first Headmasters Report to the Governors, there were 63 pupils (including 7 new ones), 8 pupil teachers and 1 student teacher. Pupils were admitted from the age of 9 years (Minutes of the Governors, 1908).

THE ROYAL LATIN SCHOOL,
BUCKINGHAM.

SECONDARY SCHOOL for BOYS & GIRLS

Recognised by the Board of Education.

HEAD MASTER—**WILLIAM FULLER, B.A., CAMB.**

The aim of the School is to provide a Sound Modern Education.

THE STAFF **consists entirely of experienced and highly qualified Graduates.**
THE BUILDINGS **are replete with every Modern Convenience.**
THE FEES **are exceedingly moderate—£6 6s. per annum.** [186

Boys are received from NINE and Girls from TEN years of age.

THE HEADMASTER IS PREPARED TO RECEIVE A LIMITED NUMBER OF BOARDERS.

Buckingham Express, Nov 14, 1908

The former premises (the Master's house and St John's Chapel) which still remained the property of the Charity Trustees, had to be dealt with in some way, and it was resolved to sell off the Master's residence (erected in 1696), which had become somewhat dilapidated, and it was purchased in 1908 by CA Bennett, the adjoining owner at £330. (Harrison, 1909, p442).

In 1909 the girls from Buckingham Council school had their cookery lessons at the Royal Latin School (BCFSPTA, 1979, p21).

In 1909, the tuition fees were raised from £6-6s-0d to £6-12s-0d, and it was suggested that the chapel should be sold by the school governors to the National Trust for the sum of £200. The National Trust was then a relatively new organisation, first registered in 1895. An inventory of the chapel, then used as a classroom was initiated, and on 26th November 1909 the contents were:

In the main room:

Mahogany bookcase
Painted glazed bookcase
Quantity of books

Small square table with drawer
Two carved oak desks
Carved oak reading desk
Offertory box
10 Honours boards
Restoration board
Quantity of old maps
Blackboard
Step Ladder
Electric light fittings and 6 lamps
Gas fittings and lamp and pole
Door and frame

In the Gallery

Three deal stands
Six easels
Globe (no stand)

In the Turret

Bell and bell ropes

The school bell was used to announce the beginning of morning and afternoon school (RLSM, 1931-1932, p97), and in 1909 the Governors decided to remove and rehang it in the new school, to give the carved oak desks, reading desk and offertory box to the Vicar and churchwardens of Buckingham in recognition of the long association between the school and the church, and to remove useful items to the new school and to auction the remainder (Governors Minutes, 1909).

In 1911, the school had 90 pupils, including boarders (Kellys 1911). The headmaster and the boarders lived at 6 West Street, Buckingham. In 1912, Lady Verney resigned as a Governor, but the other Governors particularly Dr Cheesman, Baroness Kinloss (see *Biography*) and Messrs Osborne, Hawes and Denchfield were as active as ever (Governors Minutes, 1912).

In 1914, the First World War came to Buckingham, and the events are best related in the words of Mr Fuller himself:

> *'In 1914 came the Great War, and during the next four years we had a most weird history. Of course, the first difficulty was with the masters. These joined up, one after another, and it was impossible to replace them. As the war went on they all disappeared, and we had to carry on with five ladies and myself. In fact it was only an eleventh hour intervention by the Board of Education that prevented my being taken away also. I was not pleased at this, but the Board's ruling was that the school must have one man left when two thirds of its pupils were boys. These lads also kept disappearing suddenly. Many of them were at school on a certain Friday and in the Army on the next Monday. And oh! that Roll of Honour! It seems far off now, but you of the present day cannot understand what we felt, when one after another of those whom we remembered as boys here (and as little ones too some of them) passed into the Beyond' (RLSM, Summer 1931, p22).*

> *'Another memory of this period is that of the influx of seventeen Belgian boys and girls, who had been driven from their homes by the German advance through their country. These really fitted into our school life wonderfully well. I saw three of them last summer and they all have the happiest recollections of their time here' (RLSM, Summer 1931, p22).*

In 1920, the school comprised about 90 pupils including boarders, and the school had ten entrance scholarships. In addition to the Headmaster, there were five teachers (Kelly, 1920, p57). The 'Old Boys Prize Fund' founded by the Harrison brothers (RLSOLA, 1932) developed into the 'Royal Latin School

Old Pupils Association' and had its first meeting on July 28th 1920, where Dr Cheesman was elected President, and William Fuller Vice President; the committee comprised 6 men and 6 women perhaps reflecting the make-up of the mixed school, or because women had won the right to vote only two years earlier. The first years of the association were spent arranging whist drives, Old Pupils events, membership details and raising money for school purchases (a piano, flag, War memorial). There were some 61 members. The term 'Old Latonians' was abbreviated to 'Old Latins', and the society became known as the 'Old Latins Association' (RLSOLA, 1920-1931).

In the 1920s only 16 pupils were from Buckingham town. Some pupils travelled in by train from Verney Junction, Grandborough and Winslow, but the majority travelled in by bicycle from Charndon, Hillesdon, Gawcott, Maids Moreton, Thornborough, Tingewick and Marsh Gibbon. Thus Agriculture was not only important to the general population at this time, but most of the pupils lived on farms. In 1922 a school Calf Club was started (RLSM, Dec 1930, p62), sponsored by the Buckinghamshire Agricultural Society. Prospective young farmers selected a calf, took it home and reared it until show day, when prizes were awarded (Morton, 1988).

In 1921, the financial constraints imposed by the 1907 Board of Education scheme had to be revised so that the annual tuition fees could be raised to £10-10s. It was again revised in 1923, allowing the maximum tuition fees to be exceeded 'with the approval in writing of the Board of Education'. In 1924 further revisions took place, allowing the transfer of one Newton scholarship to Denton.

In 1998 Jack Adams recalled his experiences at the school as a pupil in the 1920s: 'Pa' Fuller was an academic 'Mr Pastry' with a dog and cane, who lived opposite the Bakery on the Brackley Road. He remembered being a member of the elite 'Tadpole Eleven' cricket team and wrote about the children waving the Union Jack as Queen Mary visited Buckingham to open Stowe school: 'If we showed enthusiasm for the Queen we showed no enthusiasm whatsoever for the Stowe boys. They wore neat light grey suits with long trousers and were the sons of the aristocracy. We were the sons of the soil and would have only been too pleased to have rubbed their noses in it' (Adams, 1998). Eric Morton, a pupil from 1921-1926, recalls that boys and girls were not allowed to speak to each other, except when inclement weather prevented sports afternoons, and 'pump-handle style' ballroom dancing was organised - even then a boy could not ask a girl to dance more than once. The House system comprised three houses: Stratton, Denton and Newton and members of the respective houses had to wear their house emblems on Founders Day: a Clover Leaf; Garden Sorrell; and Lambs wool (Morton, 1988).

In the years 1928 to 1931 there were some 130 pupils (Kellys, 1928 & 1931). On Founders Day (24th June) 1928, the Rev NR Ramsay unveiled the Brass memorial to those members of the school who had died in the First World War (RLSM, 1934-6, P475).

In 1929-30, it appears that there were ten teachers, five male and five female the latter were all unmarried. Boys and girls were received from 10 years of age, and the fees were now £11 per annum inclusive of books and games (Buckingham Advertiser 3/8/1929), although it was noted that 'there was a deficiency of girls' books in the school library' (RLSM, Summer 1931,

THE ROYAL LATIN SCHOOL

BUCKINGHAM.

A Secondary School for Boys and Girls recognised by the Board of Education.

Head Master—WILLIAM FULLER, M A., Camb.

ASSISTANT STAFF:

Miss D. Merry, M.A.	Mr. S. G. Williams, B.A.
Miss E. Staveley, B.A.	Mr. G. H. Jones, B.Sc.
Miss G. M. V. Lowe, B.A.	Mr. H. Mairs.
Miss R. W. Locke (Domestic Subjects).	Mr. W. Buckingham, A.R.C.A.
Miss Z. Full (Physical Exercises).	Mr. R. A. Edwards (Handicraft).

THE AIM OF THE SCHOOL IS TO PROVIDE A SOUND MODERN EDUCATION.

The Buildings are replete with every modern convenience.

BOYS AND GIRLS ARE RECEIVED FROM TEN YEARS OF AGE.

FEES:—£11 per annum inclusive of books and games, with (1) a reduction of £2 per annum on reaching the age of 16 and a further reduction of £2 per annum on reaching the age of 17; (2) a reduction of 25 per cent. for each fee paying pupil, after the first, in the case of brothers and sisters attending at the same time.

APPLICATION FOR ADMISSION MAY BE MADE TO THE HEADMASTER.

p32). The aim of the school was to provide a sound modern education (Buckingham Advertiser Aug 3,1929). In the Headteachers Report of 1929-1930, there were 146, 143 and 148 pupils in the Autumn, Spring and Summer terms, with 152 pupils entering for Autumn 1930, which was the first time in the history of the school that the numbers had exceeded 150 (Governors Minutes, 1930). It is notable that the school now taught 50 pupils more than it was originally designed to accommodate some 25 years earlier. Only 10 of the 32 candidates for the Entrance Scholarships reached the required standard. The sixth form had expanded from 5 to 9 pupils.

At the end of the Summer term 1931, Fuller retired having been in post for 23 years, then being 60 years of age. He was presented with a wireless set by the Old Latins Association (RLSOLA, 1931). During the Second World War, he took up a full-time post lecturing at Magdalen College, Oxford, to help replace younger masters who had gone into war service. At the end of the war, he retired again, to give private tuition at his home in Lonsdale Road, Oxford (RLSM, Jul 1947, p33). He died in 1948 (RLSOLA, 9 Jan 1948).

1931-1935

Maurice Walton Thomas, was a graduate of the School of Modern History at Keble College, Oxford in 1922. He was at Grays Inn (1923-1926), became a Barrister at Law, and achieved his LL.M in 1929 from University College, London. He was appointed headmaster on 1st September 1931.

In 1932 a wooden building was constructed which housed a Dining Hall, Sixth Form room, Library and Mistresses room. Thus hot School Dinners were introduced - a major change as pupils previously had had to bring in packed lunches, and the only hot dinners had been those illegally cooked on a shovel in the school furnace (Morton, 1988). On Founders Day 1932, in accordance with custom, a pilgrimage was made to the Old Latin School (RLSM, 1931-1932, p84).

The school had active societies - the Lecture Society, the Musical Society, the Debating Club, Play-Reading Society, the Young Farmers Club and the Scouts. The majority of parents were still connected with Agriculture. The Debating Society argued that 'Foxhunting should be abolished' - and the motion was carried. The Sixth form asked for an electric light to be fitted in their room (RLSM, 1932, p12). In June 1933, the school gathered to watch the Prince of Wales inspect the British legion; and in the same term the school scouts went to see the Chief Scout, Lord Baden Powell at Livingstone Dayrell.

The school had 130 pupils and 10 entrance scholarships (Kellys, 1931). There were approximately 25 pupils in each form group: VI, Va, Vb, IV, III, and II. Form III boys were called 'The Outcasts', and Form II 'The Tadpoles' (RLSM, 1932).

His Headmasters Report of 1934-35 showed a breakdown of pupils:

	Boy	**Girl**	**Total**
Scholarship Holders	39	26	65
Fee Payers	53	41	94
Student Teachers	2		2
Total	94	67	161

In 1934-6 there were still three houses: Newton, Stratton and Denton. The latest technology - a Murphy wireless set (a radio) was purchased. The Tuck shop was inundated by requests for 'Milky Ways' and ice-creams. The three supporting pillars of the 'Latin culture' were the 'sovereignty of God, the life of the family, and the freedom of the individual' (RLSM, 1935, p354). Until this time, only silent films had been available, and now 'talkie' films began to be introduced (RLSM, 1934-6, p458).

In December 1934, a visiting lecturer told pupils of the current incursion by Japan into Manchuria, the breach of the Treaty of Versailles by Hitler, and concluded that 'all of Europe is in a state of tension and is looking forward to January 1935, which will undoubtedly prove a crisis in her affairs' (RLSM, 1934, p272). Thus the scene was set for World War II.

MW Thomas left in December 1935, after four and a half years of 'wise and able administration of his office', to take up the position of Headmaster of Tottenham County School (RLSM, 1934-1936, p372).

1936-1939

Stanley Arthur Dyment had graduated with Honours at Bristol in 1924, and achieved an MSc from University College London in 1930. He was appointed Headmaster on 1st January 1936, then being 35 years of age. He was a friend and former colleague of Thomas (RLSM, 1934-1936, p372), presumably as they were both at University College at the same time.

The Rev NR Ramsay retired in 1936 after serving 27 years as Governor of the school (RLSM, Dec 1939, p129). Matthew Cox, ex-headmaster, presented the prizes on Speech Day in 1937 (RLSM, Oct 1937, p69). In the same year, a hard tennis court was built which was also used for gymnastics and netball (RLSM, Oct 1937, p45). A school photograph dated 1937 shows 10 teachers (five male, five female), the Headteacher, and possibly a matron. There were 137 pupils, 75 boys and 62 girls. Despite all the efforts of the Old Latins Association in arranging a flurry of events, its membership had dwindled to 38 members (RLSOLA, 1939).

Refugees from Europe sought schooling for their children and Buckinghamshire County Education Committee had no objection to the RLS admitting refugee children so long as: there were places available; and that they were able to pay their fees (RLS Archives, July 1939). It would appear that Bucks County Education Committee offered travelling allowances to children who lived more than two and a half miles from the school - which sometimes included providing bicycles or storage for bicycles at railway stations (RLS Archives, April 1939).

In 1938, Dyment lived at Fairview, Bourton Road, Buckingham and was on the War Office list of the Territorial reserve of Officers. He was also a trained Air Raid Precautions (ARP) Warden and his correspondence with British Gas Masks Ltd requesting masks for the children still survives (RLS Archives, Dec 1938).

Dyment left in the Summer of 1939, to take up the post of Headmaster at Glendale County School, Wood Green, Middlesex (RLS, Staff Register). Mr WGN Emerton JP, known as the 'Sergeant' to generations of children, died after 30 years service as caretaker to the school.

1939-1941

Henry Bert Toft, was born on Oct 2nd 1909, attended Manchester Grammar school, and graduated with Honours in the General Sciences (Mathematics, Physics, Biology) at Manchester University in 1931. He achieved his Teaching Diploma in Manchester in 1932 and became Assistant Master at Manchester Grammar School. He also played rugby for England on ten occasions between 1936 and 1939

(The Times, Jul 11th 1987). In September 1939 he was appointed Headmaster of the Royal Latin School, at which time there were 170 pupils (Kellys, 1935).

In June 1939, prior to his first term, Bucks County Education Committee wrote to Toft at his residence at 12 Shaftesbury Avenue, Cheadle Hulme in Cheshire, confirming that: 'The Royal Latin School is an aided school ... has a Governing Body appointed under a Scheme approved by the Board of Education, on which the County Council and various other local or Educational Bodies are represented'. The letter explains that the County Council insist on the annual expenditure being in accordance with budgets, and that the Governors are in charge of budgeted expenditure; and that the County controls pupil intake through its Secondary School Entrance Examination (RLS Archives, June 1939).

The declaration of the Second World War introduced a number of changes, not least the carrying of gas masks by pupils and staff, and an influx of new 'evacuee' pupils from Birmingham and London which swelled the school to more than 250 pupils (RLSM, July 1947, p3). Chemicals that could be used for making explosives had to be locked in cupboards (RLA Archives, March 1939). The school timetable was changed with the seven lessons being shortened from 45 to 40 minutes to allow the children to cycle home in daylight and avoid the Black-Out. However this caused problems for children travelling home to Marsh Gibbon by train, as the London Midland and Scottish Railway changed their own timetable. Thus arrangements were made for six RLS children to travel home on the Elementary school bus (RLS Archives, Nov 1939) and a car was hired for the seven Steeple Claydon children during the winter and spring terms (RLS Archives, April 1940).

As the War continued, everything became scarce, and the school railings were appropriated for the war effort, although the RLS gates were spared. Bomb shelters were placed in both the boys and girls playgrounds (RLSM, July 1947, p3). The RLS served as the Headquarters for the Buckingham Air Training Corps (ATC) Squadron, with RLS teacher Tom Allitt as the Commanding Officer (RLSM, July 1947, p5).

Both pupils and senior staff served in the Air Raid Precautions (ARP)

Report Centre, and 'Dug for Victory' by the cricket nets. Even the tennis courts and football field were ploughed up (RLSM, July 1947, p3). In April 1940 Buckinghamshire War Agricultural Executive Committee asked if any boy volunteers were available to help with the forthcoming harvest, due to a shortage of labour. By harvest 1941, schoolboy harvest centres were organised - camps of 20 to 30 boys aged 15+ that were supervised by farmers. The boys under 16 were paid 5d per hour, and if over 16 were paid 6d per hour. The boys usually provided their own food and transport (bicycles), though sometimes catering was offered by the WVS and Women's Institutes, with rationed food being supplied by the Ministry of Food. Special courses on 'Food Education' were run for Domestic Science staff on 'War-time Cookery and Catering and how to make the most of rationed foods' (RLS Archives, May 1940). Petrol was also rationed, and it was common to see Toft riding his bicycle around the town (RLS Archives, September 1940).

Some teachers were 'called up' for war service (RLSM, Dec 1939, p128 & 131), and graduate women with no previous teaching experience were recruited to replace them (RLS Archives, Sep 1940). The RAF were also recruiting boys aged between 15 and 17 as RAF Aircraft Apprentices (RLS Archives, Oct 1939).

In 1941, Toft himself joined the RAF as a signals specialist and was posted to the Shetlands where he became involved in the 'battle of the beams' against the German bombers (Times, Jul 11th 1987).

1941

Donald E. Morgan, Headmaster of Wolverton Secondary School, became Acting Headmaster of the Royal Latin School for one term from October to December 1941, whilst Toft was serving his War Service.

1942-1945

Charles Foster, was born at Willesden in 1907, the son of a school master. His BSc (Kings College, London) was in Physics and Mathematics; his MA (Bristol) and PhD (Kings College, London) were in Education. He was the Senior Science Master at Aylesbury Grammar School (1936-1941), and became Acting Headmaster of the Royal Latin School from January 1942 until August 1945 (Bucks Bibliographies, BRO).

In 1943 a parental survey was conducted, with some 50 replies. Ten parents objected to their children peeling potatoes, and six objected to the chore of washing the dishes (RLS Archives).

Dr Foster left to become an Inspector at the Ministry of Education (1946-54), when Toft returned to take up his post. Foster then entered the church and rose to Diocesan Director of Religious Education (1959-68), Canon of Portsmouth Cathedral (1964-68), and Senior lecturer in Divinity at King Alfred College, Winchester (1968-71). He died in June 1972 (Bucks Bibliographies, BRO).

1945-1948

Henry Bert Toft returned to the Royal Latin in the Summer of 1945 to serve another three years.

The work of the RLS Old Latins Association continued until 1941, where the Minutes show that major plans were being deferred until after the war (RLSOLA, 1941). At this time, the school emblem, as printed on the school magazine by the Old Latins Association, was a wild free swan on a 'spade' shield - a shape popular in the 19th century. War not only interrupted the meetings of the Association from 1941-1946, but also the RLS magazine (due to a shortage of paper) from Spring 1940 until July 1947 (RLSM, July 1947, p5). The Association reconvened in November 1946 which also coincided with Toft's return from War service. In 1947, Buckinghamshire County Council received the designs for a new coat of arms for County use (BCC, 1997) and following their lead, the school emblem was changed to the county design of a Ducally chained swan on a 'heater' shield - a shape more popular in the 20th century (Friar, 1997, p171).

The Education Act 1944

The Education Act of 1944 substantially affected British secondary education: fees were abolished in maintained schools and free secondary education was to be made available to all children; the Board of Education was to be converted to the Ministry of Education; Local Education Authorities had to provide medical checks, school meals, free milk, access to swimming pools and playing fields for all school children; school leaving age was to be raised to 15 years; schools had to provide religious instruction and minimum accommodation facilities were specified.

A meeting of the Governing Body held on June 13th 1945 resulted in an application to change the status of the school from 'assisted' by the LEA to being 'Voluntary Controlled' under the provision of the 1944 Act (ED 162/220). This meant that more than 50 percent of the funding of the school was to be provided by the LEA and two-thirds of the governors had to be appointed by the authority (Curtis, 1968, p384). This is detailed in the Instrument and Articles of Government dated 12th August 1946 specifically for the Royal Latin School (RLSOLA, 1946) which states that the Governors of the Royal Latin School should comprise 18 people:

Six Foundation Governors :
4 from the Trustees of the General Charities,
1 from the Hebdominal Council of Oxford University
1 from the Old Latins Association

Twelve Representative Governors :
12 to be appointed by the LEA, of which:
3 from Buckingham Borough Council
3 from Buckingham Rural District Council

The instrument also states that governors could not have any financial interest in property, goods or services supplied to the school; that masters could not be governors; that any meeting had to have 6 governors to be quorate. These Governing Body conditions remained unchanged until the Education Act of 1980. Separate sections set out the authority and duties of the Governors, LEA and Head; and procedures for appointing and dismissing the Head, Assistant masters and non-teaching staff; pupil admissions; holidays and curriculum.

In March 1947 the school was subject to a three day inspection by the Ministry of Education (ED162/220). They found that on leaving the school, girls pursued clerical occupations, and boys favoured agriculture, industry and engineering. Only 1 boy and 1 girl had proceeded to University within the past 3 years. The facilities for providing meals and Physical Education were criticised, but the Library was said to be a 'great asset'. The staff comprised the Head, four Masters and four Mistresses, and half the staff had only served for less than one year. There were 74 boys and 90 girls; 18 pupils in the Sixth Form, and an average of 30 pupils in the other five year groups. The school comprised a Hall, 5 classrooms, 1 science lab, 1 lecture room, 1 domestic science room, and a canteen hut. Presumably spurred by this report, and the highlighted need for improved accommodation, in September 1948, Buckinghamshire County Council purchased on behalf of the school Grenville Cottage, comprising house, 2 acres of land for £4,800, as recorded in the books of the Ministry of Education under the Education Act of 1944 (ED 162/220).

Toft left to become Principal of Bath Technical College, and he retained his interest in Rugby Union. Following his appointment as South-East Berkshire College of Further Education in 1962, he retired, and died in 1987 (Times, Jul 11th 1987).

In writing the history of this school, the long-lost past is in danger of catching up with memories of the present. To ensure that this author does not commit this offence it seems best to follow the Buckingham tradition: to cease the detailed history at this point; to merely list Headteachers and notable events; and to leave the recent past and present for future historians to record.

1948-1979

George K. Embleton gained his MA from Cambridge, and spent his war years in the Navy. He joined the Royal Latin School on 6th September 1948 at the age of 34. He had plans for the school and was instrumental in moving the school to the Brookfield estate and creating two separate boarding houses for boys and girls (Grimsdale, 2000).

In 1963, the school relocated to another site further down Chandos Road, which was also accessible by Brookfield lane. On 10th June 1963 'Queen Elizabeth the Queen Mother ... this afternoon visited Buckingham and opened the new buildings of the Royal Latin School' (Times, 11 June

1963), at which time HM The Queen Mother also inspected the guard of honour - the Buckingham Squadron of the Air Training Corp. The Queen Mother unveiled a marble plaque, and the new buildings were dedicated by the Bishop of Buckingham. In its new location, the school could accommodate 360 pupils (Elliott, 1975, p180). When the Royal Latin School relocated, the old school became Buckingham County Junior school. In the 1970s it became known as Chandos Middle school, and in 1991 it became Grenville Combined school.

Embleton left in the school in 1979, leaving three times as many pupils as he had inherited from Toft (Grimsdale, 2000).

1979-1992

Peter Luff gained an Honours degree in history at Durham, became Head of History at a Derbyshire Grammar school and Deputy Head at Sir Henry Floyd in Aylesbury before he began his headship in September 1979. The school had 566 pupils on roll, of which 86 pupils were in the sixth form, and there were some 34 girl boarders and 25 boy boarders (September 1980).

In 1988, the Royal Latin School ceased teaching Latin after more than 500 years. At this time the numbers of pupils was 660 (Daily Telegraph, 11/07/1988). As a result of the newspaper article, Eric F. Morton, MBE sent a substantial scrapbook to the school, entitled 'An Ancient Foundation' recalling his memories as a boy at the RLS from 1921 to 1926 (RLS Archives). In 1989 Rotherfield Sixth Form centre opened, and 1991 the RLS Boarding House closed.

Mrs Edna D. Embleton, widow of the previous Headmaster, and school secretary for many years, was a strong ambassador for the school, and became Chairman of Governors.

1992-date

Cecilia Galloway, MSc, BSc(Hons), CChem, FRSC, PGCE became the first female Headteacher in the history of the school. Formerly science teacher at Wolverhampton Grammar, then at Grays, Essex; Head of Chemistry and then Science at St Bernards, Slough; and Deputy Head at Ryeish Green Comprehensive, Reading.

In 1992 there were 672 pupils on roll; today (September 2000) there are 1220+ pupils. To cater for this rise in numbers there have been extensive changes to the school buildings and organisation. She was presented with a Plato Award for Outstanding Leadership in June 2000, and received the corresponding Certificate in the Millennium Dome in October 2000.

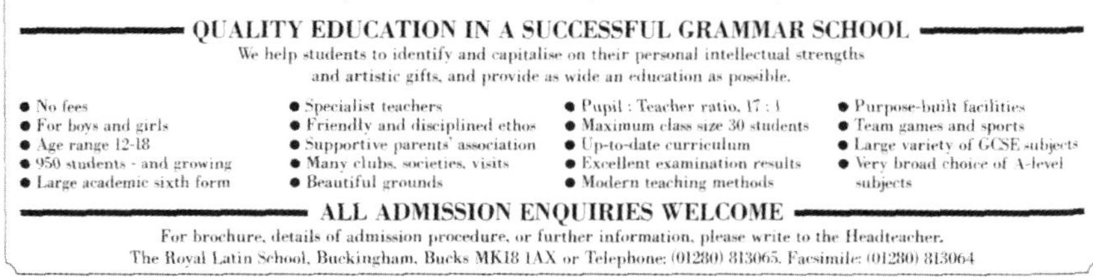

INVESTOR IN PEOPLE
THE ROYAL LATIN SCHOOL
Buckingham
founded 1423
ROYAL LATIN SCHOOL
A 1423 D
MISSION
To prepare young people to succeed in a rapidly changing world and to make the learning process as happy and secure as possible.
AIMS
To foster academic, spiritual, moral and personal development. To provide a caring and challenging environment. To encourage excellence. To develop students to become responsible citizens.
QUALITY EDUCATION IN A SUCCESSFUL GRAMMAR SCHOOL
We help students to identify and capitalise on their personal intellectual strengths and artistic gifts, and provide as wide an education as possible.
• No fees
• For boys and girls
• Age range 12-18
• 950 students - and growing
• Large academic sixth form
• Specialist teachers
• Friendly and disciplined ethos
• Supportive parents' association
• Many clubs, societies, visits
• Beautiful grounds
• Pupil : Teacher ratio, 17 : 1
• Maximum class size 30 students
• Up-to-date curriculum
• Excellent examination results
• Modern teaching methods
• Purpose-built facilities
• Team games and sports
• Large variety of GCSE subjects
• Very broad choice of A-level subjects
ALL ADMISSION ENQUIRIES WELCOME
For brochure, details of admission procedure, or further information, please write to the Headteacher.
The Royal Latin School, Buckingham, Bucks MK18 1AX or Telephone: (01280) 813065. Facsimile: (01280) 813064

RLS advertisement from 1998

The Masters house attached to the old Royal Latin School.

The RLS at Brookfield (2000)

The old Royal Latin School as it appears today

BIOGRAPHY

The purpose of this section is to give further information about the people and the organisations already mentioned.

Bartone, Henry

Henry Bartone was the master of Higham Ferrers grammar school from 1372 to 1399, and he educated Henry Chichele (who was later to become Archbishop of Canterbury). Bartone served several terms as mayor of Higham Ferrers, alternating with Thomas Chichele (the father of Henry Chichele) (Leach, 1969, p253).

It is possible that this Henry Bartone, mayor and schoolmaster, was a relative of John Barton (Roskell, 1992, p136 & VCH, Bucks, iv, p148). Another Henry Barton was Mayor of London in 1417, and again it is not known if he was a relative of John Barton (VCH, Bucks, iv, p147 & Elvey, i, 136 & 155).

Barton, William

William Barton was Coroner of the northern Hundreds of Buckingham from c1372 (Jenkins, 1934, p 163) and Justice of the Peace. William had two sons, both of whom were called John Barton and both of whom became lawyers and members of Lincoln's Inn (Roskell, 1992, p138-143). He lived in Castle House in Buckingham. William died on Sunday July 11th 1389 and was buried in Thornborough church where there is a memorial to him and his wife. A flagstone in the nave is inlaid with brass and depicts two figures dressed in long cloaks; he wears a hood, and his wife a veiled head-dress; beneath which is the inscription:

> *'Hic jacet Will[iel]mus Barton qui obiit festo Translat[io]nis S[an]c[t]i Benedicti Abb[a]tis anno d[o]m[ini] Mill[esim]o CCCLXXXIX et Regni Regis Ric[ard]i Sec[und]i xiii incipiente quando dies d[om]in[i]calis accidit sup[er] l[ite]ram C hora vesp[er]arum cujus a[n]i[m]e p[ro]picietur d[eu]s Amen'.*

('Here lies William Barton who died on the feast of the translation of St Benedict, Abbot, in the year of our Lord 1389, at the beginning of the thirteenth year of King Richard II, and on whose soul God will have mercy by one hundred masses at the hour of Vespers every Sunday. Amen').

His son, John Barton (junior), erected a memorial to his father, mother and elder brother in Thornton church, but this has long since disappeared. Willis (1755, p301) recorded it as:

> *'At the bottom of North window of Thornton church was this legend: Orate pro bono Statu Wilhelmi Barton et Emmote, Uroris ejus, necnon, Johannis Barton, senioris, quondam Recordatoris London. Quorum Animabus propicietur Deus'.*

Thornton church showing the North windows

Barton (senior), John

John Barton (senior) had become a lawyer by 1395, although he may possibly have originally entered holy orders as a rector of Foscott in 1390 when he was presented by Alan Ayette (Lipscombe, iii, p14). As a lawyer, he was extremely successful; he was a Knight of Buckinghamshire and attended parliament in 1397 and again in 1401, 1404 and 1408 (Willis, 1755, p26). He became the 1st Duke of Exeter's attorney in 1399 (Goodman, 1961, p350-355), and later became Recorder of the City of London (VCH, Bucks, ii, p145). Probably because his father, William, was steward to Richard de Molyns, John Barton senior was able to continue the connection with this wealthy family by becoming the lawyer for Sir William Molyns (Boatwright, 1994, pxxxvii). John acquired various properties in the county including Addington, Skerritts Manor, Bourton, Moreton, Gawcott, Foscott, Stone Manor, and properties in Buckingham, Oxford and Oxfordshire. He also had use of two houses in London (Roskell, 1992, p138-143). His home residence was Castle House in Buckingham, which he had inherited on the death of his father, William, in 1389. Castle House was eventually left to the Fowlers and then the Lambard family. Here Catherine of Aragon was entertained in 1514, and Charles I in 1644 (Kelly, 1920, pp55; Sheahan, 1862, p232; Elliot, 1975, pp42, 59).

John Barton (senior) was present at the celebration mass and procession for the victory at Agincourt, held in the Guildhall Chapel, London on the 13th Oct 1415 with the Mayor of London, Richard (Dick) Whityngtone, Robert Chichele, William Chichele, Henry Barton (see *Biography*) and other Aldermen of the City of London (Riley, 1868, p620).

John Barton's will, dated 5th June 1431, directed that: his body be buried in the St Peters Church in Buckingham in St Rumwold's (see *Biography*) aisle; he gave £16-13s-4d for 4000 Masses to be said immediately after his death for his soul and 6s-8d to a person to ensure that the Masses were faithfully and speedily performed; and gave numerous legacies including 40s to the Masters and brethren of the Hospital of St Bartholomew's, Smithfield; 40s to the Masters and brethren of the Hospital of St Thomas of Acon, London to pray for his soul, the souls of his parents, his Benefactors and friends etc; and gave all his tenements in Buckingham to his younger brother, John Barton, on condition that he shall find one fit Chaplain to say daily Mass for his soul, the souls of his parents, his Benefactors and friends at St James Altar in the Church of St Peter. The terms of engagement for the chaplain appointed by the master of St Thomas of Acon stated that: 'Salary was 10 marks per annum with which he should acquiesce, and be content, and have no other stipend; he had to be present at Matins and Vespers, in the Choir of the Church on all festivals and that he should say the whole Psalter of David throughout every week'; he was allowed 15 days for holidays; he had to deputise another Chaplain when he was ill or on holiday or forfeit 1d per day for every day that Mass was not said, to be paid to some poor person in Buckingham town; and that the Chaplain and his successors should be appointed by the Master and brethren of the Hospital of St Thomas of Acon. If the chaplain neglected his duty, then the master of St Thomas of Acon, should replace him without interference from the Bishop of Lincoln. His will also founded Barton's Hospital for six poor persons. He left all the tenements, rents, services to his brother, and after his brothers death, to his sisters, and after their deaths to William Fowler and his heirs. If the income from his Buckingham property was insufficient to maintain the services or maintenance of his houses, then he gave authority for them to make use of the income from his properties in Boreton, Moreton, Gawcott, Lenborough, Thornborough, Hillesdon, Water Stratford, Shaldeston and Foxcot in Buckingham, and Worton in Oxfordshire (VCH, Bucks, ii, p145; & Willis, MS22, p68 & Willis, 1755, p54-57).

John Barton senior died on 7th Feb 1432 and was buried in Buckingham church (Boatwright, 1994, pxxxvii).

Bartons Chantry, Buckingham

Bartons Chantry was founded by the will of John Barton (senior). It was located in St Rumwold's Aisle at the church of St Peter and St Paul, and was founded to ensure that a Priest said Mass for the souls of John Barton (senior), his parents and friends; and to pay six poor men and women to be the congregation 'every one of the said to have 4d the Week, and to keep an obit there, 2 tapers of six pound wax, also to find a torch, Wine and Wax yearly' (see Appendix II). At the Reformation, Elys was the chantry priest here and was appointed by the Hospital of St Thomas of Acon, and was awarded a pension of £4 per annum (Hodgett, 1959, p13). The chantry ornaments were also listed:

> *'Item: there be certeine implimentes belonging to the said chauntrie viz ij peire of vestments one of olde redd and blewe velvett thother white sarcenet and blewe chamblett and a chalice all gylte waing xv unces etc' (Brown, 1908, p12).*

Elys may have been the priest named as William Elys, chaplain in Buckingham in 1522 (Chibnall, 1973, p29) and in 1526 (Salter, 1909, p243).

Barton (junior), John and Isabel

In 1412 John the younger refused a promotion to the Order of the Coif - the elite group of barristers called Serjeants-at-Law who were entitled to wear a white silk head cap (coif) in court. Most judges had to be members of Serjeants' Inn, and therefore members were expected to work for the Crown. His penalty for continued refusal was to spend nine days imprisoned in the Tower of London (Roskell, 1992). Presumably Crown work was less lucrative and/or politically more dangerous than private commissions. He worked almost exclusively for the nobility, and managed to build a complicated property portfolio.

Alabaster effigies of William and Elizabeth Wilcotes, parents of Isabel Barton, in North Leigh church, Oxfordshire

John Barton Junior, was MP of Buckinghamshire from 1413 to 1423 (Elliott, 1975, p59). He married Isabel, daughter of William Wilcotes, an Oxfordshire lawyer, knight of Oxfordshire and royal justice. In the process, he also gained a brother-in-law, Sir Thomas Wykeham, a great-nephew and heir of William Wykeham (see *Biography*). So it is not surprising that from 1415 to 1431, John Barton was a trustee of the Wykeham estates in Hampshire, Oxfordshire & Somerset (Roskell, 1992).[21]

Isabel Barton died in 1457, having been married a second time (like her mother) to Sir Robert Shotesbrook (Russell, 1897, p53). By the terms of her husband's will money was left to William Fowler, to give to the churches of Thornton, Padbury etc, but as he had failed to do so, it was left to his son Richard Fowler, Chancellor of the Duchy of Lancaster, to honour her wishes by means of his will proved 19th November 1477 (VCH, Bucks iv, p244/5). His will refers to her as 'Dame Isabel Shotesbroke'. Sir Robert 'Shottisbrook' was alive and at Thornton in 1453 (Willis, 1755, p308).

Bartons Chantry, Thornton

John Barton (junior) left a will dated 1433, and died c1434:

> *' Ego, Johannes Barton, condo testamentum meum in hunc modum: lego corpus meum ad sepeliendum in capella Annuntiationis B.M.Virginis in Eccl de Thornton. Item volo, quod predicta capella de novo edificetur bonis et catellis meis. Item lego fabricie eccl. predict. 10 Marcas et cancello 5 marcas' (Willis, 1755, p301).*
>
> [I will that my body be buried in the chapel of the Annunciation

---

21. William Wilcote's wife was Elizabeth, and they had five daughters: Elizabeth, Philippa, Margaret, Isabel and Anne (VCH, Berks, iv, p422). When William Wilcotes died, Elizabeth married Sir John Blacket (died 1430) of Icomb (Glos), and she herself died in 1445. Her heirs were her daughters by William Wilcotes: Elizabeth had married into the Wykeham family, Isabel had married John Barton, and Anne had married into the Conyers family ((VCH, Berks, iv, p422) & (VCH, Oxon, 1990, xii, p221)). The inheritance included the estates at North Leigh and Seacourt Manor near Wytham.

of the Blessed Virgin Mary in the church at Thornton. I will 10 marks to the fabric of the church and 5 marks for the chancel].

The will of John Barton (junior), directed that his wife Isabel should enjoy the Manor of Thornton for life. Thornton was placed into the hands of trustees to the use of Isabel, and in 1440 she made an agreement with Henry Chichele, Archbishop and founder of All Souls College that in exchange for lands in Long Crendon and Maid's Moreton, she would receive 200 marks and the college would provide a chantry priest for the chapel at Thornton, and two priests in the college itself to sing daily masses for the souls of John Barton and others. Further land deals were made in exchange for an annuity of 28 marks. After her death in 1455/6, the college received the revenues from Long Crendon & Maids Moreton of £22 and £6 respectively, of which the £6 from Maids Moreton was used to support the chantry priest at Thornton (Catto et al, Vol ii, 1992, p651-653).

The alabaster effigies of John Barton and his wife Isabel at Thornton were identified and described by Willis in 1755 may still be seen today (see pages 22-23), although they have since been moved in various church restorations (Tricker, 1996). Willis thought that John Barton's feet rested on a dog, but the original intention was probably a lion, which matches his 'Lion of March' pendant representing his allegiance to Richard, Duke of York (Tricker, 1996). Isabel is beautifully dressed in a sleeveless gown and long cloak. Thus it is thought that the chapel of the Annunciation of the Blessed Virgin Mary housed Chastillon's chantry, was rebuilt by Robert Ingleton, in accordance with the will of John Barton junior (VCH, Bucks, iv, p247).

Braose

The family name Braose is also spelled Breaux, Brus or Bruce. The family originally came from France in the time of William the Conqueror. One branch of the family became the Lords of Bramber. William de Braose, the 4th Lord of Bramber was a Marcher lord who subdued the Welsh: he was known as the 'Ogre of Abergavenny' because in 1175 he invited three Welsh princes and their families to a feast in his castle, and then massacred them all. William married Maud de Saint Valery who herself, was not averse to fighting the Welsh. As William was a rebel baron, in 1208 King John asked for their son, William, to be a hostage to ensure their loyalty and obedience; and Maud refused. Consequently Maud and her son died of starvation in Windsor Castle in 1210. Her husband William died the following year in exile in France.

The Braose family gained Buckingham when William and Maud's son, William, married Matilda de Clare, daughter of Richard de Clare who held the manor and castle of Buckingham. Their first son, John, was born in 1198 and was called 'Tadody' (the bastard) by the Welsh because his father and grandmother had been killed. John was Lord of Bramber and Gower and was present at the signing of the Magna Carta in 1215. He married Margaret and their first son, William, was born in 1220. John died in 1232 due to a riding accident. William was only 12 years old so wardship was first given to Peter des Rievaux the sheriff of Buckingham, and when the latter died in 1234, wardship passed to the King's brother, Richard Earl of Cornwall.[22] William married Alina, and their first son was called William.

In summary, the line of inheritance is believed to be as follows:
William Braose (died 1211), married Maud de St Valery (died 1210),
and their son
William Braose (junior) (died 1210), married Matilda de Clare,
and their son
John Braose (1198-1232) married Margaret,
and their son
William Braose (1220-1284) married Alina,
and their son
William Braose married Mary
(Thompson, 2000 & VCH, Bucks, iii, p480-481)

---

22. It is not known why the Earl of Cornwall still held so much land in the inquisition document of 1289/90.

Some sources state that another branch of the family settled in Scotland, thus the eighth Robert the Bruce (1274-1329) who became King of Scotland may possibly have been a Braose, but this link is believed to be tenuous.

Brome

Dame Isabel Denton appears to have been born Isabel Brome of Badsley Clinton. Isabel married Philip Purefoy, and gained a mother-in-law, Marion the daughter and heiress of Alan Aete. Isabel and Philip and had four offspring: John, Nicholas, William and Alice. Philip Purefoy died c1466 (Lipscombe, iii, 1847, p71). In 1472 Isabel married John Denton of Blackthorn, Oxon (also referred to as John Denton of Wightam in Berkshire (Harleian Soc, 1871, p228-9) and purchased the Manors of Foxcote, Buckinghamshire and Burton Hastings, Warwickshire, from the Purefoys. By 1491, all Isabel's sons by Philip Purefoy had died, and the only Purefoy heir was a young cousin, Nicholas; and John Denton was given the wardship together with the keeping of the Purefoy lands in Berkshire, Buckinghamshire, Leicestershire & Warwickshire (VCH, Warwicks, vi, p58).

John Denton and Isabel had a number of children, and in his will of 1497-8, John Denton bequeathed the manor of Foxcote to his wife Isabel Denton, with instructions to look after his youngest son Thomas (a minor). Isabel was his executor who possessed Foxcote and according to Willis, (1755, p187) survived him for some 40 years and died about 1540. This was the Denton family that was later to become the Lords of Hillesden.

The Muster Certificates for 1522 show that Isabella Denton possessed property in Westbury, Shalstone and Foxcote, and was liable for significant taxes, £2, £18-15s-0d, & £10 respectively. She was alive in Shalstone in January 1523 (Willis, 1755, p266), but had probably died by 1535 as she does not appear in the Musters of that date. Thus, assuming that Isabel married Purefoy no later than 1463 (3 years before he died, in order to have had his three children) and assuming she was then 16 years old, she must have been born in 1447 at the latest. Thus she outlived most of her children and two husbands, and would have been at least 76 years of age in 1523.

Chastillon

The chantry at Thornton was first initiated in 1348 by John Chastillon, for the souls of his wives Alice and Joan, and for the souls of his father and mother, Malcolm and Sibill. He endowed the chantry with 2 messuages and a croft and 100 acres of land in Thornton to found the chantry of St Mary in Michael's church at Thornton. Five marks were paid for a licence to Edward III's hanaper (Willis, MS22, p48-49 & Cal.Pat. 1348, p47). Eight years later, in 1356, this chantry was apparently ordained by licence of the bishop of Lincoln (VCH, Bucks, iv, p248).

Cheesman

Dr Cheesman of Castle Street, was a local family doctor, and benefactor of the school. He 'generously provided the refreshments for the annual Christmas party. On these occasions the out-of-town pupils were put up for the night by the town pupils. The doctor had a warm spot for young people' (Crook, 1975, p26). He was described by William Fuller, the Headmaster as 'the kindly, humorous old chairman who has been connected with the Governing Body for forty years. He was one of the best friends the school ever had ...' (RLSM, Summer 1931, p22).

Chichele

It is possible that the Barton and Chichele (or Chicheley) families were known to each other for more than a century, as both family names appear in Thornborough as witnesses on several legal documents c1300 (Elvey, ii, 1975, p328). In the 14th century, Thomas Chichele, mayor of Higham Ferrers, had three sons: William (a Grocer), Robert (a Grocer, Mayor of London in 1412), and Henry.

Henry Chichele (c1362-1443) was born at Higham Ferrers, Northamptonshire, and educated by Henry Bartone (see *Biography*) the master of Higham Ferrers grammar school. He attended New College, Oxford in c1387 only eight years after its foundation (in 1379) by William of Wykeham, Chancellor of England and Bishop of Winchester. New College was a chantry chapel with the purpose of supplying parish priests to make up for all those who had died in 1349/50 during the Black Death. Thus Chichele has been described as a protege of Wykeham (New College, Aligrafix, 1995). Chichele became an advocate (like the Bartons) and occupied numerous ecclesiastical posts.

The lives of the Bartons and Henry Chichele were entwined from 1402, when both John Bartons provided security in Chancery on behalf of Henry Chichele, helping to defend him against a Crown prosecution charge of contempt (Roskell, 1992). In 1414, Henry Chichele became the Archbishop of Canterbury, and in the following year, John Barton (junior) became a trustee of the William Wykeham estates. In 1422, Chichele went back to his grammar school and founded a hospital and secular college at Higham Ferrers for eight chaplains and six choristers (VCH, Northants, iii, p266), and appointed both John Bartons as trustees (Catto et al, Vol II, 1992, p651-653 & Roskell, 1992). In 1427, Henry Chichele and John Barton (junior) were joint owners of Chesterton, Huntingdonshire (Roskell, 1992). Following in the footsteps of his patron, Wykeham, Henry Chichele furthered his commitment to education by founding All Souls College in Oxford in 1437, just six years before his death in 1443.

It is thought that the brothers John Barton were also well acquainted with Henry Chichele's brothers, Robert and William who may have been Aldermen of London in 1415. They had much in common: they lived relatively close and they moved within the same social and legal circles.

Cox

Richard Cox (c1500-1581) was born at Whaddon in Buckinghamshire educated at Eton, Cambridge and Oxford, and became headmaster of Eton.

He was one of the clergymen who annulled the marriage of Henry VIII to Anne of Cleeves. He had a number of clerical posts, was an eminent theologian, and was Prebendary of Lincoln in 1542-1547. He was almoner and tutor to Prince Edward 1544-50. In 1547 he surrendered the Manor of the Prebend End of Sutton-cum-Buckingham. From 1547-1549 he visited schools and colleges and destroyed books and manuscripts which were based on pre-1534 religious beliefs (ie. books written before Henry VIII displaced the Pope as Supreme head of the church in England) (Smith, 1892 & 1969). He became vice-chancellor of Oxford, 1547-1552, when his destruction of books, statues, pictures and manuscripts to 'eradicate Popery' earned him the title of 'Cancellor' of the University. After Queen Mary instituted the Heresy laws (c1553) he went into exile until Elizabeth I came to the throne (in 1558). He became bishop of Norwich in 1559, and 'anti-Roman Bishop of Ely' 1559-1580 (Smith, 1969; & Cross, 1958; & Bowker, 1981, p100; & Routh, 1964, p276-280).

Denton

According to the Victoria County History of Berkshire (iv, p338), the Dentons originally came from Fyfield, whereas other sources state that they originated from Cumberland. It appears that John Denton of Wytham held Appleton Manor in 1496, and it is believed that this John Denton married Isabel Brome, and his son and heir, was Thomas.

Thomas held Besselsleigh, Berkshire in 1547, Tynteyns (Tyntons) from 1515-1564, Sandford Manor in the parish of St Helens from 1545-1556, and he and his wife Margaret held the manor and overlordship of Weston in Abingdon (which was formerly part of the Abbey of Abingdon) from 1544-1552 (VCH, Berks, iv, p119 & p338). On 2nd August 1547 the Manor of Hillesden was granted to Thomas Denton Esq. by Edward VI, following the attainder of Edward Courtenay, Marquess of Exeter (Cocks, 1897, p418). Thomas Denton was knighted and became Sir Thomas Denton, Knight of Hillesdon, an eminent Bencher of the Middle Temple, Knight of Buckinghamshire in 1553 and Treasurer of the Temple. In 1511 he leased

Effigies of Alexander and Anne Denton in Hereford Cathedral

the manor of Caversfield from Richard Langston, Lord of Bucknell (VCH, Bucks, p159); and his will dated 27th December 1533 directed that his body should be buried at Caversfield church (Willis, 1755 p169-170). He died on 30th October 1558 (Lipscombe, 1847, p576).

Alexander Denton (1543-1574), son of Thomas Denton and Margaret Mordant, married Anne Willisone (1548-1566) of Hereford, an heiress (Weaver, 1886, p77); and their very ornate effigies lie in the South Transept of Hereford Cathedral, which states that Anne was the Great Niece of Bishop Skippe, and that she died in childbirth aged 18. Apparently Alexander then married Mary daughter of Sir Roger Martin and had a son, Thomas.

In 1614 Thomas Denton brought into the House of Commons a bill to fix the summer assizes at Buckingham. He married Susan third daughter of

John Temple Esq of Stowe. He is presumed to have resided at Stowe from 1594-1611 (Lipscombe, 1847, p576). His son Alexander, died in 1644/5, shortly after the sacking of Hillesden House in the Civil War. His son, Edmund, died in 1657, leaving his inheritance to Alexander.

Alexander married Hester, a granddaughter of Edmund Harman who was barber surgeon to Henry VIII (Balfour, 1988). Hester Harman was left the manor of Middleton Stoney, Oxfordshire by her father. Three of Alexander's children were born at Hillesdon (1675-1679), and John was born at Middleton Stoney in 1680. It was this Alexander who rebuilt the schoolmaster's house at Buckingham. Alexander's son Edmund built, in 1720, a new house on the site of the old manor house at Middleton Stoney and called it Middleton Park House (Blomfield, Bicester, 1887, p34-35, & 1893, p10-12).

In summary, the line of inheritance is believed to be as follows:

John Denton (died 1497) married Isabel Brome,
and their son
Thomas Denton (died 1558) married Margaret Mordant,
and their son
Alexander Denton (1542-1574) married Anne Willisone then Mary Martin,
and their son
Thomas Denton (died 1633) married Susan Temple
and their son
Alexander Denton (1596-1645) married Mary Hampden
and their son
Edmund Denton (died 1657) married Elizabeth Rogers
and their son
Alexander Denton (1654-1698) married Hester Harman
(Cocks, 1897, p419).

The Dentons were dedicated to Buckingham and represented the County as Members of Parliament for a continuous period of 32 years:

Alexander Denton 1690-1698; his eldest son, Edmund, 1698-1708 and second son, Alexander, 1708-1722.

Eyre

After the death of William Eyre in 1830, his son William T. Eyre became vicar of Padbury. At Aylesbury Quarter sessions, he and a Mr Benjamin D'Israeli of Bradenham, qualified as magistrates for the county (Bucks Herald, Aug 6, 1836).

Fortescue

Sir John Fortescue (1531?-1607) succeeded Walter Mildmay as Chancellor of the Exchequer and privy councillor in 1589. He was tutor to Princess Elizabeth, and MP for the county and borough of Buckingham for many years, Chancellor of the Duchy of Lancaster in 1601. He was well connected with Burghley, Bacon, Raleigh and Essex (Smith, 1969). It is said that he walked in the corridors of power for many years, but always remained in the background (Smith, 1892).

Fowler

William Fowler inherited the estates of his uncle, John Barton (junior). William was succeeded by Richard Fowler in 1452, a Yorkist lawyer who was made Chancellor of the Duchy of Lancaster by King Edward IV, and later a Knight of the Shire. Richard died in 1477 and was succeeded by his son Richard who is said to have entertained Catherine of Aragon at Castle House in 1514. Edward Fowler then inherited in 1528 (Kelly, 1920, pp55; Sheahan, 1862, p232; Elliot, 1975, pp 42 & 59).

Gresham

Sir Richard Gresham (1485-1549) was a well-known merchant and financier, warden of the Mercers Company in 1525, sheriff of London in 1531, Lord Mayor of London in 1537 (Routh, 1964, p230). Despite his role as a commissioner in valuing abbeys for the *Valor ecclesiasticus*, he tried to exempt several London hospitals from closure. He was often employed by the Crown and even gave financial loans to King Henry VIII (Smith, 1969). He was the father of Sir Thomas Gresham.

Thomas Gresham (1518-1579) was elected as a Freeman of the Mercers Company in 1543 and was at that time employed by the Crown to purchase gunpowder. In 1551-2, Thomas became the Kings agent based in Antwerp which was then the centre of the International money market. He worked for Henry VIII, Edward VI, Mary and Elizabeth. Thomas founded the Royal Exchange in 1568, and Gresham College in 1575 (Routh, 1964, p230-7).

Kinloss

The Baroness of Kinloss of Stowe was the eldest of the three daughters of the 3rd and last Duke of Buckingham (1823-1889). She was 'a kindly benefactor of the school ... who was especially interested in the welfare of the Royal Latin School, and year by year during her residence she extended an invitation to the school to visit Stowe on Commemoration Day. Such visits on the Feast of St John the Baptist (June 24th) were 'happy occasions' (Crook, 1975, p26). In 1884 she married Major LFHC Morgan. Following the death of her father in 1889, she took the additional name of Grenville to become the 8th Baroness May Morgan-Grenville (Who's Who, 1941-1950) and succeeded to the Scottish Barony of Kinloss. She sold Stowe estate in 1907, and the Baroness moved to Maids Moreton where she lived to an advanced age (Crook, 1975, p26).

Knight Templars

In c1120 Hugues de Payens led some 8 knights to protect the lives of pilgrims to the Holy Land from bands of Muslims, and formed a religious/military community for that purpose. They were directly under the authority of the Pope and were exempt from any local religious control. By 1291, at the fall of Acre, the Knight Templars numbered some 20,000 members and were a wealthy organisation. As Acre had been brought under control, the Knights

Templars had effectively put themselves out of a job (as had St Thomas of Acon). As they were rich with nothing to do, and only responsible to the Pope, they were perceived to be powerful and dangerous. Rumours of secret ceremonies circulated and they were accused of heresy and immorality. King Philip IV of France voiced his concerns, and in 1307 the Pope ordered their arrest. The Pope officially suppressed the Order in November 1312 and their property was transferred to the Order of St John of Jerusalem or confiscated. In 1314, the last Grand Master, Jacques de Molay was burned at the stake at Notre Dame, Paris.

Layton

Richard Layton (1500?-1544) was archdeacon of Buckingham in c1534-1538 and was not given the Prebend (Bowker, 1981, p100). He was a regional inquisitor in charge of the suppression of the monasteries. He visited and investigated monasteries prior to and during dissolution. His reports to Thomas Cromwell still survive, and it is said that he was a 'notorious clerk who had a coarse and evil mind; if he could find evidence of impropriety he reported it, if not, he accused them of concealing it' (Cook, p5, 1965). He visited Oxford University in 1535 to make reforms, and started visiting monasteries in the same year. He was at the trial of Anne Boleyn in 1536; and Dean of York in 1539 (Smith, 1969).

Leach

Arthur Francis Leach (1851-1915), the son of a Barrister, was educated at Winchester and All Souls, Oxford. He became a Barrister himself in 1874, and Assistant Charity Commissioner (Endowed Schools Department) in 1884. In 1901 he was Administrative Examiner of the Board of Education. He was a prolific author and wrote two major books on the history of medieval schools (see Bibliography) as well as eighteen county histories of schools for the Victoria County History (Black,1962). The works of this 'energetic and controversial writer have been thoroughly examined (Miner, 1990).

Lowndes

William Lowndes (1652-1724) was born at Winslow, the son of Robert (1619-1683) who had taken refuge in America at the outbreak of the Civil War, but returned after the execution of the King. His mother was Elizabeth FitzWilliam. Lowndes was educated at the Free School in Buckingham (Willis, 1755), and in 1679 at the age of 27, began his lifelong association with the Treasury. He was already chief clerk when he was promoted to Secretary in 1695, and his share of the fees for the first year of office approached £2,400. He had a great part to play in the re-coinage of silver currency and shared his ideas with Isaac Newton (Stephen, 1888). He was one of the original board members of the Bank of England - and the founder of the National Debt. He built Winslow Hall between 1698 to 1702, and his hand-written account books of the construction totalling £6,585-10s-2¾d still survive (Telegraph, Jan 30, 1999, T29). Lowndes died on 20th January 1724 and is buried in the family vault at Winslow (Stephen, 1888). On 6th November 1747, Lord Chesterfield, letter-writer and political journalist, wrote of him as 'a very covetous, sordid fellow' who used to say 'Take care of the pence and the pounds will take care of themselves' (Stephenson, p1998, 1946).

Mercers

'The name Mercer is derived from the Latin, mercator, a merchant. He was no simple pedlar or small tradesman, but a merchant who dealt in a varied assortment of goods such as linen cloths, satins, jewels, silk, wood, oil, copper, wine, lead and salt' (Ditchfield, 1904, p18). The Fraternity of the Worshipful Company of Mercers is a Livery Company, which started in the reign of Henry II (1154-1189). In 1347 the company was officially recognised (Ditchfield, 1904, pp17-22), and in 1394 it received its incorporation. Their 'mission' was to: provide for the poverty of their members whether caused by 'shipwreck and other misfortunes'; to maintain a chantry priest to say mass for the souls of the King and Queen, and for the souls of all mercers past and present; and to provide charity for poor Mercers (Cal.Pat, 1394, p425). In 1396, they were allowed to buy property for investment purposes, and by 1561, the Mercers had evolved into a trading company. The members of the Mercers company have always been closely associated with public duty in the city of London and many have been Mayor, Sheriffs and Aldermen. Approximately 70 members have served as Mayor of London, including Richard (Dick) Whittington (see *Biography*) in the 15th century who was mayor on three occasions (Ditchfield, 1904, pp17-22).

The Mercers Company assembled and worshipped in the Hospital of St Thomas of Acon, probably from the early 14th century. One such annual meeting was recorded in 1390, 'where all the Livery were to sup together on the Sunday before the Feast of St John the Baptist (24th June) when the new Masters were chosen and the poor of the mistery sustained with its alms by common consent'.[23] On the Feast of St Thomas the Martyr (29th December) the Mayor, aldermen and sheriffs of London attended services at the Hospital of St Thomas of Acon (Forey, 1977, p502). From 1407, the Mercers company made use of a meeting room in the Hospital, as well as a chapel in their church. They purchased the meeting room in 1413, and this became the first Mercers Hall. In 1442, the Mercers made annual payments to the monks at the hospital to say masses for their deceased brothers and sisters (Watney, 1892, p43). The Order had property and holy monks. The Mercers had money and by their foundation needed to maintain a chantry priest to protect their souls. The synergy was obvious. In 1444 the hospital was incorporated by Act of Parliament (Watney, 1892, p43), and by 1459 the Mercers had even 'purchased the right' to short list candidates for the Master of St Thomas of Acon, from which the brethren would make the final selection (Hill, 1852,p4). The financial considerations appear to have been considerable as the Hospital received from the Mercers £66-13s-4d in 1502, £100 in 1511, and loans of £40 and £100 in 1513 and 1514. From 1514, the master of St Thomas of Acon had to give an annual account of his administration to the Mercers Company (VCH, London, 1974,

---

23. It is also of note that, throughout living memory, the Royal Latin School has celebrated 'Founders Day' on the Feast of St John the Baptist.

p494). Thus the College of St Thomas of Acon, a religious house, became very intimately connected with the Mercers Company. Even the school started by John Neel, the Master of the Hospital of St Thomas of Acon in 1447, became known as the Mercers School after the Reformation, and 'was attached to this London hospital for the education of those children, who were the acolyths employed in the ministration of the services of the Church' (Hill, 1852, p1).

Thus it would appear that the Mercers directly supported the Order of St Thomas of Acon from c1442 to the Reformation. It is also apparent that both the Mercers and the Order had an interest in promoting education. It is not beyond the realms of possibility that because of this background, the boys at Buckingham had to be sons of local tradesmen.

Mildmay

Thomas Mildmay was a commissioner and auditor of the Court of Augmentations, founded in 1537 for handling the money received from the dissolution of the monasteries. Thomas obviously paved the way for his fourth and youngest son, Walter, born c1520 to become, in 1545, one of the two surveyors-general of the Court of Augmentations. Thus Thomas the father was a senior figure in the dissolution of the monasteries, and Walter the son was a senior figure in the dissolution of the chantries.

Walter was knighted in the last year of the reign of Henry VIII, and two weeks after the death of Henry, he was appointed commissioner of crown revenues. In 1548 he was on Edward VI's commission for the continuance of the grammar schools which had belonged to dissolved chantries. He was in charge of establishing the new mint at York in 1551, and for the accounting of the receipt of jewels, plate and other valuables surrendered by the chantries. Thus Mildmay was at the Court of Augmentations from 1547/8 to 1553/4 and had authority to sell those college lands, chantries, free chapels, guilds etc surrendered to Edward VI by the Acts of Parliaments of 1545/6 & 1547/8. He became a Member of Parliament and became involved in a census of royal farms under Elizabeth I, selling crown lands etc, and in 1566 was appointed Chancellor of the Exchequer. In 1585 he founded Emmanuel College, Cambridge. He informed Mary Queen of Scots of her forthcoming trial in 1586, and was a special commissioner at her trial. He died in 1589 (Smith, 1969).

Thomas Mildmay dissolved the Hospital of St Thomas of Acon, and his son Walter Mildmay agreed that the Bartons chantry school at Thornton should be continued.

Minshull

Richard Minshull was the grandson of Sir Richard Minshull, knight for Charles I, who lived at Bourton House which was taken and sacked in 1642. Richard lived 'in great splendour, keeping a Coach and six horses, falling into Gaming and other Extravagances' (Elliott, 1975, p35). He was imprisoned as a debtor in 1712 and died in 1729/30.

Newton

Gabriel Newton was born in 1683, was admitted to the freedom of the borough of Leicester in 1702, became Alderman of Leicester in 1726, and Mayor and Justice of the Peace in 1732. His family were mainly schoolmasters and clergy and thus he was a stout "Church and King" man. In 1746, having no sons to leave his fortune, estimated at £14,000, he decided to devote the greater part of it to the 'religious education of children'. In 1760-1762 he conveyed substantial land holdings in Leicestershire for charitable purposes with the Corporation acting as Trustees. Under the terms of the Trust, dated 15th March 1760, the Trust had to pay £26 per annum to the Corporation of Buckingham, as well as to other beneficiaries. These payments were to be used for the clothing and education of sons of indigent parents belonging to the Established Church of England. The stipulated colour of their coats was green - hence the establishment of the Green Coat school in Buckingham, and the proliferation of Green Coat schools elsewhere. It is recorded that James Jones was elected schoolmaster of the 'Gabriel Newton' charity school at Buckingham on 2nd July 1781 (Harrison, 1909, p26). Finally, by Newton's will of 1761, he left

£3,250 to be invested to generate income for the Clothing, Schooling and Educating of thirty-five boys ... without any regard to any particular parish. He died on 26th October 1762, aged 79. In 1784 the first school in Leicester was set up, followed by another in 1808. 'A chronic problem for the charity schools was the difficulty of getting suitable masters, the salaries being generally too low' (Greaves, p367). In 1833 the Leicester charity committee visited the Green Coat school at Buckingham to check the usage of their funding and the report stated that: 'the school was well run, and good use was made of the accumulated surplus of funds; though the master was allowed to teach twenty more day scholars, other than those on Newton's foundation' (Greaves, p348-375).

Pix

Mary Griffiths, daughter of Roger Griffiths the headmaster of the Royal Latin School (1665-1682), was born c1666 and married George Pix, a Merchant Tailor in 1684. In 1696, Mary Pix made her debut and produced a play 'Ibrahim, the 13th Emperor of the Turks' at the Dorset Garden, London - a blank verse tragedy which she dedicated to Richard Minshull of Bourton. She published a novel, a farce and wrote several plays. She was 'devoid of learning and notorious for her fatness and love of good wine', an acclamation which would have, no doubt, upset her father (Smith, 1969).

Ruding

In June 1451 Ruding was a professional scribe and compiler of legal documents in the diocese of Worcester, and was neither married nor in Holy Orders (Papal Letters, x, 552). In 1454 he was a Bachelor of Law and Prebendary of Ewherst and Holyngton in the free chapel of St Mary's within Hastings Castle in the Chichester diocese (Cal.Pat.Henry VI, vi, 162). In 1455-6 he was also rector of St Michaels in Gloucester (Worcester diocese). By 1457 he had relinquished his benefices in Chichester diocese (Cal.Pat. Henry VI, vi, 362); but still held Gloucester until 1468 (brass inscription). In 1455-6 he was Archdeacon of Stowe then Archdeacon of Bedfordshire in 1460, Prebendary of Biggleswade in 1467

Drawing of Ruding's memorial brass at Biggleswade

Reproduced with the kind permission of the Society of Antiquaries (Griffin, 1936).

which he relinquished the following year, when he became Archdeacon of Northamptonshire (Willis, 1730), and latterly Archdeacon of Lincoln and Prebendary of Sutton-cum-Buckingham in 1471 (Willis, 1755, p57). It is thought that Ruding's extensive use of the scallop shell symbolises a pilgrimage to the tomb of St James in Santiago de Compostela, Spain. Ruding died in 1481/2 (Willis, 1755, p75), when he was buried at Buckingham church as directed by his will (Gibbons, 1888).

Rumwold

The legend of St Rumwold of Buckingham, which dates from the 11th century, is that he was the son of Rumwold, King of Northumberland, and that his mother was the daughter of Penda, King of Mercia. As soon as he was born it is said that he announced himself to be a Christian and demanded to be baptised. He preached on wisdom and the Trinity, predicted his own death in three days time and gave instructions for his burial at three locations. His body was buried at Kings Sutton, then after a year reinterred at Brackley, and then after two years reinterred in the church of St Peter and St Paul at Buckingham church. Rumwold was canonised as a Saint, and his shrine became the focus of pilgrimage (Lipscombe, 1847, p580). The life of Rumwold has been brilliantly analysed, by examination of medieval documents (Love, 1996).[24]

Scott

Sir George Gilbert Scott (1811-1878) was a famous English architect, born at Gawcott, near Buckingham to Thomas Scott, Reverend of Holy Trinity Church. In Buckingham, in 1837 he advised on alterations to Castle House; in 1839 he provided drawings for the extension to Buckingham Gaol ; in 1860 he advised on a subsidence problem at Buckingham Church; in 1862 he designed a Workhouse in Buckingham for the accommodation of 125 paupers; in 1857 he designed a bell turret for the Royal Latin School. After 1840 he became the leading practical architect in the Gothic revival, and he was awarded many commissions to restore or build civil and ecclesiastical public buildings. His works include: the Martyrs Memorial, Oxford (1841); St Nicholas, Hamburg (1844); St George's, Doncaster; the India Office; the Home & Colonial Offices (1858); the Albert Memorial (1862-63); St Pancreas Station & Hotel, London (1865); Glasgow University (1865); the chapels of Exeter & St John's Colleges, Oxford. He was elected A.R.A.(1855), R.A.(1861), P.R.I.BA(1873-1876), Professor of Architecture at the Royal Academy (1868), and was knighted in 1872 (Chambers, 1972, p1150). In all, he 'designed, restored or otherwise influenced' 850 buildings (Encyclopaedia Britannica, 1994-1999).

Sackville

Thomas Sackville, first Earl of Dorset and Baron Buckhurst (1536-1608), was a barrister; poet & playwright; grand master of freemasons 1561-1567; knighted in 1567; privy councillor; commissioner of state trials and broke the news of her Death sentence to Mary Queen of Scots in 1586; treaty

---

[24]. Rumwold's Aisle was where John Barton (senior) elected to be buried and site his chantry in 1432.

negotiator with France; lord treasurer 1599 until his death; lord high steward at Essex's trial; chancellor of Oxford University in 1591 (Smith, 1969, p1147).

Stratton

Matthew Stratton was the Archdeacon of Buckingham for almost 50 years, from c1219 (Willis, 1755, p73). He also held the Prebend of Sutton-cum-Buckingham (VCH, Bucks, i, p290). The Prebendal Church of Buckingham and the Church of King's Sutton in Northamptonshire, were appropriated to the Cathedral of Lincoln in 1090 and formed one of its earliest and richest endowments, not least because of the benefits conferred by the numerous contributions by pilgrims to the Shrine of St Rumwold (Lipscombe, 1847, p572). It is recorded that the Prebend of Sutton-cum-Buckingham was the second most valuable in England [the most valuable being Massam in Yorkshire] (Harrison, 1909, p123). The value of the Prebend meant that Stratton was engaged in several legal battles about the benefices he held, and seems once to have upset Bishop Grosseteste by refusing to accept his arbitration (VCH, Bucks, i, p290).

The archdeacon of Buckingham was instructed by the Pope, to restore Buckingham church in 1239 and 1244 (Papal Letters, x). In 1245, in the 3rd year of Pope Innocent IV, it was confirmed that the parish church of St Peter and St Paul in Buckingham belonged to the Prebend of Sutton-cum-Buckingham, which was held by Matthew Stratton.[25]

Matthew de Stratton died about 1268 and willed his body to be buried in the Abbey of Osney in Oxford (Willis, MS22, p168).

---

25. Sutton-cum-Buckingham was the original name of the Archdeaconry of Buckingham; and from 1265 to 1675 the Prebendaries of Sutton-cum-Buckingham were the Incumbents of Buckingham (Sheahan, 1862,p234). The church at King's Sutton is called St Peter and St Paul, the same name as the church in Buckingham, and the wall arcading in the chancel dates from 1100. As the altar is dedicated to St Thomas of Canterbury (St Thomas of Acon), it is possible that Archbishop Thomas a Becket prayed in this church on his way to Northampton Castle to meet King Henry II, on the 5th or 6th October 1164. In 1170 Archbishop Thomas was killed in his Cathedral at Canterbury by four knights and was soon afterwards proclaimed a martyr.

Temple

Sir Peter Temple (1592-1653), was the second baronet of Stowe, an MP for Buckingham and knighted in 1641. He was a Parliamentarian (Smith, 1969).

Sir Richard Temple (1634-1697) was the third baronet of Stowe, son of Sir Peter Temple, and MP for Buckingham in 1659, 1660-1678, 1680-1697; and High Steward of the Borough of Buckingham, 1653-1687, -1697. He was a secret Royalist (Smith, 1969).

Sir Richard Temple (1669?-1749) was the fourth baronet of Stowe, MP for Buckingham in 1708 and 1710, and the shire in 1704-1705; he rebuilt Stowe and instituted the gardens.

Whitgift

John Whitgift (1530-1604) educated at Cambridge in 1550 where Bradford, was his tutor.[26] He obtained his BA in 1553/4, MA in 1557, and was ordained in 1560. He became Chaplain to Richard Cox in 1560 (Garrett, 1938, p134), and with this background had a 'strong desire for a unified Church of England' (Cross, 1958). In 1571 Whitgift became Dean of Lincoln, 1577 Bishop of Worcester, and Archbishop of Canterbury, 1583-1604. Later he founded and endowed schools and almshouses in Croyden (Cross, 1958).

Whittington

Richard (Dick) Whittington (c1340-1423), was probably the third son of Sir William Whittington of Pauntley in Gloucestershire. He married Alice daughter of Sir Ivo Fitzwaryn, a Dorset knight of considerable property. He was a mercer by trade, and became one of the most eminent members of the Mercers Company and a commercial magnate (Ditchfield, 1904, pp17-22). Thus he was well acquainted with the Barton and Chichele families. He made frequent large loans to Richard II, Henry IV and Henry V. He was sheriff of London in 1394, and mayor of London 1397-98, 1406-07, and

---

26. Bradford (1510-1555) was burnt at the stake for his Protestant beliefs.

1419-20. He left no children, so the greater part of his vast fortune was left for charitable and public purposes, that were administered by the Mercers (Ditchfield, 1904, pp17-22): the rebuilding of Newgate prison; founding an almshouse and college (Cross, 1958 & Encyclopaedia Brittanica, 1910, p615).

Willis

Browne Willis (1682-1760) was born in Dorset, and was educated at Westminster and Christ Church, Oxford. He was an avid and eccentric historian, without whom much of the history of the Royal Latin School would have been lost. He was elected MP for Buckingham, 1705-1708, being at that time resident of Whaddon. He used his influence to promote the prosperity of Buckingham, and succeeded in bringing the assizes back to Buckingham from Aylesbury, initiated the building of the gaol in the market square, and collected a large sum for the repair to the old church. He wrote a number of books, the best known of which is the 'History of Buckingham' published in 1755. He was active in building, restoring and maintaining churches and schools for the poor.

Wykeham

William de Wykeham (1324-1404), educated at Winchester, became the King's chaplain in 1347 and chief warden and surveyor of a number of royal castles. He took up numerous ecclesiastical posts at various locations including Prebendary of: Lichfield in 1359; St Paul's London; Hereford; Salisbury; Beverley; Bromyard; York; Wells; and Hastings. He was archdeacon of Lincoln in 1363, Prebendary of Buckingham in 1365, Bishop of Winchester 1367-1404, Chancellor of Winchester 1368-1371, and founded New College in 1379 (Smith, 1969). A chantry chapel was built for him at Winchester Cathedral.

BIBLIOGRAPHY

Adams, J.	*'To be a Farmers Boy'*, Private Communication, 1998.
Allison, K.J. Beresford, M.W. & Hurst, J.G.	*'The deserted Villages of Oxfordshire'*, Dept. English Local History, Occasional papers No.17, Leicester University Press.
Balfour, M.	*'Edmund Harman - Barber and Gentleman'*, Tolsey Paper No.6, The Tolsey Museum, Burford, 1988.
BCC	*'Buckinghamshire County Guide'*, The British Publishing Company, 1997.
BCFSPTA	*'Memories of a school in Buckingham'*, Buckinghamshire County First Parent Teacher Association,1979.
Beckett, I.F.W.	*'Posse Comitatus 1798'*, Buckinghamshire Record Society, No.22, 1985.
Beckett, J.	*'The Rise and Fall of the Grenvilles'*, Manchester University Press, 1994.
Belloc, H.	*'How the Reformation Happened'*, Cape, London, 1934.
Black, A & C.	*'Who was Who, 1897-1915'*, London: 1962.
Blomfield, J.C.	*'History of Deanery of Bicester'*, Bristol, 1887.
Blomfield, J.C.	*'History of Deanery of Bicester'*, Parts 7-8, London: Elliot Stock, 1893.
Blomfield, J.C.	*'History of Finmere', Walford*, Advertiser Office, 1887.

BM Lansd 572	Lansdowne Charters, fol 572, British Museum (now at the British Library).
Boase, C.W.	*'Register of Oxford University'*, Oxford History Society, Clarendon Press, 1885.
Boatwright, L.	'Inquests and Indictments from the late 14th Century Buckinghamshire', *Bucks. Rec. Soc. 29,* 1994.
Bowker, M.	*'The Henrican Reformation - the Diocese of Lincoln under John Longland, 1521-1547'*, Cambridge University Press, 1981.
BRO	Buckinghamshire Record Office, Aylesbury.
Broad, J.	'Buckinghamshire Dissent and Parish Life, 1669-1712', Editor: John Broad, *Bucks Record Soc*, No.28, 1993.
Brown, J.E.	*'The Edwardian Inventories of Buckinghamshire'*, Editor: Eeles, F.C., 1908.
Bucks Advert.	Newspapers: 'Buckingham Advertiser & North Bucks Free Press' or 'Buckingham Advertiser & Winslow & Brackley Record', various dates.
Bucks District Councils	*'Catalogue of Records of the borough of Buckingham: District Councils. 1554-1974'*
Bucks Herald	Newspaper: 'Bucks Herald', various dates.
Burke, A.P.	*'Family Records'*, Heraldic Publishing Co. Inc.: New York, 1965.
C143	'Inqusitions ad quod Damnum' Henry III to Richard III, Chancery Records at the Public Records Office, Kew.
Cal.Chart Rolls	*'Calendar of Charter Rolls'*, HMSO, various dates.

Cal Pat — *'Calendar of Letters Patent Rolls'*, HMSO, 1891-1986.

Carlisle, N. — *'A concise description of the Endowed Grammar Schools in England and Wales'*, Baldwin Craddock & Joy, 1818.

Catto, J.I. & Evans, R. — *'The History of the University of Oxford'*: Clarendon Press, Oxford, 1992.

Chambers, W.R. — *'Bibliographical Dictionary'*, Editor: J.O.Thorne, London: W. & R. Chambers Ltd, 1972

Chapman, C. R. — *'The Growth of British Education and its records'*, Lochin Publishing, Dursley, Gloucestershire, 1992.

Charity Commission — *'Commissioners Reports of 1819-1837'*, Clowes, London.

Charity Commission — *'Analytical digest of the Commissioners Reports of the Digest printed in 1832'*, Clowes, London, 1835.

Charity Commission — *'The 14th Report of the Charity Commissioners of Endowed Charities'*, 1868.

Charity Trustees — *'Minutes of the Charity Trustees at Buckingham'*, Aylesbury Record Office, CH34/AM1, 1838-1877.

Chibnall, A.C. — *'Certificate of Muster for Buckinghamshire 1522'* by The Royal Commission on Historical Manuscripts, Edited by A.C.Chibnall, HMSO, 1973.

Clarke, John — *'The book of Buckingham'*, Barracuda Books Ltd., Buckingham, 1984.

Cocks, A.H. — *'The Church Bells of Buckinghamshire'*, London: Jarrold & Sons, 1897.

Constant, G. — *'The Reformation in England, the English Schism'*, Sheed & Ward, London, 1934.

Cook, G.H. *'Letters to Cromwell and others on the Suppression of the Monasteries'*, London: J.Baker, 1965.

Crockford *'Crockford's Clerical Directory'*, Horace Cox, London.

Crook, W.G.S. 'A long tradition of learning in Buckingham', *Buckinghamshire and Berkshire Countryside*, March 1975.

Cross, F.L. *'The Oxford Dictionary of the Christian Church'*, Oxford University Press, London, 1958.

Curtis, S.J. *'History of Education in Great Britain'*, University Tutorial Press Ltd., London, 1968.

Curtis, S.J. & Boultwood, M.E.A. *'An Introductory History of English Education since 1800'*, University Tutorial Press Ltd, London, 1970.

Dickens, A.G. *'The English Reformation'*, London: B.T.Batsford Ltd, 1989.

Ditchfield, P.H. *'The City Companies of London'*, London: J.M.Dent, 1904.

Dominey, J.H. *'Biggleswade Parish Church, through seven centuries,1276-1976'*, 1976.

Douglas, D.C. *'English Historical Documents 1833-1874'*, Eds Young, G.M. & Handcock, W.D., London: Eyre & Spottiswoode, 1956.

Dutton, Allen & Co *'Buckinghamshire Directory'*, 1863.

E301 'Augmentations Office: Chantry Certificates', Exchequer Records at the Public Records Office, Kew.

E322 'Augmentations Office: Surrender by the larger monasteries' Exchequer Records at the Public Records Office, Kew.

ED162 — 'Education Records: secondary schools' at the Public Records Office, Kew.

Elliott, D.J. — *'Buckingham - The Loyal and Ancient Borough'*, London: Phillimore, 1975.

Elvey, G.R. — *'Luffield Priory Charters'*, Buckinghamshire & Northamptonshire Record Societies, 1975.

Emden, A.B. — *'A Biographical Register of the University of Oxford to AD 1500'*, Oxford, 1959.

Emden, A.B. — *'A Biographical Register of the University of Oxford 1501 to 1540'*, Oxford, 1974.

Encyclopaedia Britannica — *'Encyclopaedia Britannica - A Dictionary of Arts, Sciences, Literature and General Information'*, Cambridge University Press, 1911.

Ford, T. — 'Letter to Browne Willis', *MS22*, p58-59, 1733. Bodleian Library.

Forey, A.J. — 'The Military Order of St Thomas of Acre', *English Historical Review*, Vol XCII, No.CCCLXIV, July 1977.

Foster, C.W. & Thompson, H.A. — *'Chantry Certificates for Lincoln and Lincolnshire, 1548'*, Architectural & Archaeological Society of Lincoln, 1927.

Fowler, G.H. — *'Rolls from the office of the Sheriff of Bedfordshire and Buckinghamshire, 1332-1334'* , The County Museum, Aylesbury, & Bedfordshire Record Society, 1929.

Friar, S. — *'Heraldry for the Local Historian and Genealogist'*, Grange Books, London, 1992.

Garrett, C.H. — *'The Marian Exiles, 1553-1559'*, Cambridge University Press, 1938.

Genealogist	*'Genealogist Magazine'*, Quarterly Journal of the Society of Genealogists, London, new series. Various dates.
Gentleman's Magazine	*'Gentleman's Magazine'*, published monthly from 1731-1868.
Gibbs, R.	'Buckinghamshire local occurances 1400-1700', *Buckinghamshire Local Records,* Aylesbury, 1878.
Gibbons, A.	*'Early Lincoln wills'*, 1888.
Giles, J.A.	*'Matthew Paris's English History 1235-1273'*, H.Bohn, London, 1852.
Goodman, A.	'Richard II servants & the Missenden Inheritance', in *Records of Buckinghamshire or papers and notes on the History, Antiquities, and Architecture of the county*: Architectural and Archaeological Society, Aylesbury, Vol 17, 1961-1965, p350-355.
Gough, R.	*'Sepulchral Monuments of Great Britain'*, 1786-1796, pl.102, Vol ii, p272*n*.
Greaves, R.W.	*'The origins and early history of Alderman Newton's Foundation'*, Leicestershire Archaeological Society.
Grimsdale, E.	'Personal communication', 1999 & 2000, Deputy Head of the Royal Latin School.
Griffin, R.	'A brass once in Biggleswade church', *Journal of the Society of Antiquaries of London*, XVI, 1936, p284-290.
Halstead, W.	'Letter to Browne Willis', *MS22*, p60. 1734. Bodleian Library.
Harrison, J.T.	'The Royal Latin School, Buckingham', in *Records of Buckinghamshire or papers and notes on the History,*

Antiquities, and Architecture of the county: Architectural and Archaeological Society, Aylesbury, 1909.

Hey, D. *'The Oxford Dictionary of Local and Family History'*, Oxford University Press, 1997.

Hill, Rev T. *'The History of the Mercers School, London'*, London: R.Clay, 1852.

Hodgett, G.A.J. 'Pensions assigned to former incumbents of Dissolved Chantries, 1547-1574', *Lincolnshire Record Society,* No.53, 1959.

Hughes, M.W. 'Calendar of Feet of Fines for the County of Buckingham', *Records of Buckinghamshire or papers and notes on the History, Antiquities, and Architecture of the county: Architectural and Archaeological Society*, Aylesbury, Vol 4, 1940.

Hundred Rolls *'Rotuli Hundredorum',* 1812

Jenkins, J.G. 'Calendar of the Roll of the Justices of Eyre, 1227', in *Records of Buckinghamshire or papers and notes on the History, Antiquities, and Architecture of the county: Architectural and Archaeological Society*, Aylesbury, 1945.

Jenkins, J.G. 'An Early Coroners Roll for Buckinghamshire' in *Records of Buckinghamshire or papers and notes on the History, Antiquities, and Architecture of the county: Architectural and Archaeological Society*, Aylesbury, 13, p163-185, 1934-1940.

Johnson, R.M. 'Buckinghamshire 1640-1660 - a study in county politics' a thesis lodged at Aylesbury Reference Library, written in 1962-63.

Kelke, Rev W.H. — 'The Destroyed and Desecrated churches of Buckinghamshire', in *Records of Buckinghamshire or papers and notes on the History, Antiquities, and Architecture of the county: Architectural and Archaeological Society*: James Pickburn, Aylesbury, Vol 1, 1858.

Kellys — 'Post Office Directory of Buckinghamshire', various dates.

Kennet, W. — *'Parochial Antiquities, attempted in the history of Ambrosden, Burchester and other adjacent parts in the Counties of Oxford and Buckingham'*, The Theater, Oxford, 1695.

Kennet, W. — *'Parochial Antiquities, attempted in the history of Ambrosden, Burchester and other adjacent parts in the Counties of Oxford and Buckingham'*, Clarendon Press, Oxford, enlarged from the authors manuscript notes of 1685, printed in 1818.

Knowles, D & Hadcock, R.N. — *'Medieval Religious Houses in England and Wales'*, London: Longman, 1971.

Kohn, G.C. — *'Dictionary of Historic Documents'*, Facts on File Inc, New York, 1991.

Lathan,R. & Matthews,W. — *'The diary of Samuel Pepys'*, Vol ix, 1668-1669, London: G.Bell & Sons Ltd., 1976.

L&P Hen VIII — *''Letters and Patents, Foreign and Domestic of Henry VIII'*, HMSO, 1862-1932.

Laugharne Indenture — 'Laugharne Indenture', 1855, Buckinghamshire Record Office.

Leach, A.F. — *'The Schools of Medieval England'*, London: Methuen Co. Ltd.1969.

Leach, A.F. *'English Schools at the Reformation'*, Westminster: Archibald Constable & Co. 1896.

Lipscombe, G. *'History and Antiquities of the County of Buckinghamshire'*, 1847.

Long, C.E. 'Dairy of the marches of the royal army [1664-5]' Editor C.E.Long, *Camden Soc*, 1859.

Longden, Rev H.I. *'Northamptonshire & Rutland Clergy from 1500'*, Northampton: Archer & Goodman, 1939.

Love, R.C. *'Three Eleventh-century Anglo-Latin Saints' Lives'*, Clarendon Press, Oxford, 1996.

McLaughlin, E. 'Notley Abbey', in *Bucks Ancestor*, June 1997: Buckinghamshire Genealogy Society, Vol 6, No.2, pp66-68.

Mercer & Crocker *'Mercer & Crocker's Directory'*, Mercer & Crocker: Leicester, 1871.

Midmer, R. *'English Mediaeval Monasteries 1066-1540'*, Heinemann: London, 1979.

Miner, J.N. *'The Grammar Schools of Medieval England, A.F.Leach in Historiographical Perspective'*, McGill-Queen's Press, London, 1990.

Morton, E. F. M.B.E. 'An Ancient Foundation', Manuscript in Royal Latin School Archive, 1988.

Musson & Craven *'Musson & Craven's Commercial Directory'*, Nottingham, 1853.

New College 'New College', Internet, http://193.123.31.186/new.html, Aligrafix 1995.

Nichols, W — *'An alphabetical list of the names of the several persons who voted at the election of the knights of the shire for the county of Buckingham ... at Aylesbury on Wednesday 21st April to Thursday 6th May 1784'*, Nicholls, 1785.

Osborn — *'Osborn's Concise Law Dictionary'*, 8th edition, Eds: L.Rutherford & S.Bone, London: Sweet & Maxwell, 1994.

Papal Letters — *'Calendar of Papal Letters relating to the British Isles, from 1198 to1492'*, HMSO, 1893-1960 at the Public Records Office, Kew.

Pigot — *'Pigot and Company's London and New Commercial Directory*, 1823-24.

Pigot — *'Pigot and Company's National Commercial Directory'*, 1830.

Pigot — *'Pigot and Company's National Commercial Directory'*, 1831-32.

Pigot — *'Pigot and Company's National Commercial Directory'*, 1842.

Powicke, F.M. — *'Medieval books of Merton'*, Clarendon Press, Oxford, 1931.

Ramsay, G.D. — *'John Isham, Mercer and Merchant Adventurer'*, Northamptonshire Record Society, Vol XXI, Northumberland Press, Durham, 1962.

Rashdall, H. — *'The Universities of Europe in the Middle Ages'*, London: Oxford University Press, 1951.

Rayner-Smith, C. — *'Hardwick-cum-Tusmore'*, Oxford: Oliver & Son, 1972.

REQ2 — 'Court of Requests', Chancery Records at the Public Records Office, Kew.

Richardson, J. *'The Local Historians Encyclopaedia'*, Historical Publications Ltd, New Barnet, Herts, 1993.

Riley, H.T. *'Memorials of London in the 13th 14th & 15th centuries'*, Longmans, London, 1868.

RLSM *'Royal Latin School Magazine'*, RLS Archives.

RLSOLA 'Royal Latin School Old Latins Association', RLS Archives.

Roskell, J.S. *'The House of Commons 1386-1421'*, 1992.

Roundell, H. *'Some account of the town of Buckingham'*, Chandler: Buckingham, 1857.

Roundell, H. *'Buckingham town, Buckingham people and their Neighbours during the Civil Wars'*, Buckingham, 1864.

Routh, C.R.N. *'Who's who in history 1485-1603'*, Oxford: Basil Blackwell, 1964.

Roy, I. 'Royalist Ordnance Papers 1642-1646', Part 2, Ed Ian Roy, Vol xlix, *Oxfordshire Record Soc.*, 1975.

Russell, R.H. 'The Monuments at Thornton, Bucks' in *Records of Buckinghamshire or papers and notes on the History, Antiquities, and Architecture of the county: Architectural and Archaeological Society*, Aylesbury, Vol 7, 1897.

Salter, Rev H. *'Subsidy collected in the Diocese of Lincoln in 1526'*, Blackwell: Oxford, 1909.

Salter, H.E. *'A Cartulary of the Hospital of St John the Baptist'*, Oxford Historical Soc., Oxford, 1917.

SFO 'Fire Insurance Index, Sun Fire Office', 1725. The Guildhall, London.

Sheahan, J.J. *'History and Topography of Buckinghamshire comprising a general survey of the county'*, London: Longman, Green, Longman and Roberts, 1862.

Smith, G. *'The Dictionary of National Biography'*, Oxford University Press, 1892.

Smith, G. *'The Dictionary of National Biography, The Concise Dictionary'*, Oxford University Press, 1969.

Smith, W.H. 'The Borough Guides - Buckingham', No.65.

Stalker, C. *'The Universal British Directory of Trade and Commerce'*, London, 1790.

Stalker, C. *'The Universal British Directory'* London, 1791.

Stephen, L. *'Dictionary of National Biography'*, London: Smith, Elder & Co., 1888.

Stephenson, B. *'Stephenson's Book of Quotations'*, London: Cassell, 1946.

Thompson, D. 'The Braose Web', www.freespace.virgin.net/doug.thompson/Braoseweb/, 1998-2000.

Tricker, R. *'The Church of St Michael and All Angels, Thornton, Buckinghamshire'*, The Churches Conservation Trust, Series 4, no.25, 1996.

Ussher, Rev R. *'A history of the Parish of Westbury'*. Undated. Bucks RO.

VCH. *'Buckinghamshire'*, Victoria County History.

VCH. *'Berkshire'*, Victoria County History.

VCH. *'London'*, Victoria County History.

VCH. *'Northamptonshire'*, Victoria County History

VCH. '*Oxfordshire*', Victoria County History.

VCH. '*Warwickshire*', Victoria County History

Watney, Sir J. '*Some account of the Hospital of St Thomas of Acon*', London: Blades, East & Blades, London, 1892.

Watney, Sir J. '*Some account of the Hospital of St Thomas of Acon*', London: Blades, East & Blades, London, 1906.

Weaver, F.W. '*The Visitation of Herefordshire made by R.Cooke in 1569*', Exeter: William Pollard, 1886.

Willis, Browne '*An history of the Mitred Parliamentary Abbeys and Continental Cathedral churches*' London, 1719.

Willis, Browne. '*Survey of the cathedrals of Lincoln etc*', London, 1730.

Willis, Browne. '*The History and Antiquities of the Town, Hundred and Deanery of Buckingham*', London, 1755.

Willis, Browne. *MS 22*, Bodleian Library, Oxford.

APPENDIX I

Writ for Inquisition ad quod damnum 1289/90 (C143/14 No5)

C143/14 No 5. Reproduced with kind permission of the Public Records Office

The letter from King Edward I to the Sheriff of Buckingham

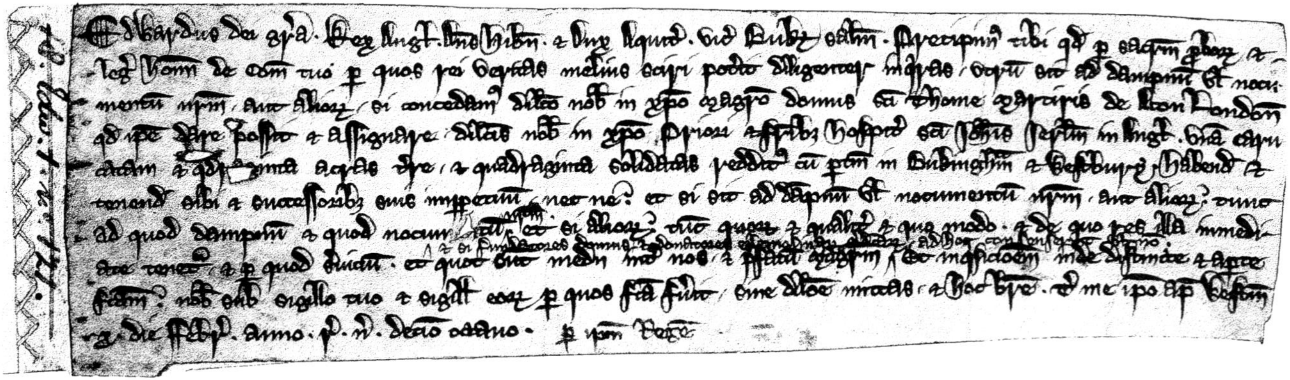

Transcription of the letter from King Edward I to the Sheriff of Buckingham

EdWardus dei gra[cia] Rex Angl[ie], D[omi]n[u]s Hib[er]n[ie] et Dux Aquit[anie] vic[ecomiti] Buk[ingham] sal[ute]m. Precipim[us] tibi q[uo]d p[er] sacr[amentu]m p[ro]bo[rum] et

leg[alium] homi[num] de Com[itatu] tuo p[er] quos rei veritas melius sciri pot[er]it diligenter inq[ui]ras vtru[m] sit ad dampnu[m] vel

nocument[um] n[ost]r[u]m aut alior[um] si concedam[us] dil[e]c[t]o nob[is] in [Christ]o mag[ist]ro domus s[an]c[t]i Thome martiris de Acon London[ie] q[uo]d ip[s]e dare possit et assignare dil[ec]tis nob[is] in [Christ]o Priori et fr[atr]ib[us] Hospit[alis] s[an]c[t]i Joh[ann]is Jer[usale]m in Angl[ia]. vna[m] carucatam

et q[ua]draginta acras t[er]re et quadraginta solidatas reddit[us] cu[m] p[er]tin[enciis] in Bukingh[a]m et Westbury Habend[as] et

tened[as] sibi et successorib[us] suis imp[er]petuu[m] nec ne; et si sit ad da[m]pnu[m] u[e]l nocumentu[m] n[ost]r[u]m aut alior[um] tunc

ad quod dampnu[m] et quod nocumentu[m] n[ost]r[u]m et si alior[um] t[u]nc quor[um] et qual[i]t[er] et quo modo, et de quo res illa immediate

tenet[ur], et p[er] quod s[er]uiciu[m] et quot s[u]nt medii int[er] nos et p[re]fatu[m] mag[ist]r[u]m, et si fundatores domus et donatores elemosina[rum]

eiusdem adhoc consenserant v[e]l no[n]; Et inq[ui]sicio[n]em inde distincte et ap[er]te f[ac]tam nob[is] sub sigillo tuo et sigill[is] eor[um] p[er] quos f[ac]ta

fu[er]it sine dil[aci]o[n]e mittas et Hoc br[ev]e. T[este] me ip[s]o ap[ud] Westm[onasterio] x die Febr[uarii] anno r[egni] n[ostri] deci[m]o octauo.

p[er] ip[su]m Rege[m].

Translation of the letter from King Edward I to the Sheriff of Buckingham

Edward by the grace of God, King of England, Lord of Ireland, and Duke of Aquitaine, Sends greetings to the Sheriff of Buckingham. We command you that, by the oaths of honest and

law-abiding men of your county, by whom the truth of the matter may be best known, you should diligently inquire, whether it would be to the loss or

harm of us, or of other people, if we were to grant, to our beloved in Christ the Master of the Hospital of St Thomas the Martyr of Acon in London,

That he might give and assign, to our beloved in Christ the Prior and brethren of the Hospital of St John of Jerusalem in England, One carucate and

forty acres of land and forty shillings in rents, with their appurtenances, in Buckingham and Westbury, To have and

to hold to them and their successors for ever or not; And if it would be to the loss or harm of us, or of other people, then

to what loss or harm of us, and if that of others, then of whom, and of what kind and in what manner, And of whom that property is immediately

held, and by what service, and how many mesne tenants there might be between us and the aforesaid Master, and whether the founders of the house and the donors of free alms consent to this or not. And you should send the inquisition thereof, clearly and openly made, and this writ, to us, under your seal and the seals of those by whom it was made, without delay. Witness myself at Westminster on the 10th day of February in the eighteenth year of our reign.

by the King himself.

The reply from the Sheriff of Buckingham to King Edward I

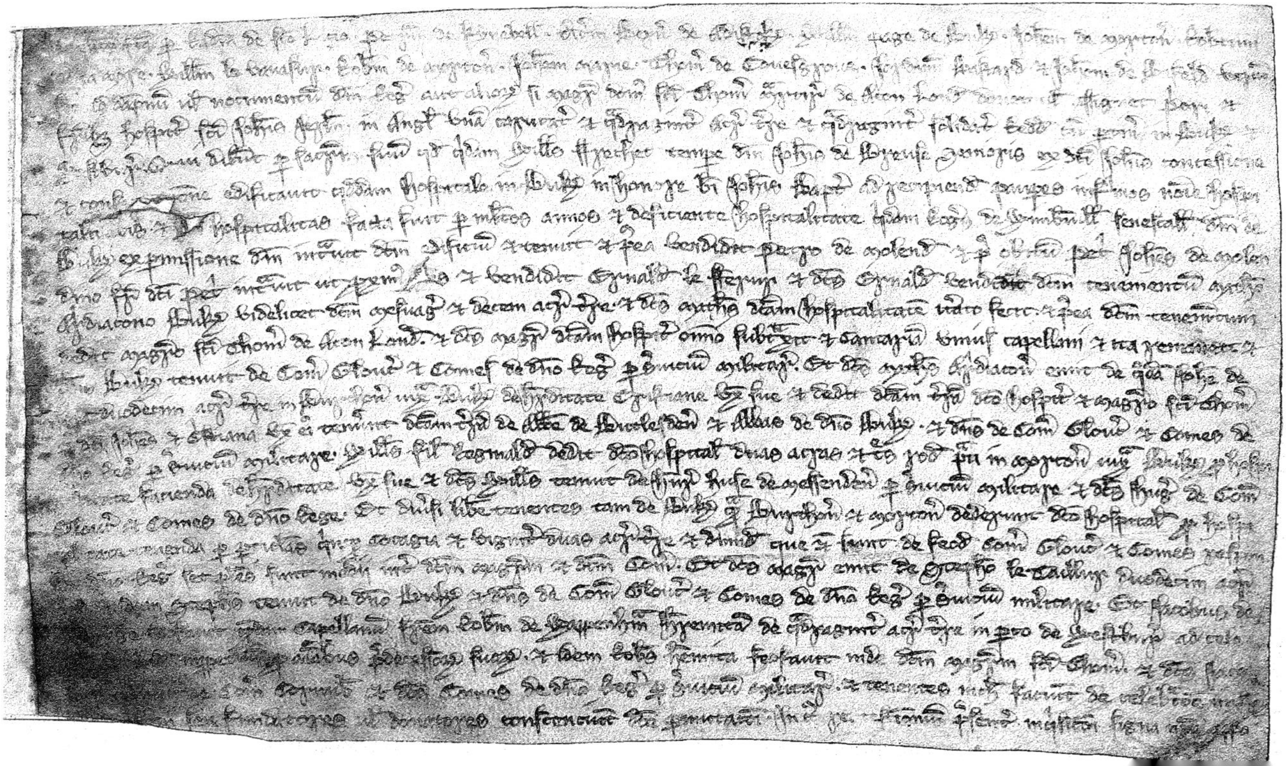

Transcription of the letter from the Sheriff of Buckingham to King Edward I

Inquisitio f[ac]ta p[er] Rad[ulfu]m de s[anc]to Lucio, Petr[u]m de Kynebell, Ric[hardu]m Bern[er] de Adistoke, Will[elmu]m page de Buk[ingham], Joh[ann]em de morton, Rob[er]tum

de la mare, Will[elmu]m le vauasur, Rob[ertu]m de morton' Joh[ann]em marie, Thom[as] de Couesgroue, Jorda[nu]m Bastard et Joh[ann]em de Bifeld vtr[u]m

sit ad da[m]pnu[m] ut nocumentu[m] d[o]m[ini] Reg[is] aut alior[um] si mag[iste]r dom[us] s[an]c[t]i Thom[e] m[a]rtiri[s] de Acon Lond[onii] donet u[e]l assignet P[ri]ori et

fra[tri]b[us] hospit[alis] s[an]c[t]i Joh[ann]is Jer[usa]l[e]m in Angl[ia] vna[m] carucat[am] et q[ua]dragint[a] acr[as] t[er]re et q[ua]dragint[a] solidat[as] redd[ituum] cu[m] p[er]tin[enciis] in Buk[inghania] et

Westbur' Qui dic[u]nt p[er] sacr[ament]um suu[m] q[uo]d q[ui]dam Wille[lmu]s Frethet temp[or]e d[o]m[ini] Joh[ann]is de Breuse senioris ex d[ic]ti Joh[ann]is concessione

et consi[derati]one edificauit q[uo]ddam hospitale in Buk[inghania] in honore b[eat]i Joh[ann]is Bapt[iste] ad recipiend[um] paup[er]es inf[ir]mos no[m]i[n]e hospitalitatis

et [quod] hospitalitas facta fuit p[er] m[u]ltos annos et deficiente hospitalitate q[ui]dam Rog[eru]s de Wimb[er]uill senescall[us] d[o]m[ini] de

Buk[inghania] ex p[er]missione d[o]m[ini] int[ra]uit d[i]c[tu]m edificiu[m] et tenuit et p[ost]ea vendidit Petro de molend[ino] et p[ost] obitu[m] Pet[ri] Joh[ann]es de molendino

fra[ter] d[i]c[t]i petri int[ra]uit ut p[ro]xim[us] [he]res et vendidit Ernald[o] le Ferur et d[ic]t[u]s Ernald[us] vendidit d[i]c[tu]m tenementu[m] Math[e]o

Ar[chi]diacono Buk[inghania] videlicet d[i]c[tu]m mesuag[ium] et decem acra[s] t[er]re, et d[i]c[tu]s math[eu]s d[i]c[t]am hospitalitatem it[er]ato fecit et p[ost]ea d[i]c[tu]m tenem[en]tum

dedit mag[ist]ro s[anc]ti Thom[e] de Acon Lond[onie], et d[i]c[tu]s mag[iste]r d[ic]tam hospit[alitem] om[n]i[n]o subt[ra]xit et cantaria[m] vnius capellani et ita remanet et

d[omi]n[u]s Buk[ingham] tenuit de Comi[te] Glouc[estrie] et Comes de d[omi]no Reg[e] p[er] s[er]uiciu[m] militar[e]; Et d[i]c[tu]s math[eu]s Ar[chi]diacon[us] emit de q[uo]da[m] Joh[anne] de

leys duodecim acra[s] t[er]re in Burthon iux[ta] Buk[inghania] de h[e]r[e]ditate Cristiane vx[oris] sue et dedit d[i]c[t]am t[er]ra[m] d[i]c[t]o hospit[ali] et mag[ist]ro s[an]c[t]i Thom[e],

et d[ic]ti Joh[ann]es et C[ri]stiana ux[or] ei[us] tenu[er]unt d[i]c[t]am t[er]ra[m] de Abb[at]e de Bittlesden et Abbas de d[omi]no Buk[inghania], et d[omi]n[u]s de Com[ite] Glouc[estrie] et Comes de

d[omi]no Reg[e] p[er] s[er]uiciu[m] militare. Will[elmu]s fil[ius] Reginald[i] dedit d[ic]to Hospital[i] duas acras et t[re]s rod[as] p[ra]ti in morton' iux[ta] Buk[inghania] p[ro] hospitalitate

facienda de h[e]r[e]ditate vx[oris] sue et d[i]c[tu]s Will[elmu]s tenuit de H[e]nr[ico] Huse de messenden p[er] s[er]uiciu[m] militare et d[i]c[tu]s Hugo de Comite

Glouc[estrie] et Comes de d[omi]no Rege; Et diu[er]si lib[er]e tenentes tam de Buk[inghania] q[uam] Burthon et morton dederunt d[i]c[t]o hospital[i] p[ro] hospitalite tenenda p[er] p[er]tic[u]las qu[inque] cotagia et vigint[i] duas acra[s] t[er]re et dimid[iam] que et[iam] sunt de feod[o] Com[itis] Glouc[estrie] et Comes respondit

d[omi]no Reg[e], set pl[ur]es sunt medii int[er] d[i]c[tu]m mag[ist]r[u]m et d[i]c[tu]m Com[item]; Et d[i]c[tu]s mag[iste]r emit de Steph[an]o le Taillur duodecim acras

[illegible] et idem Steph[anu]s tenuit de d[omi]no Buk[ingham] et d[omi]n[u]s de Com[ite] Glouc[estrie] et Comes de d[omi]no Reg[e] p[er] s[er]uiciu[m] militare; Et Jacobus de

[illegible] feofauit ip[s]um capellanu[m] fr[atr]em Rob[ertu]m de Wappenh[a]m, h[e]remita[m], de q[uad]ragint[a] acris t[er]re in p[ar]co de Westburi ad cele[brandum]

[illegible] imperpetuum p[ro] an[im]abus p[re]decesso[rum] suo[rum] et idem Rob[ertu]s h[er]emita feofauit inde d[i]c[tu]m mag[ist]r[u]m s[an]c[t]i Thom[e], et d[i]c[tu]s Jaco

bus [tenuit] de Com[ite] Cornubie, et d[i]c[tu]s Comes de d[omi]ne Reg[e] p[er] s[er]uicium militar[e], et tenentes nich[il] faci[u]nt de celeb[ra]c[i]o[n]e [illegible] *

[illegible] seu fundatores u[e]l donatores conscenciunt d[ict]i p[re]mictac[i]o[n]i[s]. In c[uius] rei testi[m]oniu[m] p[re]sent[i] inq[ui]sic[i]o[n]i signa n[ost]ra appo[suimus].

* Possibly miss[arum]

Translation of the letter from the Sheriff of Buckingham to King Edward I

Inquisition taken by Ralph de Saint Lucius, Peter de Kynebell, Richard Berner of Adistock, William Page of Buckingham, John de Morton, Robert

de la Mare, William le Vauasur, Robert de Morton, John Marie, Thomas de Covesgrove, Jordan Bastard, and John de Bifeld, whether

it would be to the loss or harm to our Lord the King, or to others, if the Master of the House of Saint Thomas the Martyr of Acon in London should give or assign, to the Prior and

brethren of the Hospital of Saint John of Jerusalem in England, one carucate and forty acres of land and forty shillings in rent, with their appurtenances, in Buckingham and

Westbury; and [the said jurors] say, on their oath, that a certain William Frethet, in the time of our Lord John de Braose senior, by the grant and decision of the said John,

built a certain hospital in Buckingham in honour of Saint John the Baptist, to receive poor sick people in the name of hospitality,

and it provided hospitality for many years. And when the hospitality ceased, a certain Roger de Wimbervill, steward of our Lord of

Buckingham, by permission of the Lord, entered and held the said building, and afterwards sold it to Peter Miller, and after the death of Peter, John Miller, the brother of the said Peter, entered it as next heir, and sold it to Ernald le Ferur, and the said Ernald sold the said tenement to Matthew,

Archdeacon of Buckingham, namely, the said messuage and ten acres of land. And the said Matthew made the hospital begin again, and afterwards gave the said tenement

to the Master of Saint Thomas of Acon in London, and the said Master of the said hospital removed everything and a chantry of one chaplain, and thus it remains. And

the Lord of Buckingham held it of the Earl of Gloucester, and the Earl held it of our lord the King by knight service. And the said Matthew the Archdeacon bought, of a certain John de

Leys, twelve acres of land in Bourton near Buckingham, out of the inheritance of Christiana his wife, and he gave the said land to the said hospital and to the Master of Saint Thomas.

And the said John and Christiana his wife held the said land of the Abbot of Bittlesden, and the Abbot held it of the lord of Buckingham, and the lord held it of the Earl of Gloucester, and the Earl held it of

the lord King by knight service. William son of Reginald gave to the said hospital two acres and three roods of meadow in Morton near Buckingham, to make a hospital,

out of the inheritance of his wife, And the said William held it of Henry Huse of Messenden by knight service, and the said Hugh held it of the Earl of

Gloucester, and the Earl held it of our lord the King. And various free tenants, both of Buckingham and of Bourton and Moreton, gave to the said hospital, for hospitality, five cottages held separately and twenty-two and a half acres of land, which are of the fee of the Earl of Gloucester. And the Earl held them of

the lord King, but there are several mesne tenants between the said Master and the said Earl. And the said Master bought of Stephen Taylor [le Taillur] twelve acres

[illegible] [which] the same Stephen held of the Lord of Buckingham. And the lord held it of the Earl of Gloucester, and the Earl held it of the lord King by knight service. And James de

[illegible] enfeoffed a certain chaplain, Brother Robert de Wappenham a hermit, of forty acres of land in the park of Westbury, for celebrating

[illegible] [mass] for ever for the souls of his ancestors, and the same Robert the hermit enfeoffed thereof the Master of Saint Thomas. And the said James

held it of the Earl of Cornwall, and the said Earl held it of the lord King by knight service. And the tenants do nothing about the celebration [illegible] [of masses],

[illegible] whether the benefactors or the founders or donors consent to the said arrangement. In witness whereof to this present inquisition we have set our seals.

Footnotes to the Inquisition ad quod damnum

a. Ralph de Saint Lucius is probably Ralph de St Lys of Westbury and rector of Radclive, whose family held the St Walery Honour in Westbury. This property was also said to be held by the Earls of Cornwall between 1240 and 1335 (VCH, Bucks, iv, p263-265). At the beginning of the reign of Edward I, Joanne de Someri was Lady of Westbury and with Simon St Lys held one Knights fee called the honour of St Wallery, of the Earl of Cornwall, and the Earl of the king, in capite, and paid scutage and 4 marks per annum to the Earl of Cornwall (Lipscombe, iii, p142). William de Kynebelle was a chaplain and baliff of the Liberty of St Walery (Fowler, p7, 1929).

b. A Roger de Wymbervill appears in the Calendar of Roll for the Justices of Eyre in 1227, as a man who is able to give his pledge on behalf of others, and is named in legal cases regarding lands in Deniton & Fulebroc (Jenkins, 1945).

c. Most of the names of these witnesses also appear as witnesses or jurors in the Luffield Priory Charters. For example: Peter de Kynebell, Ralph de Saint Lucius and John Morton are witnesses in 1292 (Elvey, 1975, no735); Ralph de Saint Lucius, Jordan Bastard and John Morton in 1294 (Elvey, 1975, no511); William Page and John Marie in 1307 (Elvey, 1975, no.430); Jordan Bastard and Robert de la More in 1294 (Elvey, 1975, n512). William le Vavasur owned land in Leckhampstead (Elvey, 1975, no 706), and was present at an inquisition following the hanging of a felon in Thornborough in 1303 (Elvey, 1975, no 712).

d. Robert de Morton and John de Moreton who were presumably present because their father, William son of Reginald, gave property directly to Matthew Stratton to contribute to the hospital.

e. The only other 'Ferur' that has been located is Nicholas le Ferur who in 1293 was a servant of the King that was 'now incapable of work', and the King requested that the Hospital of St John the Baptist at Oxford should provide him 'with the necessities of life for as long as he lives' (Salter, 1917, pxxxii).

f. Luffield Priory was a Benedictine establishment located at Syresham, near Brackley and was active from c1118. The Black Death (1348-1382) is thought to have killed all the monks at Luffield. In 1494, due to lack of funds, the priory was annexed to Windsor by Henry VII (Midmer, 1979, p210).

APPENDIX II

Chantry Certificate No 4, sub-section 9

- Buckingham dated 4th February 1545/6. (E301/4)

This document lists three chantries in Buckingham: the Brotherhood of the Trinity and Our Lady; Barton's chantry; and Matthew Stratton's chantry of St John the Baptist and St Thomas of Acon.

E301/4. Reproduced with kind permission of the Public Records Office

Overview

For ease of display, the certificate is shown on the following pages divided into the three sections (a,b & c) indicated below

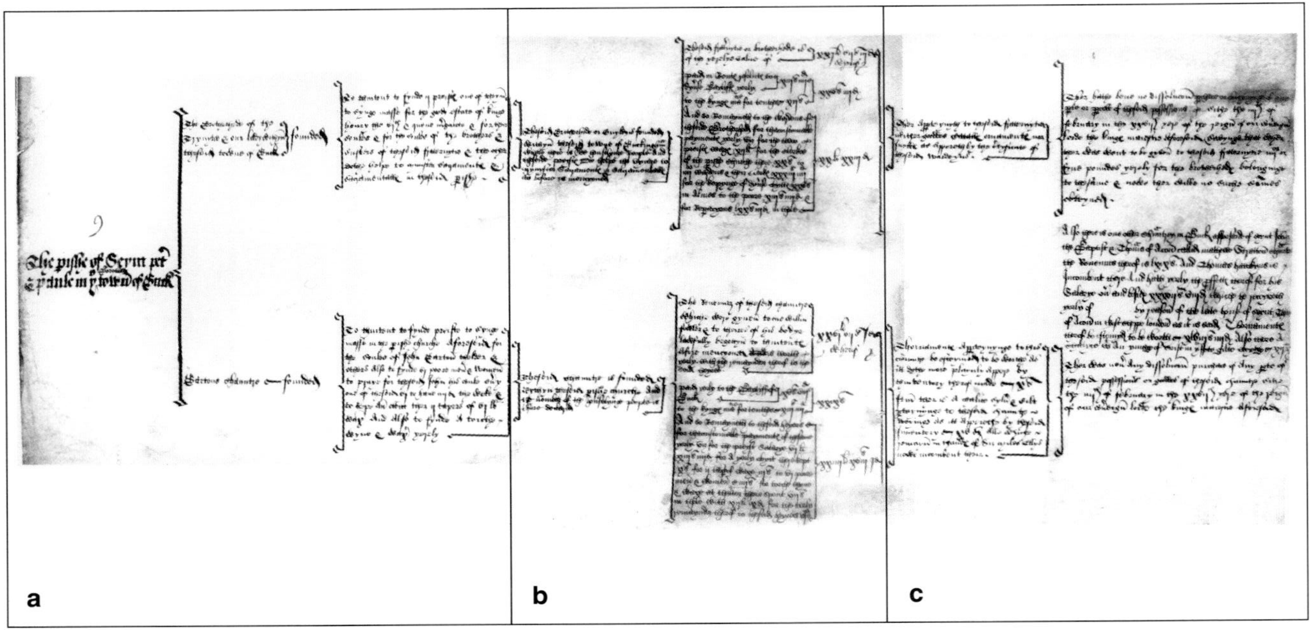

The parisshe of Seynt Peter & Paule in ye towne of Sudb[ury]

The Brotherhede of the Trynitie & our lady [illegible] in the said towne of Sudb[ury] — founded

To thentent to fynde a prieste one of them to synge masse for the good estate of Kynge Henry the vjth & quene margarete & for their soules & for the soules of the brothers & sisters of the said fraternytie & the other [illegible] helpe to amynister sacramentes & sacramentalles in the said parisshe.

Ectone chauntrye — founded

To thentent to fynde a prieste to synge masse in the parisshe churche aforesaid for the soules of John Ectone [illegible] & others Also to fynde vij poore men & women to praye for the said John his soule every one of the said vij to have [illegible] the weke & to kepe an obitt there [illegible] tapers of vj lb wax And also to fynde A torche [illegible] wyne & wax yerely

The Brotherhede of the Trynytie & our lady Withyn theseid toWne of Buck[ingham]	founded	To thintent to fynde ij preiste[s] one of theym to synge masse for the good state of kinge henry the vi[th] & quene m[ar]garete & for their soules & for the soules of the brothers & sisters of theseid fraternytie & the other dothe helpe to minister sacramente[s] & sacramentalle[s] in theseid p[ar]ishe.

The p[ar]ishe of Seynt pet[er] & paule in t[h]e BoroWe town of Buck[ingham]

Bartons Chauntre ———	founded	To thintent to fynde preiste to synge masse in the p[ar]ishe churche Aforesaid for the soules of John Barton thelder & others Also to fynde vi poore men & Women to praye for theseid John his soule eu[er]y one of theseid vi to haue iiiid the Weke & to kepe An obbitt ther ii tapers of vi lb Wax And Also to fynde A torche, Wyne & Wax yerely.

Footnote: Henry VI (1421-1471) married Margaret of Anjou in 1445.

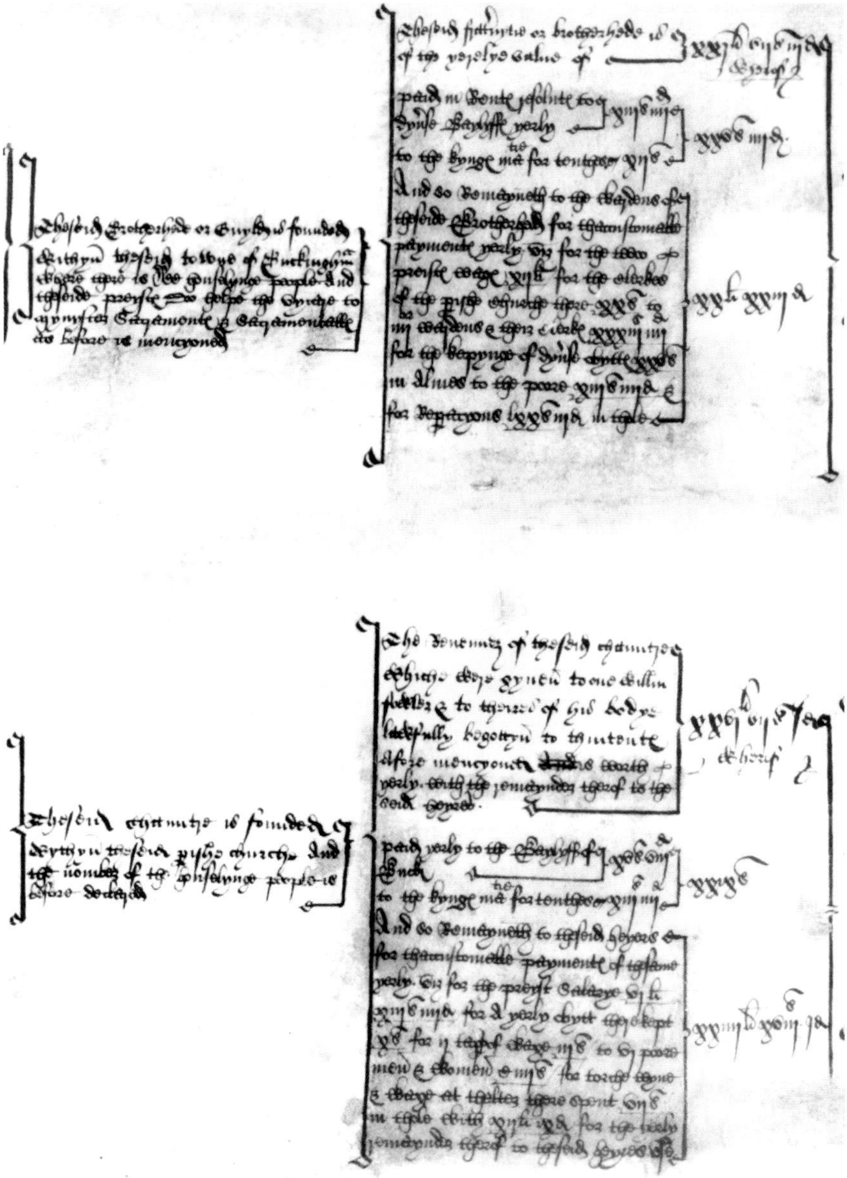

Thesaid Brotherhede or Guylde is founded within thesaid towne of Buckingham where there is [illegible] howselynge people And thesaid preiste doo helpe the curate to mynister Sacramentes & Sacramentalles as before is menc[i]oned

Thesaid ffraternitie or brotherhede is of the yerelye value of — [illegible] whereof

paid in Rente resolute to [illegible] yerely — [illegible]
to the kynge Ma[jes]tie for tenthes [illegible]

And so Remayneth to the wardens of thesaid Brotherhed for thaccustomede paymente yerely viz for the [illegible] preiste wage [illegible] for the clerkes of the parisshe churche there [illegible] to [illegible] wardens & their clerke [illegible] for the kepynge of dyuerse obittes [illegible] in Almes to the poore [illegible] for Reparac[i]ons [illegible] in thole — [illegible]

Thesaid chauntrie is founded within thesaid parisshe churche And the nomber of the howselynge people is before declared

The Revenues of thesaid chauntrye which was gyuen to one Willm [illegible] & to theires of his bodye lawfully begotten to thintente afore menc[i]oned [illegible] yerely with the remaynder thereof to the said heyres. — [illegible] whereof

paid yerely to the Bayliff of [illegible] — [illegible]
to the kynge Ma[jes]tie for tenthes [illegible]

And so Remayneth to thesaid heyres for thaccustomede payment of the same yerely viz for the preist Salarye [illegible] for a yerely obitt there kept [illegible] for [illegible] to [illegible] poore men & women [illegible] for [illegible] there spent [illegible] in thole [illegible] for the yerly remaynder thereof to thesaid heyres [illegible]

	Theseid fratt[er]nytie or brotherhede is of the yerelye value of	xxjli vijs iijd Wherof
	paid in Rente[s] resolute[s] to xiijs iiijd dyu[er]se Baylyffe[s] yerly to the kinge[s] ma[ies]tie for tenthes xijs	xxvs iiijd
Theseid Brotherhede or Guyld is founded Withyn theseid toWne of Buckingham where there is 700 houselynge people And theseid preyste[s] Doo helpe the vycare to mynyster sacramente[s] & sacramentalle[s] as before is mencyoned.	And so Remayneth to the Wardens of theseid Brotherhed for thaccustomable paymente[s] yerly viz for the tWoo preiste[s] Wage[s] xii li for the clerkes of the p[ar]ishe churche there xxs to iiii Wardens & their clerke[s] xxxiiis iiiid for the kepynge of dyu[er]se obytte[s] xxvs in Almes to the poore xiiis iiiid for Rep[ar]acyons lxxs iiid in thole	xx li xxiiid
	The Reuenuez of theseid chauntre Whiche Were gyuen to one Will[ia]m FoWler & to theires of his bodye laWfully begottyn to thintente[s] Afore mencyond ~~And~~ is Worth yerly with the remaynder therof to the seid heyres	xxvi li viis id Wherof
Theseid chauntre is founded Wythyn theseid p[ar]ishe churche And the nomber of the houselynge people is before declard	paid yerly to the Baylyff of xvs viiid Buck[ingham] to the kinge[s] ma[ies]tie for tenthes xiiis iiiid	xxxixs
	And so Remayneth to theseid heyers for thaccustomable paymente[s] of thesame yerly viz for the preyst salarye vi li xiiis iiiid for A yerly obytt ther, & kept xs for ii tap[ar]s of Waxe iiis to vi poore men & Women ciiiis for torche Wyne & Waxe at thalter there spent viis in thole With xii li ixd for the yerly remaynder therof to theseid heyres vse	xxiiii li xviiis id

Ther hath bene no dissolucon purchase or chaungynge of any
pte or prcell of the seid possessions sith the iiijth of
februarye in the xxvijth yere of the reign of our soveraign
lorde the kinge maiestie aforesaid. Excepte that ther
ther was wont to be gyven to the seid fraternytie iiijor or
fyve poundes yerely for the brotherhode belongynge
to the same & nowe ther wilbe no suche somes
obteyned.

Ther apperteynith to the seid fraternytie
sylver goodes cattalle ornamentes nor
nothe as apperith by the certificate of
the seid wardeyns.

Also there is one other chauntrye in Buckellersbury of seynt John
the Baptiste & Thomas of Acon called Mathew Stratton chaunt
the Revenues therof is lxjs. And Thomas hawkyns is
Incombent there And hath yerly the proffitt therof for his
Salarye ... and beside xxxvjs viijd which he receyveth
yerly of by reason of the late house of saint Thom
of Acon in the seid cytye of London as it is seid. Ornamentes
therof be estemed to be worth xls viijd. Also there a
chalice & an ymage of Crist in plate gilte weyinge ... xij

Ther was non any dissolucon purchase of any pte of
the seid possessions or goodes of the seid chauntrye sith
the iiijth of februarye in the xxviijth yere of the reign
of our soveraign lorde the kinge maiestie aforesaid.

Ornamentes apperteynynge to this
chauntrye be estemed to be worthe as
it doth more playnly appere by
an inventory therof made — xs
And there is a chalice sylver & gilt
perteynynge to the seid chauntrye
weyinge as it apperith by the seid
inventory — xvj oz all whiche
remayn in thandes of Sir myles Ellys
nowe incumbent there.

Ther hathe bene no dissolucon p[ar]chase or obteynynge of any p[ar]te or p[ar]cell of theseid possessions of sithe the iiii[th] of february in the xxvii[th] yere of the reign of our sou[er]eign lorde the kinge[s] maiestie aforeseid Savynge that ether ther Was Wont to be gyven to theseid fraternytie iiii[or] or fyve poundes yerely for the brotherhede[s] belongnge to the same & noWe ther Wilbe no suche sum[m]es obteyned.

Ther App[er]teynyth to theseid fraternytie neither gooddes chatalle[s] ornamente[s] nor Juelle[s] as appereth by the c[er]tyficate of theseid Wardeyns.

Also there is one other chauntrey in Buck[ingham] afforesaid of seynt John the Baptist & Thomas of Acon called matheWe Stratton chauntrey the Reuenues thereof is lxixs And Thomas HaWkyns is Incombent there And hath yerly the p[ro]fette[s] thereof for his Salarye, ou[er] and beside[s] xxxviis viiid Whiche he receyveth yerly of [blank] by reason of the late house of Seynt Thomas of Acon in Westcheppe, London as it is said Thornamente[s] thereof be estemyd to be Worth - xlviiis iiiid. Also there A chalyce w[i]t[h] An ymage of crist, in t[h]e fote gilte, Weynge 12 oz Ther Was neu[er] Any dissolucon purchase of Any p[ar]te of theseid possessions or gooddes of theseid chauntre sithe the iiii[th] of february in the xxvii[th] yere of the reign of our sou[er]eign lorde the kinge[s] maiestie aforeseid.

Thornamente[s] App[ar]teynynge to this chauntre be estymed to be Worthe As itt dothe more playnly Appere by thinventory therof made — xs It[e]m ther is A chalice sylu[er] & gilt p[ar]teynynge to theseid chauntre - Weyinge As itt Apperethe by theseid Inventory — xs oz Alle Whiche remayn in thande[s] of Sir miles Ellys noWe incombent their.

Footnote: The 27th year of King Henry VIII was 1535/6.

APPENDIX III

Chantry Certificate No 4, sub-section 10

- Thornton dated 4th February 1545/6. (E301/4).

E301/4. Reproduced with kind permission of the Public Records Office

Overview

For ease of display, the certificate is shown on the following pages divided into the three sections (a,b & c) indicated below

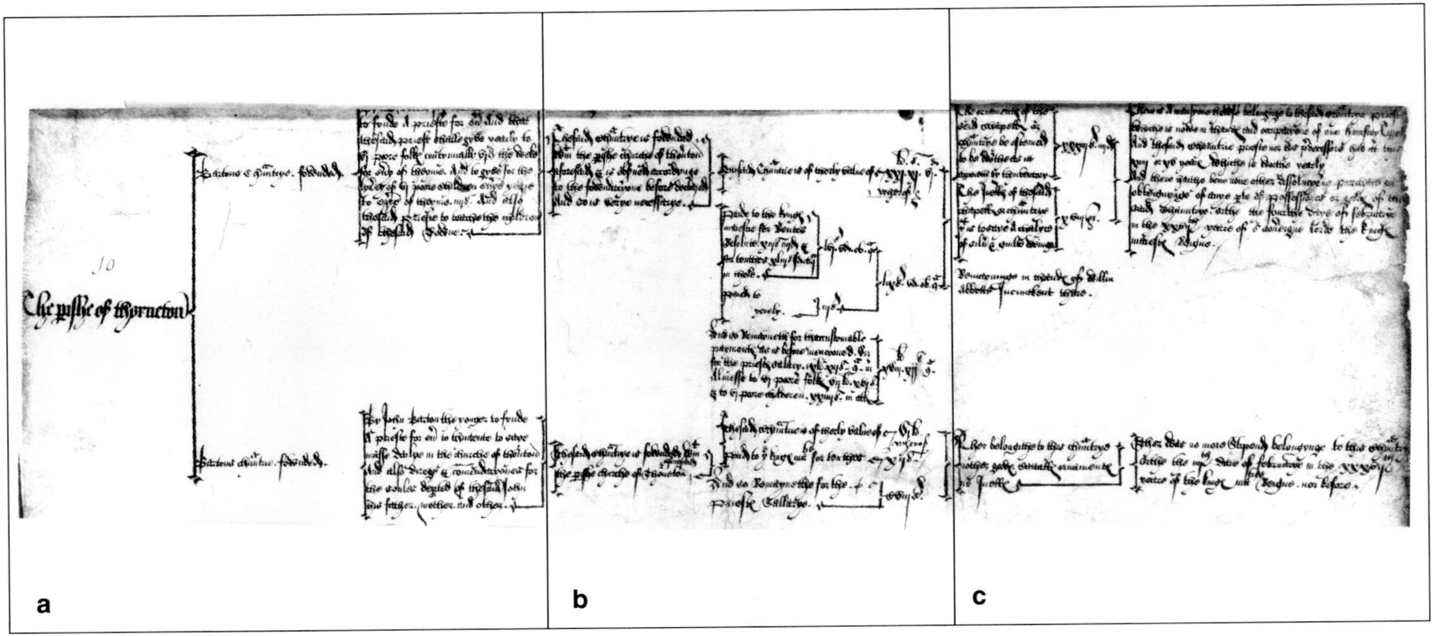

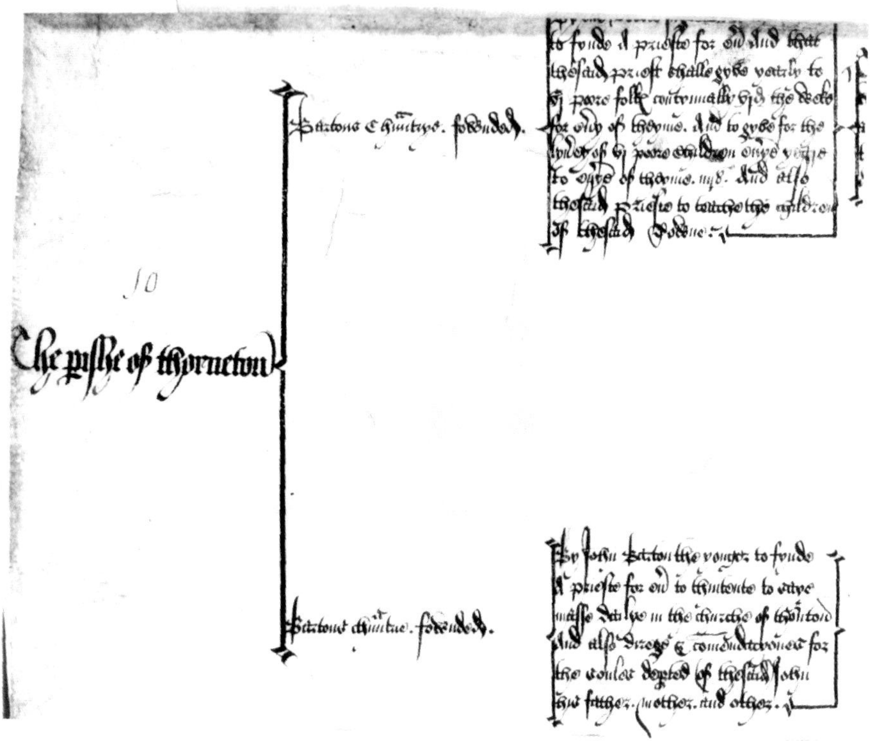

10

The parishe of Thornton

Suttons Chauntrye. foundede.

[illegible]
to founde a prieste for ever And that
the said prieste shalle gyve yerely to
vj poore folke continually vjd. the weke
for ever of theyme. And to gyve for the
wyder of vj poore children eche yere
to eche of theyme iiijs. And also
the said prieste to teache the childern
of the said towne.

Suttons chauntrie. foundede.

By John Sutton the yonger to founde
a prieste for ever to continue to saye
masse dailye in the churche of Thornton
And also dirige & comendaciones for
the soules departed of the said John
his father. mother. and other.

Bartons Chauntrye foWnded

by Robert Ingleton to the intente
to fynde A prieste for eu[er] And that
thesaid priest shalle gyve yearly to
vi poore folke[s] contynually vid the Weke
for eu[er]y of theyme. And to gyve for the
lyu[er]ey of vi poore children eu[er]ye yeure
to eu[er]ye of theyme iiiis And also
thesaid prieste to teache the children
of thesaid ToWne.

The p[ar]ish of thorneton

Bartons chauntrie foWnded

By John Barton the yonger to fynde
a prieste for eu[er] to thintente to saye
masse dailye in the churche of thornton
And also direge & com[m]endacyones for
the soules dep[ar]ted (of thesaid) John,
his father, mother and other

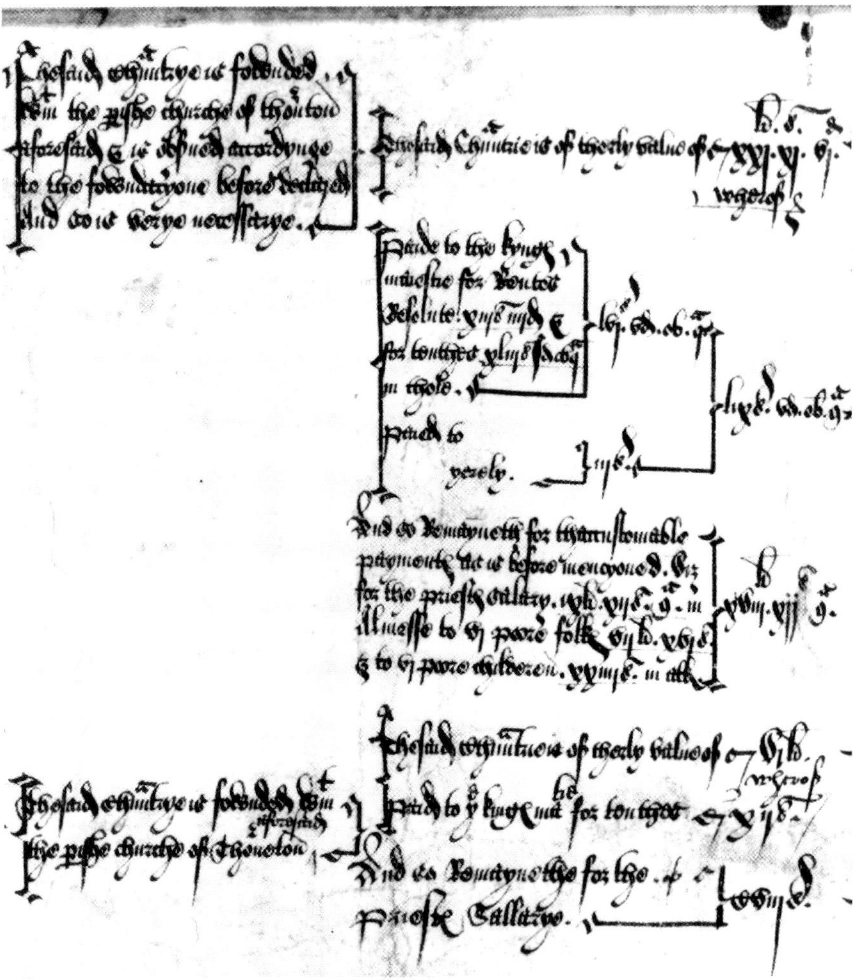
The said chauntrye is founded within the parishe churche of Thornton aforesaid & is ordeyned accordynge to the foundacyone before declared And so is verye necessitye.

The said Chauntrie is of the yerly value of xxj.li. vj.s. vj.d. wherof

Paide to the kynges maiestie for Rentes Resolute xiiij.s. iiij.d. & for tenthes xlij.s. vij.d. in whole lvj.s. xj.d. ob. qr.

Paied to yerely iiij.s.

lx.s. xj.d. ob. qr.

And so Remayneth for the accustomable paymentes as is before mencyoned viz for the priestes sallary xvj.li. xiij.s. iiij.d. in allmesse to the pore folke xlj.s. viij.d. & to the pore chyldren xxiiij.s. in all xviij.li. vij.s. iiij.d.

The said chauntrye is founded within the parishe churche of Thornton aforesaid

The said Chauntrie is of the yerly value of vj.li. wherof

Paied to the kinges maiestie for tenthes xij.s.

And so Remayneth for the Priestes Sallarye cviij.s.

Thesaid chauntrye is foWnded W[i]t[h]in the p[ar]ishe churche of thornton aforesaid & is obs[er]ued accordynge to the foWndacyone before declared And so is verye necessarye	Thesaid chauntrie is of therly value of xxi li xis vid whereof		
	paide to the kynge[s] maiestie for Rentes Resolute xiiis iiiid & for tenthes xliiis id ob qa in thole.	lvi li vd ob qa	lixs vd ob qa
	paid to yerely	iiis	
	And so Remayneth for thaccustomable paymente[s] as is before mencyoned. Viz for the prieste[s] salary ix li xiis qa in Almesse to vi poore folke[s] vii li xvis & to vi poore childeren xxiiiis in all		xviii li xiis qa
Thesaid chauntrye is foWnded w[i]t[h]in the p[ar]ishe churche of Thorneton aforesaid	Thesaid chauntrie is of therly value of ——		vi li wherof
	paid to t[h]e kinge[s] ma[ies]tie for tenthes —		xiis
	And so Remaynethe for the prieste[s] sallarye		Cviii s

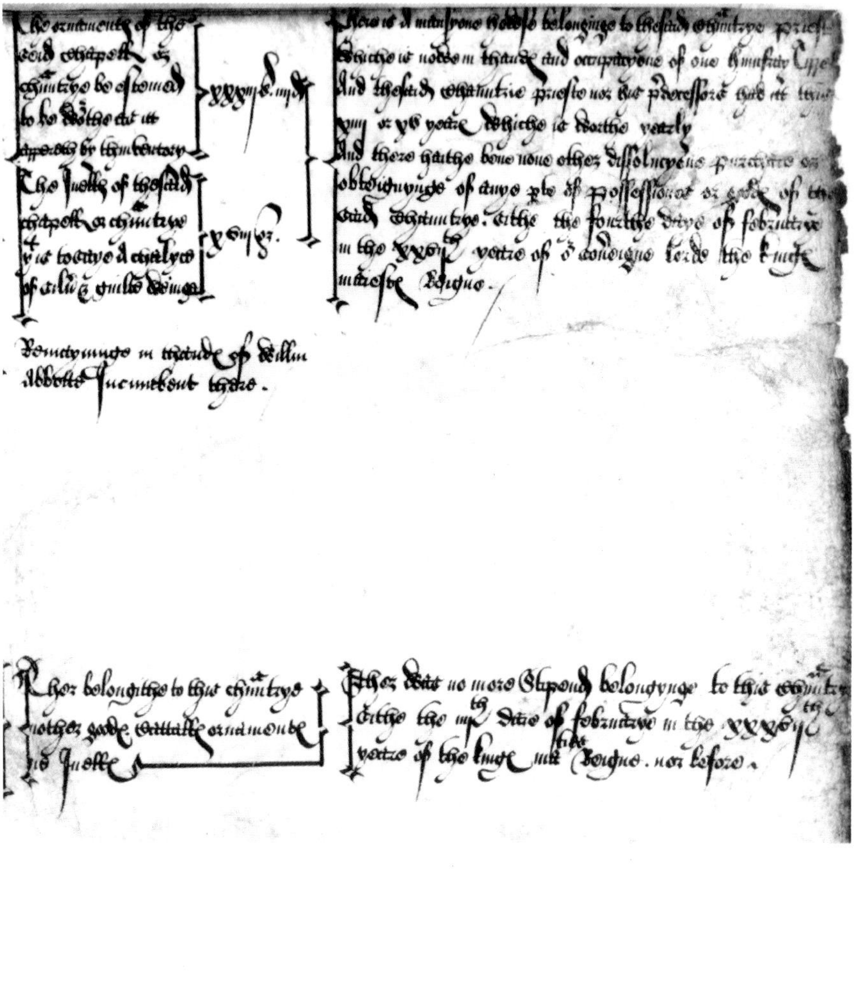
The ornamentes of the seid chapell or chauntrye be estemed to be worthe att ther apprysed by thinventory
xxxvjs. viijd
The Juelles of the said chapell or chauntrye yt is wrought a chalyce of silver & guilte weinge
x oz.
Remaynynge in the hande of Willm Abbotte Incumbent there.
There is a mansyone howse belonginge to the said chauntrye priest whiche is nowe in the hande and occupacyone of one Christofer Tyzer And the said chauntrie prieste nor his predecessors have it this xiiij or xvj yeres whiche is worthe yerely
And there hathe bene none other dissolucyone purchase or obteynynge of any p[ar]te of possessions or goodes of the said chauntrye. Sithe the fourthe daye of februarie in the xxxvijth yere of or soveraigne lorde the kinge maiestie reigne.
Ther belongithe to that chauntrye nother goode cattalle ornamente nor Juelle
Ther was no more Stipend belongynge to this chauntrye Sithe the iiijth daye of februarye in the xxxvijth yere of the kinge maties reigne. nor before.

The ornamente[s] of the seid chapell or chauntrye be estemed to be Wo[r]the as itt appereth by thinventory	xxxiiis iiiid	There is A mansyone hoWse belonginge to thesaid chauntrye prieste Whiche is noWe in thande[s] and occupacyone of one humfray Tirrell And thesaid chauntrie prieste nor his p[re]decessors had itt thier xiiii or xv yeare[s] Whiche is Worthe yearly [blank] And there haithe bene none other dissolucyene purchase or obteignynge of anye p[ar]te of possessiones or goode[s] of the said chauntrye sithe the fourthe daye of februarye in the xxvii[th] yeare of o[u]r sou[er]eigne Lorde the kinge[s] maiestie[s] Reigne.
The Juelle[s] of thesaid chapell or chauntrye th[a]t is tosaye A chalyce of silu[er] & guilte Weinge	xviii oz	
Remayninge in thande[s] of Will[ia]m Abbotte Incumbent there		

Ther belongithe to this chauntrye nother goode[s] cattalle[s] ornamente[s] nay Juelle[s]	Ther Was no more Stipend belongynge to this chauntrye sithe the iiiith daie of februarye in the xxxviith yeare of the kinge[s] mai[es]ties Reigne nor before.

APPENDIX IV

Transcription of Chantry Certificate No 5, sub-section 14

- Thornton c 1548/9

E301/5. Reproduced with kind permission of the Public Records Office

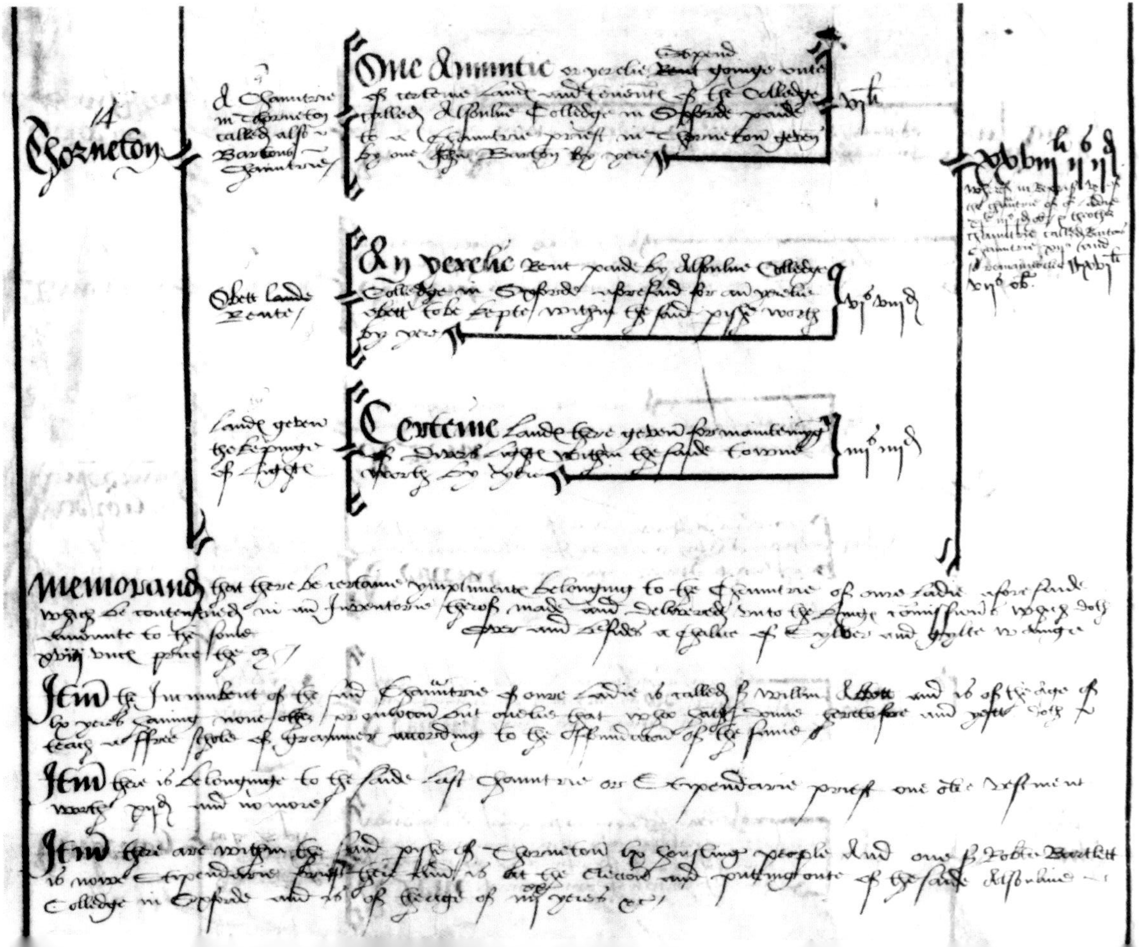

14 Thorneton	A Chauntrie in Thorneton called also Bartons Chauntrie	One Annuitie or yerelie Stipend (Rent) goinge oute of certeine landes and tenementes of the Colledge called Allsoulne Colledge in Oxforde paide to a Chauntrie priest in Thorneton aforesaid by one John Barton by yere	vjli	xvjli vjs vjd [illegible]
	Obett landes Rentes	Ayn yerelie Rent paide by Allsoulne Colledge Colledge in Oxforde aforesaid for an yerelie obett to be keple within the said parishe worth by yere	vjs viijd	
	landes geven the kepinge of lighte	Certeine landes there geven for mainteyninge of [illegible] within the saide towne worth by yere	iiijs iiijd	

Memorandum that there be certaine ornamentes belonginge to the Chauntrie of our Ladie aforesaide whiche be contenyned in an Inventorie therof made and delivered unto the kinges commissioners whiche doth amounte to the some of viij li [illegible] and besides a chalice of silver and gilte weinge xviij unce price the oz [illegible]

Item the Incumbent of the said Chauntrie of our Ladie is called Sir William Abbott and is of the age of lx yeres havinge none other promotion but onelie that whiche he hath doune heretofore and yett doth teache a free schole of Grammer accordinge to the ffoundacion of the same

Item there is belonginge to the saide last Chauntrie or Stipendarie priest one olde vestment worth xxd and no more

Item there are within the said parishe of Thorneton [illegible] houselinge people And one Sir Robert Bartlett is nowe Stipendarie priest there [illegible] at the election and puttingoute of the saide Allsoulne Colledge in Oxforde and is of thage of [illegible] yeres &c

Thorneton	A Chauntrie in Thorneton called also Bartons Chauntrie :	**One Annuitie** or yerelie Stipend goinge oute of certeine lande[s] and tene[me]nte[s] of the Colledge called Alsoulne Colledge in Oxforde paide to a Chauntrie preist in Thorneton geven by one John Barton by yere	vi li	**xxviii li iis iid** whereof in Repriser v[i]z of the chaunterie of o[u]r Ladie xi li iiis id ob & theother chauntrie called Bartons chauntrie xiis and id remaines cler xvi li viis ob
	Obett Rente :	**An yerelie** Rent paid by Alsoulne Colledge Colledge in Oxforde aforesaid for an yerelie obett to be kepte within the said p[ar]ishe worth by yere	vis viiid	
	Lande[s] geven the kepinge of Lighte[s] :	**Certeine** lande[s] there geven for maintenyng of divers lighte[s] within the saide towne worth by yere	iiiis iiiid	

MEMORAND[UM] that there be certaine ymplimente[s] belonging to the Chauntrie of oure Ladie aforesaide which be contenaned in an Inventorie therof made and Delivered vnto the kinge[s] com[m]ission[er]s which doth amounte to the some Over and besides a Chalice of Sylver and gylte wainge xxiii unce[s] price the oz

IT[E]**M** the Incumbent of the said Chauntrie of oure Ladie is called Sir Will[elmu]m Abbott and is of the Age of lx yeres hauing none other promoc[i]on but onelie that whoo hath donne heretofore and yett doth teach a Free schole of grammer according to the Foundac[i]on of the same

IT[E]**M** thae is belonginge to the saide last chauntrie or Stipendarie priest one olde vestment worthe xiid and no more

IT[E]**M** there are withyn the said p[ar]ishe of Thorneton lx housling people And one Sir Rob[er]te Bartlett is nowe Stipendarie preist there and is at the elecc[i]on and puting oute of the saide Alsouline Colledge in Oxforde and is of theage of iiij[xx] yeres &c

APPENDIX V

Chantry Certificate for the Provision of Pensions & Continuance of Schools

- Buckingham Hundred (E301/77) dated 1548/9.

This document is important for three reasons: firstly it confirms that the sum 'x^{li} viii^{s} ob' from Thornton was the £10-8s-0½d that eventually endowed the Royal Latin School; secondly it confirms that the Thornton school was continued (with the note in the margin); and thirdly the following page of this document was the one that misled Browne Willis, and that Isabel Denton actually endowed a school in Shalston.

This document is dated 1549 and lists the names of the chantry priests, their approximate ages, and income by County, so that they can be awarded a pension. Under the heading of the Hundred of Buckingham, the first page gives the details on two chantries in Thornton. The chantry of Our Lady is also called Barton's, and the incumbent is William Abbott, who 'doth teach a gram[mer] Schole according to the fundac[i]on and hath no other lyving but this saide Chantrie'.

The top half of the second page concerns Hundred of Buckingham, the lower half concerns the Hundred of 'Chilterne'. In Buckingham town there are two chantries: the Fraternity of the Trinity; and Barton's chantry. Buckingham Hundred includes Shalston.

Com Buck

A brief abstracte or declaracion perticulerly of the names of all the late Colledges
Chauntries Fraternities Freechappelles Guyldes Brotherhedds Stipendaries and such others within the said Countie of Buck
nowe in the Kinges maiesties handes by vertue of the late Acte of parliament had and provided for the same, declaring
the names and Surnames of the masters Governors prestes Incumbentes ministers and others whiche enioyde the same
livinges as intitled unto by the said late [illegible] As also all the Scoles Preachers Academy [illegible] having [illegible]
[illegible] oute of the premisses for [illegible] parte [illegible] made in the second yere of the Reigne of our Soueraigne
Lord Edwarde the sixt by the grace of god kinge of Englonde Fraunce and Irelonde defendor of the faith and in erth
of the Churche of Englonde and also Irelonde supreme hedd as hereafter followeth [illegible] that is to saye

Hundred de Buck

Thornton	The Chauntrie of our Ladie in Thornton otherwise called Bartons Chauntrie worthe by yere over and besides certeine reprises	xix li viij s ob	Sir William Abbott incumbente of the said Chauntrie	The said Incumbent of the age of [illegible] yeres hath yerelie [illegible] of the said Chauntrie over and besides all reprises by yere [illegible]	[illegible] li viij s ob	The said Incumbent [illegible] Scole [illegible] and [illegible] the said Chauntrie
	Memorand there is paide oute of the said Chauntrie by yere unto [illegible] weekelie to [illegible] whiche doth amounte unto the yerelie some of				vij li [illegible]	
	Item paide also to [illegible] yerelie for [illegible] of the [illegible] whiche doth amounte to the yerelie some of				xiij s iiij d	
	The Chauntrie in Thornton called [illegible] Chauntrie maintened by Allsoulne Colledge in Oxforde over and besides certeine reprises worthe by yere	lxvj s	Sir [illegible] incumbent of said Chauntrie	The said Incumbent of the age of [illegible] yeres hath [illegible] of the said Chauntrie paide by the said Allsoulne Colledge by yere [illegible]	lxvj s	The said Incumbent hath no other [illegible] but the said [illegible] that is presented

Com[itatus] Buck[ingham]

A brief abstracte or declarac[i]on p[ar]ticularly of the names of all the late Colledges,
Chauntries Fraternities Freechappelle[s] Guildes Brotherehedes Stipendaries and such others within the said Countie of Buck[ingham] now in the kinge[s] maiestie[s] hande[s] By virtue of the Late Acte of p[ar]liament hadd and provided for the sume As well with the names and Surnames of the mast[ers] Governers prieste[s] Incumbente[s] ministers and p[er]sons whose lyvinge[s] the kinge[s] highnes is Intitled vnto by the saide act As Also all the Scholes preachers Beademen and poor foulke[s] having yerelie Relyff oute of the premiss As for one parte or p[ar]cell thereof made on the seconde yere of the Reigne of oure souraigne Lorde Edwarde the sixte by the grace of god kinge of Englonde Fraunce and Irelonde defnder of the feath and in Erth of the Church of Englonde and also Irelonde Supreme hedd as heraftre folowithe That is to saie in

Hundred de Buck[ingham]

Con[tinuatu]r the Schola quousque	**The Chauntrie of** oure Ladie in Thorneton aforesaide called Bartons Chauntrie worthe by yere ouer and bysides certeine Reprieses	**xixli viijs ob**	S[i]r Will[ia]m Abbott ys Incumbente of the saide Chauntrie	The said Incumbent of theage of lx yeres hath yerelie cominge of the saide Chauntrie over and besides all Reprises by yere cler	**xli viijs ob**	The saide Incumbent dothe teach a gram[mer] Schole according to the fundac[i]on and hath no other lyving but this saide Chauntrie

Con[tinuatu]r to the pore quousque **Memorand[um]** there is paide oute of the saide Chauntrie by yere vnto six poor foulkes wekelie to everie of theyme vid which doth amounte vnto the yerelie Some of ———— **vij li xvjs**

Item paide also to six Childerne yerelie for everie of ther lyveries iiijs which doth amounte to the yerelie som[m]e of **xxiiijs**

Thorneton

	The Chauntrie in Thorneton called bartons Chauntrie mainteined by Alsoulne Colledge in Oxforde ouer and besides Certeine Reprises Worth by yere	**Cviijs**	S[i]r Rob[er]te bartlitt clerke ys Incumbent of the saide Chauntrie	The saide Incumbent of the age of iiij xx yeres hath one annuitie or yerelie penc[i]on cominge of the saide Chauntrie paide by the said Alsouline Colledge by yere clere	**Cviijs**	The said Incumbe[nt] hath no other livy[ng] but this saide Chauntrie that is presented

Penc[i]o[n] Cviijs

Buckingham Towne

	The ffraternitie of the Trinitie in the towne of Buckingham is worth clere and besides all reprises by yere	xvj^li ij^s vj^d	There names are John Crampe & Walter Bochame Clerke	The said Incumbent of theage of lx yeres about hath yerelie coming of the said ffraternitie for salary of theyr serving clere by yere vj^li	The said Incumbent hath no other lyving but this
	Memorandum there is paide yerelie oute of the said ffraternitie of theyme [illegible] in all by yere / unto a pore Clerke there for there wages by yere	xxvj^s viij^d			
	Item there is distributed unto poore folke every yere the same	xiij^s iiij^d			
	A Chauntrie called Bartons Chauntrie within the said towne is worth over and besides certeine reprises by yere	vj^li	Sir Myles Elis is Clerke & Incumbent of the said Chauntrie	The said Incumbent of the age of lx yeres hath the yerelie coming of the said Chauntrie one annuitie of yerelie rent going oute of Gabriell [illegible] landes clere by yere	vj^li	And the said Incumbent hath no other lyving or promotion and is decrepitt and lame

Shalston

Memorandum that there is iiij marke yerelie geven for the sustentation of a prieste there to teache Children for the augmentation of [illegible] which iiij marke by yere the said Isabell [illegible] his lyving / his name is not presented /

Hundred de Chilterne

A Chauntrie called [illegible]		The said Incumbent of theage		And what other lyving

	The Fraternitie of the Trinitie in the towne of Buckingham ys worth over and besides all Repris[es] by yere there	**xvijli iijs vijd**	There names are p[re]sented John Temys & Will[ia]m Godfraie Clerke[s]	The said Incumbente[s] of theage of lx or theraboute[s] haue yerelie coming of the said Fraternitie for either of their Stipende[s] clere by yere vj li	**xij li**	The said Incumbente[s] haue no other living but this

Buckingham towne

Memorand[um] there is paid yerelie oute of the said Fraternitie unto ii p[ar]yshe clerke[s] there for their wage[s] viz to either of theyme xiijs iiijd in all by yere —— **xxvjs viijd**

It[e]m there is distributed unto poor foulke[s] everie yere on good Frydaie —— **xiijs iiijd**

	A Chauntrie called Bartons Chauntrie with in the said towne is worth ouer and besides certeine reprises by yere	**vjli**	S[i]r myles Elis clerke is Incumbent of the said Chauntrie	The saide Incumbent of the age of lx yeres hath yerelie coming of the said Chauntrie one annuitie or yerelie Rent going out of Gabriell Foles lands clere by yere	**vj li**	And the said Incumbent hath no other living or promoc[i]on and is decripitt and lame

Shalston

Memorand[um] that there is iiij marke[s] geven for the terme of xx yeres whereof viij yeres be past by Dame Isabell Denton to a prieste there to teache Children for the augmentac[i]on of his lyvinge his name is not presented.

APPENDIX VI

The Learned Tailor of Buckingham

Robert Hill, called the Learned Tailor of Buckingham, was born at Miswell, near Tring, in Hertfordshire; where an old relation having taught him his letters, he learned to read himself at home. This acquisition was so remarkable in a child, that he was sent to school, but, by some accident, prevented from going there longer than seven weeks; during which, however, he learned to write. When he was about fourteen, he was put Apprentice to a Stay-maker and Tailor at Buckingham; but his desire of knowledge being still predominant, he contrived to gratify it under every possible disadvantage. With the first money that he could scrape together, he purchased Beza's Latin Testament, and a Latin Grammar. He then applied to the boys at the Free School, and got himself employed by them, to render them such services as were in his power, having always first stipulated, that, in return, they should teach him the English of the Latin words in some rule of his Grammar. In proportion to the knowledge he acquired, he became more and more sensible of what was yet wanting; and, as soon as he was able, he added a Gradus to his Testament and Grammmar, by which he was assisted in his pronunciation. As there are few difficulties insurmountable by persevering labour, Hill, at the expiration of his apprenticeship, had not only learned his trade, but could read and understand Latin; and, now known to the neighbouring Gentlemen, one of whom, upon the death of his son, gave him some of his books, and, among others, a Greek Testament, which, being a new object of curiosity he immediately applied himself to learn Greek. In this arduous task he received some assistance from a Gentleman at Buckingham; and in about three years began to read a Greek Author with some pleasure. The same restless desire of knowledge which thus attached him to books, induced him not to follow his business at home; but instead of it, to travel as an itinerant mender of clothes. In this state of poverty and dissipation, he was still a hard student; and when he was thirty-four years of age, he began to learn Hebrew. The first book that he read, was Shindler's Grammar; but Hill found several deficiencies in Shindler, which he was at a loss to supply; and, after much labour and contrivance, he thought if he could, in his peregrinations, associate himself with some Jews, who, like himself, were travelling the country for subsistence, he might take the same route, and should be able to get such instruction as he wanted. This project he immediately put into execution; and, meeting with an itinerary Jew at Oakingham, he communicated his scheme, and stated his difficulties. The Jew was more ready to assist him than able. This inability, however, he supposed to be accidental, and therefore applied to others, but with as little success. To Hill, however, nothing was less eligible than to relinquish his purpose. He therefore had recourse to other Hebrew Grammars, of which he read eleven; but not any one of them contained all that he expected to find; though, upon the whole, he thought Mager's the best. After he had acquired the knowledge of Latin, Greek, and Hebrew, and made himself acquainted with whatever such travels as his could produce to his observation (studying half the night, that he might pursue his journey and his business in the day), he returned to Buckingham, where he remained buried in obscurity, and scarce subsisting by his labour, but perfectly contented, extremely modest, and diffident in his discourse; without any new-fangled notions in religion, which too generally distinguish smatters in learning. Among other books which accidentally fell into his hands, was an Essay on the Spirit, said to be written by the Bishop of Clogher. He had before read several Tracts on the Contraversial Points of Christianity; and, when he had read this, he wrote down his thoughts on the subject, and detected several mistakes in the quotations of that writer from the Hebrew, and his construction upon them. He also wrote a paper, to shew, that the most important and favourite Doctrines of the Church of Rome are novel inventions; and other Tracts. This extraordinary person, who died at Buckingham in 1777, is described in an interesting Tract, by Mr Spence, entitled, "A Parallel on the manner of Plutarch, between a most celebrated man of Florence, Antonio Magliabechi, and one scarcely ever heard of in England". First printed at the Hon. Horace Walpole's private press, at Strawberry-Hill, in Svo, 1757; and afterwards reprinted in Dodsley's Fugitive Pieces, 2 vols. Svo London, 1761, vol ii, p321 (note to "Letters by Eminent Persons", vol i, p271).

(Lipscombe, 1847, p586) reprint of Willis.

APPENDIX VII

All known teachers to 1948.

In the 1932-1933 Yearbook of the Royal Latin school, it was noted that 'no systematically made records' were available that listed all the masters at the school. This list has been compiled from newspapers, trade journals, staff records that survive, remembrances of former pupils, etc.

Surname	Forename	Main duties	Dates	Next post
Hawkins	Thomas	Master	1524-1553 (?)	
Webster	Henry	Master	1553-1569	
Sheppard	Alexander	Master	1574-1580	
Potter	Thomas	Master	1580-1592	
Earle		Assistant	c1591-1609	
Smith	James	Assistant	c1591-1592	
Smith	James	Master	c1592-1603	
Tomlyns	Robert	Master	1603-1609	
Nichols	John	Master	1609-1609	
Earle	Richard	Master	1609-1625	
Horne	Richard	Master	1625-1632	
Dutton	Thomas	Master	1633-1638	
Ummant	Edward	Master	1638-1660	
Paine		Assistant	c1645	
Thompson		Assistant	c1645	
Stephens		Assistant	c1645	
Stephens	Thomas	Master	1660-1664	
Warters	William	Master	1664-1665	
Griffiths	Roger	Master	1665-1682	
Griffiths	Mrs		1665-1682	
Dalby	Thomas	Master	1682-1684	

Surname	Forename	Main duties	Dates	Next post
Yeomans	Thomas	Master	1685-1690	
Noble	Mark	Master	1690-1691	
Styles	Robert	Master	1691-1696	
Ford	Thomas	Master	1696-1709	
Foster	Samuel	Master	1709-1715	
Cardwell	Richard	Master	1715-1723	
Halstead	William	Master	1723-1763	
Eyre	James	Master	1764-1785	
Eyre	William	Master	1785-1830	
Brittin	Edward	Master	1830-1855	
Britten	Manasseh	Assistant	c1851	
Laugharne	Thomas R.J.	Master	1855-1858	
Owain Jones	T.	Master	1861-1869	
Borissow	Louis	Master	1869-1871	
Cockram	Thomas	Master	1871-1891	
Sylvester	Alfred, D.	Assistant	c1881	
May	Alfred, L.	Assistant	c1881	
Lloyd	Charles	Assistant	c1887	
Stainmetz	Percy	Asssitant	c1887	
Rose	William Charles		c1890	
Wood	William Charles	Mu	c1890	
Perry	Arthur Robert	A	c1890	
Young	H.	Mu	c1890	
Nelson	Ambrose	Mu	c1890	
MacCulloch	Robert C.	Master	1891-1895	
Poll	George H.	S.A	c1892	
Wade	N.H.		c1892	
Spink	H.		c1892	
Hogg	Arthur		c1895	
Bird	Herbert		c1895	
Milsted	W.P.S	A	c1895-1898	Missouri, USA.
Cox	Walter, M.	Headmaster	1896-1908	Somerset

Surname	Forename	Main duties	Dates	Next post
Goguet-Chapuis	M.M.	F	c1896-1908	
Prevost-Brouillet		F	c1896-1908	
Lang	Georges	F	c1896-1908	
Merkau		Gm	c1896-1908	
Haubold		Gm	c1896-1908	
Hudson	T.A.G.		c1896-1908	Pontefract
Warner	A.H.		c1896-1908	
Jerrard	R.		c1896-1908	
Austin	H. (Porky)		c1896-1908	
Clarke	P.		c1896-1908	
Hall	P.S.		c1896-1908	
Parker	O.D.		c1898	
Bourgougnon	Emile	F	c1898	
Morin	M.		c1898	
Enoch	James		c1898	
Millard	Rev C.W.	Cl	c1898	
Touse	C.		c1898	
Horspool	Robert	A	c1898-1900	Bridlington
O'Flynn	F.A.	Cl,E	c1898-1901	
Lavin	Miss M.R.		c1899-1907	
Myers	J.F.		c1899	
Anderson	Herbert (Shrump)	S,M	1901-1909	Somerset
Mountain	G.	Cl,E	c1901-1903	
Morrow	F.	E,G	c1902	
Harpur	A.D.		c1902	
Haysman	F.	A	c1902	
Coulthard	C.A.	A	c1903	
Vasey	A.D.		c1903	
Gibling	Robert	E,M	1906-1908	Sherborne
Stamps	William J.	A	c1907-1911	
Clarke	Leonard C.		c1907	
Hobbs	E.William		c1907	Ackworth

Surname	Forename	Main duties	Dates	Next post
Pareham.	G.E.		c1907	
Morgans	Thomas	G,M,L,Hi	1907-1916	Killed 1918
Aveyard	Miss Ethel, A.	E,F,Dr,N	1907-1912	Marriage
Bullough	Miss Alice	E,M,Cs,Cm	1907-1912	
Richards	Fred, J.	Ag	1908-1912	Land Valuer
Fuller	William	Headmaster	1908-1931	Retired
Ogden	Alfred	F,E	1909-1910	Coleworth, Mx.
Rosen	Victor	F,E	1911-1914	Tottenham
Andrews	Percy, E.	S	1912-1919	BSc. Reading
Dawson	Lilian, I.	Hi,N,Pe	1912-1915	Marriage
Bayfield	Henry	D,A	1911-1920	Retired
Davis	Miss Ellen, M.	E,M,L	1913-1926	Leicester
Bertram-Turtle	Evelyn	E,Dr,Cs,Cm	1914-1915	Poplar
Fawcitt	Edwin, H.	F,E,L	1914-1924	Tamworth
Taylor	Ethelwyn, K.	M,S	1915-1916	Colchester
Murray	Mabel	Hi,E	1915-1922	Bahamas
Goodwin	Elsie, L.	F,M,L,Pe	1915-1919	Marriage
Dunn	Lily	Pe	1914- ?	
Smartt	Matthew, J.	L,M,F	1916-1916	Catford
Powell	Mary, W.S.	S	1916-1919	Watford
Harrison	Frank, A.	L,M	1917-1917	Resigned
Colgrove	Eleanor, M.	S,M,G	1916, 1920-1924	Marriage
Wall	Frances, V.	L,E,N	1920-1922	Kensington
Valentine	Thomas Albert	M,S	1920-1920	BSc. Liverpool
Boles	William	M,S	1920-1921	
Edwards	Edith, C.	Ds	1916-1926	Aylesbury
Laishley	James, E.	M	1922-1927	West Ham
Buckingham	William, G.	D	1920-1936	Retired
Full	Zillah, I.	Pe	1921-1940	Wolverton
Butcher	Hannah, H.	Pe	1920-1921	Marriage
Edwards-Rees	Desiree, M.M.	Hi,F,L,E	1923-1924	Durham Univ.

Surname	Forename	Main duties	Dates	Next post
Priest-Shaw	Ethel, F.	Hi,F,E	1924-1926	Married a master
Lowe	Gertrude, M.V.	G,S,M,D	1924-1929	Lincolnshire
Williams	Samuel, G.	E,F	1924-1964	
Parsons	Henry, C.	Ha	1925-1928	Hertfordshire
Staveley	Elsie, J.D.	E,Hi,F	1926-1932	Brampton
Locke	Ruth, W.	Ds	1926-1931,1938	Married
Merry	Dorothy, T.	E,N	1920-1945	London
Jones	George, H.	M,Mu,Pe	1928-1929	Middlesex
Mairs	Harry	L,M,E,F	1929-1932	Slough
Edwards	Ronald, P.	Ha	1928- ?	Died c1942
Allitt	Tom, R.	M,P	1929-1950 ?	
Labrum	Miss Helen, M.	G,S,M,Fd	1929-1936	Wakefield High
Taylor	Thomas	Hi	1931-1935	Hertfordshire
Thomas	Maurice, W.	Headmaster	1931-1935	Tottenham
Maher	Alfred, D.	S,M,Cs,Pe	1931-1931	Ilminster
Freeman	Percy	S,M,G	1932-1937	
Pickles	Winifred, M.	Ds	1931-1932	W.Riding
Jackson	Emily, K.	N	1932-1933	
Downs	Annie	Hi	1933-1937	High Wycombe
Davies	Stephanie, M.	DS,N	1932-1932	Marriage
Creer	Dorothy	Ds	1933-1933	Slough
Askins	Frances, K.	Ds	1933-1935	Buckingham
Goodger	Christopher, A.	Ha	1935-1946	
Storer	Ida, A.	Ds	1935-1939	Coventry
Dyment	Stanley, A.	Headmaster	1936-1939	Middlesex
Hough	Dorothy, M.	G,A,E	1936-1941	Lutterworth
Farmer	Melissa, A.F.	Hi,Mu,F,L	1937-1938	Littlemore, Oxon
Parkinson	John, B.	S	1937-1938	Surrey
Turner	Joseph, H.	S,Pe	1938-1946	West Bromwich
Cox	Vivien, A.M.	Hi,F,L,Cs	1938-1943	Manchester

Surname	Forename	Main duties	Dates	Next post
Barber	Auriola, M.	Ds	1939-1945	
Toft	Henry Bert	Master	1939-1941	
Foster	Charles	Acting Head	1942-1945	
Toft	Henry Bert	Master	1945-1948	Bath
McCoan	Mrs. A.		1939-1945	
Buckingham	John, F.	S,Pe,R	1939-1940	Ruthin
Tinker	Jean, P.	S,Bo,Zo	1940-1941	
Simpson	Mary, S.	L,F,E,Pe	1940-1941	Lancs
Taylor	Kathleen, J.	G,L,Hi	1941-1942	Ilford
Smith	Mrs.M.F.A.		1941-1942	
Gregory	Florence, R.	G	1941-1943	Min.of T&C
Davies	Iris, M.	S	1941-1941	
Morgan	Donald, E.	Acting Head	1941-1941	Wolverton
Atkin	Eileen, K.	S	1941-1945	
Thomas	M.C.	L,F	1941-1947	Middlesex
Foster	Charles	Acting Head	1942-1945	Min.of Educatn.
Thomson	Mary, C.	Pe	1942-1944	Buckingham
Taylor	Doris, A.	Mu	1942-1946	
Chapman	Raymond, E.	M,S	1943-1944	Chingford
Clark	Audrey, J.	Pe	1944-1946	
Maunder	Kathleen, M.	B,M	1944-1946	
Blades	Mrs K.		1944-1946	
Merritt	Mary	Hi,G	1944-1957	
Spencer	Mary	E	1945-1946	Training Coll.
Gordon	Rodica	Ds	1946- ?	
Rose	Margaret E.	Hi,G,E,Pe	1946-1948	Shropshire
Archer	E.W.	S,M,Pe,G	1946-1948 ?	
Jones	Thomas, W.T.	B,Zo,Bo,C,S	1946-1948	
Nutt	Harold, R.	Mu,	1946-1948	Wolverton
Firth	Muriel, D.	G	1947- ?	
Tole	Oscar, D	Ha	1947-1947	Royal Navy
Fox	Ethel, M.	F,L	1947-1956	Reading

Surname	Forename	Main duties	Dates	Next post
Cook	Celia, D.	Hi,E,A	1947- ?	Marriage
Usmar	Allan, O.G.	Ha	1947-1948	Oxon
Warwick	Sibyl, D.	DS,N	1948- ?	Marriage

A	Art
Ag	Agriculture
B	Biology
Bo	Botany
C	Chemistry
Cl	Classics
Cm	Clay-Modelling
Cs	Class-singing
D	Drawing
Dr	Drill
Ds	Domestic subjects (Cookery, Laundry work, Housewifery)
DS	Domestic Science
E	English
F	French
Fd	Folk Dancing
G	Geography
Gm	German
Ha	Handicraft (usually woodwork and metalwork)
Hi	History
L	Latin
M	Mathematics
Mu	Music
N	Needlework
P	Physics
Pe	Physical exercise
R	Religious instruction
S	Science
Zo	Zoology

APPENDIX VIII

Boys at the Royal Latin School.

During the compilation of this book, the names of children for the years 1839 to 1899 were recorded as and when found. This is not a complete list, but it was felt that it might prove useful to some readers.

1839

George Barratt

Edmund Pead

John Claydon

William Ridgway

George Meehan

Thomas Hedges

1840

John Claydon discharged 'for not regularly attending school.

John Meehan discharged 'for not regularly attending school.

William Stuchbery Mold

Thomas Jenkins

1842

John Owen

George Barratt, poor attendance, his father questioned.

Jenkins and Pead, poor attendance, their fathers questioned.

1843

George Barratt had left.

Thomas Mills elected.

Thomas Jenkins left.

Thomas Sloan elected.

Edmund Pead left.
Jesse Gough elected.

1844
John Hedges & William Ridgeway left.
Alfred Hedges
Thomas Wheeler
Letters of thanks were sent to the trustees from Ridgeway and Hedges.

1845
George Harrison, aged 10, son of Richard Harrison elected.

1846
George Wheeler, aged 10
Thomas Smith, aged 11

1847
William Newman Hillier, aged 10
Joseph Hughes, aged 12

1848
Robert North, aged 9
George Savry, aged 9
Joseph Sloan, aged 10

1850
George Wheeler had left,
Joseph Butcher, aged 9
Alfred Webb, aged 8

1851
Edward George Achurch aged 8

Frederick Paxton, 11
Richard Baughan Sear, 11
James Meehan, 8
Robert North, 13

1852
Thomas Archer

1853
Charles Row, 7
Edward Francis, 10
George May, 9
John Turner, 10

1855
Henry Ellborough, 11
William Hillyer Rowell, 10
Charles Rowe, 9 1/2
Alfred Thorpe, 8
John Alfred Coates, 10
Henry Meehan, 8

1857
John Alfred Coates had become ineligible to continue a scholar.
Frederick Paxton, 11
Pugh (Buckingham Advertiser, June 27th, 1857)
Charles Humphreys (Buckingham Advertiser, June 27th, 1857)

1861
Walter Webb, 11
William Turner, 10
Thomas Meehan, 8

William Taylor, 8
Charles Edward Robbins, 11
Frederick Baughan, 9

1863
Philip Inns, 11

1864
William Stowe

1865
Joseph Orchard, 8

1866
William Turner
Edward Bond, 10
Edward Wheeler, 11

1867
William Edward George Smith, 8
John Holland Jeffs, 8

1868
Charles John Meehan, 12

1870
Charles Eeley, 11
G.W.French (RLSM, Dec 1939, p140) (later governor of the RLS)

1871
Frederick Walter Bartlett, 9
Thomas Holton, 9. (He left in 1877. In 1935 he donated an original school photograph to the RLS). (RLSM, 1934-6, p476).

1872

Alfred Adcock, 9

Harry Tavener Watts, 9

1873

Ernest Henry Welch Howe, 11

Joseph Uff, 10

Francis Turner, 8

Francis Ernest Bond, 12

1875

Herbert George Jeffs, 9

William Frost, 10

1876

William Parker Varney, 9

1877

John Henry Bray, 10

1881 Census.

	Age	*Residence*
Joseph J Horwood,	13	Bicester, Oxon.
Joseph C Harwood,	14	Woolston.
Henry Horwood,	11	Somerton, Oxon.
Edward Chapman,	10	Westbury.
George Chapman,	11	Westbury.
Frank Harper,	13	Mixbury.
John H Falkner,	9	Stowe.
Tom J Hiorns,	11	Fritwell, Oxon.
Edward B Campin,	14	Bicester, Oxon.
Arthur J Campin,	13	Bicester, Oxon.

John H Lines,	13	Maidstone, Kent.
John R Harper,	12	Fritwell, Oxon.

1889-1892 (RLSM, 1934-6, p438)

	Residence:
Cecil J. Smith	Bideford
Frank H. Phipps	Marsh Gibbon
Ernest King	Fringford
Lewis King	Fringford
Fred Bond	Brill
Will Bond	Brill
Percy Wootton	Charndon
Strictus Nicholls	Wappenham
Robert Roads	Ashendon
Gerald Bird	Newport Pagnell
Charlie Vyle	Buckingham
William Jones	Edgcott

1890 (Prize-Giving 1890, RLS Archives)

Nichols R.A.
Tredwell J.
Salmon P.
Barton S.
Young N.H.
Cockram H.
Patrick L.
Cross J.W.
Smith C.J.
Turner R.V.
Turner W.C.
Arnold W.J.

Hunter E.C.
Smith S.B.
Wootton A.
Curtis J.
Hinton H.
Cockram H.J.
Gadsden C.R.
Kirby A.J.
Smith C.
Waters A.E.
Reynolds G.
Marsh W.D.
Tomkins S.C.
Hunter C.C.
Clarke F.

1893 (RLSOLA, 1932)
Harrison

1898 (RLSM, 1931-32, p53, p94-95)

	Residence:
Jim Kelly	Argentina
Henry Kelly	Argentina
Joe Enoch	Newmarket
Jim C. Enoch	Newmarket
Lewis Cantlay	Aberdeen
Jim Cantlay	Aberdeen
Vernon Cantlay	Aberdeen
Cooper CJ	Bedford
Tom Warriner	London
Bert Sibbett	London

Sam Hazlewood	Coventry
Jock MacConnal	Liverpool
Leslie MacConnal	Liverpool
Harry Byrne	
William Kitchener	
John Hensman	
Will Hensman	Newport Pagnell
Aubrey Treadwell	
George Warriner	
Bertie Roberts	
Tom W. Gibling	Thorne, Doncaster
Hughie A.L. Hughes	
Pete Collins	
Will Butcher	
Percy Gardner	Bromley
Cecil V. Gardner	Bromley
Arthur Gardner	
A.F.Tomlin	
Henry Deverell	
Edgar (Billy) Deverell	
Aubrey L. Chapman	
Fred Marchant	
Harry Starsmores	Wicken
Fred Starsmores	Wicken
W. Starsmores	Wicken
G. Starsmores	Wicken
Willie Warr	Chetewode
Arthur (Jumbo) Warr	Chetewode
Pete Hinton	
Robert Tompkins	East Claydon
Harry Tompkins	East Claydon
Alan Tompkins	East Claydon

Chris Tompkins	East Claydon
Wilfred Tompkins	East Claydon
Teddy Hawes	Bentill
Henry Hawes	Benthill
Arthur Coates	Hillesden
Leonard Hedges	Hillesden
Watkin Leadbetter	Wales
Pat Crozier	
H.J. Treen	Gravesend
S. Wallis	Woolwich
C.W. Wallis	Woolwich
C.J. Harrison	Manchester
C.M. Cannon	
Willie Pollexfen	
Charlie Pollexfen	
Fred Pollexfen	
Bob Pollexfen	
Reggie Pollexfen	
Addy Whittingham	Newcastle-under-Lyme
Harold Whittingham	Newcastle-under-Lyme
Jack Knox	Chester
Clifford Knox	Chester
Horace Lee	
Teddy Lee	
M.D. Lavell	Dulwich
J.H. (Mickey) McCarthy	
Sid Dalton	
Jack Chester	
Rowland Brake	Aldershot
Jack Brake	Aldershot
Norman D'Arcy	Hampstead
G.G. Bradley	Belfast

Harry Milsom	Claydon
R. Littlewood	Burston
E. Littlewood	Burston
Johnny Beer	
Freddy Beer	
Fred French	
Arthur Young	
Norman Young	
T.F. Watts	
W.J. Watts	
Harry Bonner	
Johnny Fisher	
W. Pargeter	
F. Pargeter	
George Turner	
T.B. Jones	
A.H. Gillam	Gawcott
Reg George	
W. Jones	
G. Stevens	Winslow
A. Stevens	Winslow
L. Stevens	Winslow
B. Stevens	Winslow
F. Stevens	Winslow
C. Stevens	Winslow
Willie Steadman	Thornborough
Harry Steadman	Thornborough
Johnny Steadman	Thornborough
C. Steadman	Thornborough
E. Godfrey	
Harold Butler	Tile House
Cecil Butler	Tile House

Archie Butler	Tile House
J.D. Gadsden	Swanbourne
F. Biddlecombe	Padbury
Georgie Bennett	
Rupert Holland	
David Mercer	
Wille Bartlett	
Fred Adams	
Johnny C.H. Illman	Wood Green
Harry Bowden	

1899 Bucks Advertiser & N.Bucks Free Press Jan 28th 1899

	Residence:
Butcher, W.H.	Buckingham
Gardner, P.	Buckingham
Cantlay, L.	Bruges, Belgium
Cantlay, J	Bruges, Belgium
Hughes, H.L	Buckingham
Gibling, T.W.	Buckingham
Cooper, C.J.	Bedford
Deverell, E.H.	Buckingham
Hensman, J.D.	Buckingham
Hazlewood, S.	Coventry
Warriner, G.F.	London
Bowden, H.L.	Marsh Gibbon
Chapman, A.L.	Buckingham
Leadbetter, W.B.C.	Wrescham
Pollexfen, C.J.	London
Treadwell, J.A.	Buckingham
Whittingham, J.A.	Newcastle
Deverell, W.E.	Buckingham

Enoch, J.C.	Newmarket
Hensman, W.	Buckingham
Adams, F.	London
Bennet, G.	Buckingham
Bonner, H.	Buckingham
Bradley, G.G.	Belfast
Gadsden, T.J.	Swanbourne
Gillam, A.H.	Gawcott
George, R.	Winslow
Holland, R.	Buckingham
Jones, W.	Winslow
Jones, T.B.	Gawcott
Knox, C.J.	Chester
Lavell, M.D.	Dulwich
McCarthy, J.W.	London
Marchant, F.	Wicken
Pollinfen, F.J.	London
Starsmore, F.	Wicken
Stevens, G.A.	Winslow
Turner, G.A.	Buckingham
Wallis, C.W.	Woolwich
Warr, W.G.	Chetwode
Cannon, C.M.	
Godfrey, E.	
Young, G.A.	
Pollexfen, F.J.	
MacConnal, C.	
Cannon, M.	

1899 Bucks Advertiser & N.Bucks Free Press & Jul 29th 1899

Whittingham, Harold (being under 6, the youngest boy in the school)
Beer, J
Beer, F.
Pollexfen, R.
Steadman, W.
Illman, T
Lee, Edward
Biddlescombe, F.
D'Arcy, N.
Gardner, C.
Littlewood, R.
Littlewood, E.
Turner, A.
Illman, J.
Adams, F.
Bradley, G.
Butler, H.
Chester, G.
Gillam, A.
Holland, R.
Jones, T.B
Knox, C.J.
Lavell, M
Stevens G.
Young, A.
Polexfen, F.
Warr, W.
Bennett, G.
McCarthy, J.
Bowden, H.
Cannon, C.

Enoch, J.
Hughes, L.
Hensman, W.
MacConnal, L
Milsom, H.
Pollexfes, W.
Warriner, G.
Cantlay, J.
Gardner, P.
Gibling, T.W.
Kelly, H.
Pollexfen, W.

APPENDIX IX

Boys and Girls in the Admissions Register 1907-1922

	Surname	First name	Entry	Left	Previous Education	Guardian
1	Denchfield	Dora	17-Sep-07	29-Jul-10	Buckingham	Frank William
2	Clarke	Stanley	01-Sep-03	29-Jul-10	Lillingstone Dayrell	Septimus
3	Stevens	William Hall	17-Sep-07	21-Dec-10	Winslow	William Hall
4	Gardner	Arthur Edwin	01-Jan-05	26-Jul-12	Buckingham	James
5	Smith	James William Ronald	5-May-04	21-Dec-10	Gawcott	James
6	Hull	Leonard William	16-Sep-08	21-Dec-10	Trowbridge, Wilts	Thomas Farwell Roper
7	Grainge	Arnold Fred	11-Sep-07	28-Jul-11	Winslow & Culworth	Frederick Stammerz
8	Foskett	Constance Mary	17-Sep-07	30-Jul-14	Winslow	William
9	Gravestock	Gladys Margaret	17-Sep-07	26-Jul-11	Buckingham	Alfred
10	Hadland	Dorothy May	17-Sep-07	19-Dec-08	Buckingham	Richard Charles George
11	Hawkins	Margaret	21-Jan-08	07-Apr-10	Botolph Claydon	George Hall
12	Jones	Ethel Hilda Lomas	01-Mar-08	19-Dec-08	Bristol	Arthur E
13	Leeming	Dorothy Margaret	21-Jan-08	26-Jul-12	Akeley	William
14	Pringle	Gladys	17-Sep-07	26-Jul-12	Buckingham	William Soden
15	Rich	Florence Noble	17-Sep-07	31-Jul-13	Great Horwood	Alfred
16	Tofield	Elsie Alice	17-Sep-07	21-Dec-10	Buckingham	Herbert Ernest
17	Bates	George William	17-Sep-07	19-Dec-08	Mursley	Joseph
18	Cubbage	Frederick Charles	21-Jan-08	07-Apr-09	Botolph Claydon	William

	Surname	First name	Entry	Left	Previous Education	Guardian
19	George	Percy	17-Sep-07	19-Dec-08	Great Horwood	J
20	Hawes	Henry	1-Jan-05	21-Dec-10	Buckingham	Thomas
21	Gregory	Charles John Edwin	21-Jan-08	26-Jul-12	Steeple Claydon	Ambrose
22	Jackman	Dennis Daniel	17-Sep-07	28-Jul-11	Gawcott	George William
23	Lester	Frank Cecil	1-May-05	29-Jul-10	Leckhamstead	Oliver
24	Nobes	Cyril	24-Sep-04	10-Nov-13	Buckingham	Richard
25	Barrett	Christine Lilian	5-May-08	30-Jul-13	Tingewick	Frederick
26	Bond	Elsie Mary	5-May-08	11-Apr-10	Thornborough	Elizabeth Bond
27	Emerton	Muriel Milton	5-May-08	30-Jul-13	Buckingham	William George North
28	Hadland	Elsie Helen	5-May-08	26-Jul-12	Buckingham	Richard Charles George
29	Underwood	Teresa Mary	5-May-08	30-Jul-13	Winslow	Homer
30	Barge	Arthur Edward	1-May-07	19-Dec-08	Twyford, Bucks	Arthur John
31	Bennett	Frank	21-Jan-08	19-Dec-08	Lillingston Dayrell	George William
32	Butler	Harvy	5-May-08	29-Jul-10	Lillingston Dayrell	Silham
33	Dawes	Louis Percy Brookholding	3-Oct-04	19-Nov-13	Swanbourne	Thomas Brookholding
34	Denchfield	Frederick Thomas	1-May-04	30-Jul-12	Buckingham	Frederick William
35	Grace	John William	21-Jan-08	07-Apr-09	Mursley	John Foster
36	Hartland	Herbert Douglas	1-May-04	21-Dec-10	Buckingham	William Herbert
37	Illing	Sydney Arthur	17-Sep-07	07-Apr-12	Winslow	Ebenezer Alfred

	Surname	First name	Entry	Left	Previous Education	Guardian
38	Perkins	Frederick William	5-May-08	28-Jul-11	Tingewick	Christopher
39	Pringle	Bruce	5-May-08	30-Jul-13	Buckingham	William Soden
40	Steadman	John Noel	1-May-05	27-Jul-09	Thornborough	Rev. William
41	Tofield	Stanley Frank	5-May-08	21-Dec-10	Buckingham	Herbert Ernest
42	Watts	Arthur	17-Sep-07	19-Dec-08	Gawcott	Thomas
43	Archer	Dorothy Annie	21-Jan-08	29-Jul-10	Banbury	Thomas
44	Clifford	Mary Rebecca	16-Sep-08	31-Jul-15	Maids Moreton	Alfred
45	Colgrove	Eleanor Mary	16-Sep-08	28-Jul-14	Winslow	Joseph
46	Ruchstuhl	Daisy Amelia	21-Jan-08	07-Apr-12	Clapham	Rev. Arthur Cannon
47	Feetham	Lily	12-Oct-08	27-Sep-11	Steeple Claydon	George
48	Sellar	Doris Rose Eunice	17-Sep-08	30-Jul-13	Winslow	Henry
49	Butler	John	5-May-08	21-Dec-11	Lillingstone Dayrell	William
50	French	George Henry	5-May-08	19-Dec-14	Buckingham	George Watson
51	Gibbs	Frederick William	5-May-08	08-Jun-11	Buckingham	George William French
52	Hartland	Eric Francis	1-Sep-05	21-Dec-11	Buckingham	William Herbert
53	Hazelton	Guy William	1-Jan-03	26-Jul-12	None	William C
54	Lester	Anthony Leslie	1-Sep-06	10-Apr-13	Leckhamstead	Oliver
55	Sheppard	Wilfred John	1-May-07	21-Dec-10	Gawcott	John
56	Stevens	Lancelot William	16-Sep-08	26-Jul-12	Preston Bissett & Redhill, Surrey	John George

	Surname	First name	Entry	Left	Previous Education	Guardian
57	Clarke	Kenneth Burleigh	1-May-06	26-Sep-12	Lillingstone Dayrell	Septimus
58	Butcher	Mabel Esther	21-Jan-08	28-Jul-09	Winslow & Steeple Claydon	Francis Elijah
59	Bunker	Marjorie	17-Sep-07	18-Jul-09	Winslow & Buckingham	Benjamin
60	Hadland	Frances Harriet	17-Sep-07	28-Jul-09	Winslow & Buckingham	Richard Charles George
61	Stevens	Gertrude Mary	17-Sep-07	28-Jul-09	Winslow	William Hall
62	Dodson	William Arthur	17-Sep-07	28-Jul-09	Winslow & Great Harwood	William Arthur
63	Underwood	Arthur Joseph	17-Sep-07	29-Jul-10	Winslow	Homer
64	Wootton	Arthur Harry	17-Sep-07	28-Jul-09	Winslow	John Henry
65	Dixon	Stanley Robert	3-Nov-08	29-Jul-09	Stoke Newington	Arthur
66	Dixon	Arthur Lionel	3-Nov-08	29-Jul-09	Stoke Newington	Arthur
67	Clifford	Arnold Samuel	1-Sep-04	29-Jul-09	Tingewick	Alfred
68	Crook	William George Seymour	9-Nov-08	30-Jul-13	Buckingham	Edward
69	Warr	William Joseph	9-Nov-08	30-Jul-13	Buckingham	William Frederick
70	Bonner	Horace Edward	19-Jan-09	28-Jul-09	Buckingham	Thomas
71	Crook	Francis Nelson	19-Jan-09	11-May-10	Buckingham	Edward
72	Haskins	Frances Marion	19-Jan-09	30-Jul-13	Home	Frank
73	Gravestock	Alfred	19-Jan-09	28-May-12	Buckingham	Alfred

	Surname	First name	Entry	Left	Previous Education	Guardian
74	Kent	Ronald Walter	19-Jan-08	07-Apr-14	Marsh Gibbon	Walter
75	Kimble	Frederick	19-Jan-09	29-Jul-10	Great Horwood	Nathan
76	Hedges	Florence Muriel May	19-Jan-09	07-Nov-12	Buckingham	Walter L
77	Winterbourne	Frances Helen	1-Mar-09	30-Jul-13	Lillingstone Dayrell	George
78	Williams	Harold	1-Mar-09	22-Dec-09	Geelong, Victoria, Australia	Gwylym
79	Williams	Frederick Charles	1-Mar-09	22-Dec-09	Geelong, Victoria, Australia	Gwylym
80	Harris	Arthur Langridge	1-Mar-09	30-Jul-13	Buckingham	Edward
81	Strickland	Reginald	1-Mar-09	28-Sep-11	Market Weighton, Yorks	William
82	Thorpe	Gertrude May	29-Apr-09	07-Apr-12	Steeple Claydon	Mark
83	Bull	Esther Evelyn	29-Apr-09	07-Apr-11	Westbury	Thomas
84	Barge	John Frederick	29-Apr-09	26-Jul-12	Twyford, Bucks	Arthur John
85	Lane	Dorothy	5-May-09	28-Sep-11	Buckingham	Edward Thomas
86	Harris	Winifred Hilda	16-Sep-09	29-Jul-10	Buckingham	Herbert
87	Sear	Winifred Grace	16-Sep-09	30-Jul-13	Adstock	George Joseph
88	Collingridge	Dorothy Lulu	16-Sep-09	31-Jul-14	Steeple Claydon	John
89	Parrott	Harry Spencer	16-Sep-09	30-Jul-13	Winslow	Ernest Edward
90	Purcell	Reginald John Henry	16-Sep-09	30-Jul-14	Buckingham	Thomas John
91	Bell	Anthony	16-Sep-09	31-Jul-15	Buckingham	Frances Kate

	Surname	First name	Entry	Left	Previous Education	Guardian
92	Franklin	Walter Harry	16-Sep-09	30-May-13	Westbury	Walter E. Harris
93	Smith	Morris John	16-Sep-09	07-Apr-12	Gawcott	James
94	Beazer	James	16-Sep-09	22-Dec-10	Great Horwood	Frederick Charles
95	Bowden	Grenville Samuel Conway	16-Sep-09	01-Feb-16	Gawcott	Herbert S.
96	Riordan	Henry	16-Sep-09	22-Jun-12	Dawlish & Buckingham	John H.
97	Marshall	John Thornton	16-Sep-09	30-Jul-13	Buckingham	John Thornton
98	Kitchener	Edith Nellie	3-Nov-09	30-Jul-13	West Ham	Samuel J
99	Cole	Hilda Blanche	5-Nov-09	21-Dec-11	Dawlish	Charles
100	Hartland	Marion	21-Jan-10	22-Dec-10	Buckingham	William Herbert
101	Hall	Albert Frank Ward	21-Jan-10	27-Jul-17	Buckingham	Albert
102	French	Charles Harrison	21-Jan-10	20-Dec-16	Buckingham	George William
103	Taylor	Edith Evelyn	21-Jan-10	07-Apr-11	Buckingham	George
104	Pitts	Joe	3-May-10	07-Apr-12	Newton Purcell	Joseph
105	Perkins	Oswald Barkley	3-May-10	28-Jul-11	Tingewick	Christopher
106	Culley	Marjory	3-May-10	30-Jul-14	Stowe	Eliza
107	Robinson	George Arnold	3-May-10	30-Jul-13	Lillingston Lovell	Eady
108	Robinson	Harry Eady	3-May-10	30-Jul-13	Lillingston Lovell	Eady
109	Theobald	Celia Marjorie	5-Mar-10	07-Apr-10	Nash	Not recorded
110	Milsom	Ronald	13-Jun-10	27-Jul-11	East Claydon	J.

	Surname	First name	Entry	Left	Previous Education	Guardian
111	Smith	Hilda Mabel	15-Sep-10	30-Jul-13	Gawcott	James
112	Hartland	Nancy	15-Sep-10	30-Jul-13	Buckingham	William Herbert
113	Freer	Louisa	15-Sep-10	26-May-15	Buckingham	William
114	Allen	Leslie Stevens	15-Sep-10	20-Dec-13	Buckingham	Thomas
115	White	Irene Kathleen	15-Sep-10	20-Dec-12	Steeple Claydon	William
116	Lane	Mabel Laura	15-Sep-10	30-Jul-13	Buckingham	Edward Thomas
117	Burton	Elsie	15-Sep-10	31-Jul-14	Padbury	J.C.B.
118	Stanley	William Edwin	15-Sep-10	21-Dec-17	Tingewick	William
119	Larking	Evelyn Florence	15-Sep-10	10-Apr-13	Home	Arthur E.
120	Mold	Cecil Edward	15-Sep-10	20-Dec-12	Buckingham	Charles Edward
121	Illing	William Ernest	15-Sep-10	13-Apr-15	Miss Bartons	Ebenezer Alfred
122	Hadland	Ella	3-May-10	07-Apr-13	Buckingham	Richard Charles George
123	Thomas	Walter Henry	2-Nov-10	27-Jul-16	Tring	William H.
124	Thomas	Gwendolin Ellen	2-Nov-10	31-Jul-15	Tring	William H.
125	Tompkins	Ursula Mary	19-Jan-11	07-Apr-12	Winslow	Walter
126	Tompkins	Walter	19-Jan-11	20-Dec-12	Steeple Claydon	Walter
127	Haskins	William Frank	19-Jan-11	27-Jul-16	Stowe	Frank
128	Foskett	Montague William	19-Jan-11	13-Apr-16	Winslow	William
129	Graves	Stanley	4-May-11	31-Jul-15	Banbury	John

	Surname	First name	Entry	Left	Previous Education	Guardian
130	Wickens	Robert Louis	4-May-11	19-Dec-14	Buckingham	William Louis
131	Kitchener	Beatrice Clarissa	4-May-11	26-Jul-12	Steeple Claydon	Samuel J.
132	Kitchener	Alice Gertrude	4-May-11	31-Jul-15	Steeple Claydon	Samuel J.
133	Nobes	Percy	14-Sep-11	27-Jul-17	Buckingham	Richard
134	White	Harry Bernard	14-Sep-11	26-Jul-12	Buckingham	Harry D.
135	Taylor	Cyril George	14-Sep-11	20-Dec-13	Buckingham	George
136	Markham	Thomas William Howe	14-Sep-11	01-Apr-18	Bournemouth	Thomas Howe
137	Attwood	Marion Alice	14-Sep-11	14-Apr-15	New Cross	Frederick W.
138	Whiting	Avice Irene	14-Sep-11	27-Jul-17	Steeple Claydon	John
139	Cadd	Elsie Martha	14-Sep-11	26-Jul-12	Hillesden	William
140	Grainge	Rex	14-Sep-11	27-Jul-17	Culworth & Buckingham	Not recorded
141	Stevens	Cyril John	14-Sep-11	27-Jan-17	Preston Bisset	John G.
142	Pollard	Dorothy Beatrice	14-Sep-11	30-Jul-14	Buckingham	Francis J
143	Easton	Mary Helen	14-Sep-11	13-Sep-12	Winslow	Robert A.
144	Fulks	Doris Evelina	24-Sep-11	Unknown	Winslow	Albert O.
145	Evans	Phyllis Lyell	14-Sep-11	27-Jul-11	Padbury	Albert
146	Thorne	Dorothy Ada Rhoda	14-Sep-11	19-Dec-14	Addington & Buckingham	Alfred
147	Grainge	Henry Francis Charlie	14-Sep-11	27-Jul-17	Winslow	Gerard
148	Ward	Robert Leslie Squires	18-Jan-12	20-Dec-12	Banbury	Charles Herbert

	Surname	First name	Entry	Left	Previous Education	Guardian
149	Hazelton	Philip	18-Jan-12	13-Apr-15	Home	William C.
150	Smout	Joseph Frederick	18-Jan-12	30-Jul-14	Home	Joseph
151	Swift	Constance Alice	29-Apr-12	07-Apr-14	Buckingham	Frederick William
152	Hilsdon	Mary	29-Apr-12	29-Jul-14	Water Stratford	William
153	King	Anstee Frank William	29-Apr-12	19-Dec-14	Home	Frank C.
154	Jackman	Dora Mary	17-May-12	27-Jul-18	Steeple Claydon	Henry
155	White	Ethel Emma	12-Sep-12	20-Dec-12	Brackley	Fred
156	Pollard	Hilda Lucy	17-Sep-12	27-Jul-16	Buckingham	F.J.
157	Blencowe	Cissie May	17-Sep-12	Unknown	Gawcott	George
158	Stevens	Chaloner Arthur	17-Sep-12	31-Jul-15	Preston Bisset	John George
159	Wootton	Elizabeth Ann	17-Sep-12	27-Jul-16	Tingewick	Alfred
160	Pratt	Marjorie Ella	17-Sep-12	Unknown	Buckingham	Frank
161	Cadd	Beatrice Hilda	17-Sep-12	07-Apr-13	Hillesden	William John
162	Bimrose	Nora	17-Sep-12	20-Dec-12	Winslow	D.
163	Hobbs	Violet Constance	17-Sep-12	27-Jul-17	Brackley	George William Hawkins
164	Hall	Samuel Walter	17-Sep-11	19-Dec-14	Harrow	Walter
165	Hall	Leonard Walter	17-Sep-11	31-Jul-15	Harrow	Walter
166	Colgrove	Joseph Lewis	17-Sep-12	20-Dec-17	Winslow	Joseph
167	Stock	Hilda Grace	17-Sep-12	31-Jul-15	Acton, London	H.C.

	Surname	First name	Entry	Left	Previous Education	Guardian
168	Cadd	Ralph Chaloner	17-Sep-12	07-Apr-13	Hillesden	William John
169	Monk	Norman Curtis	17-Sep-12	31-Jul-14	Winslow	W.R.
170	Midgley	John Herbert	17-Sep-12	22-Dec-13	Winslow	George Arthur
171	Cole	Norman Charles	17-Sep-12	19-Dec-14	Buckingham	Charles W.
172	Barton	Alfred	16-Jan-13	30-Jul-13	Hatch End, Pinner, Middlesex	Eleanor
173	Spokes	Malcolm	16-Jan-13	20-Dec-14	Banbury	Stephen
174	Wickens	William Herbert	16-Jan-13	19-Dec-14	Buckingham	W.L.
175	Smith	Cyril Francis	16-Jan-13	29-Jul-14	Gawcott	Maud
176	Godfrey	William Arthur Cyril	2-Mar-13	07-Apr-14	Devizes	Arthur W.
177	Parrott	Joseph John	2-Mar-13	31-Jul-14	Steeple Claydon	Peter
178	Howlett	Dorothy Mabel	2-Mar-13	27-Jul-17	Padbury	Frederick
179	Cubitt	Edith Alberta	1-May-13	30-May-13	Buckingham	A.G.
180	Jones	Jessie Mildred	1-May-13	31-Jul-15	Winslow	Mrs. M.
181	Monk	Frank William	1-May-13	31-Jul-15	Home	William R.
182	Laurence	Harold	1-May-13	31-Jul-15	Wallasey, Cheshire	E.H.
183	Osborne	Francis Thomas	1-May-13	06-Apr-17	Buckingham	Thomas
184	Thomas	Gerald Harry	1-May-13	13-Apr-14	Dadford	Harry
185	Tompkins	Arthur Robert Chilton	16-Jun-13	20-Dec-17	Home	Arthur R.
186	Watts	Norman Arthur	16-Jun-13	31-Jul-15	Halstead	J.

187	Godfrey	Doris	5-Apr-13	13-Apr-16	Devizes	Arthur W.
188	Dolman	Caroline Grace	18-Sep-13	10-Apr-18	Buckingham	William J.
189	Blackwell	Cicely Helena	18-Sep-13	31-Jul-15	Brackley	Edwin H.
190	Yarwood	Annie Ellen	18-Sep-13	13-Apr-16	Westbury	Alfred Thomas
191	Hedges	Blanche Olive	18-Sep-13	20-Dec-16	Buckingham	Walter L.
192	Steer	Beatrice Emily	18-Sep-13	20-Dec-18	Akeley	John
193	Wills	William George	18-Sep-13	31-Jul-15	Gawcott	William
194	Walker	Walter Cecil	18-Sep-13	27-Jul-16	Winslow	George D.
195	Salmon	Perridge William	18-Sep-13	20-Dec-16	Buckingham	Perridge
196	Beckett	Harry Edmund	18-Sep-13	19-Dec-14	Botolph Claydon	Albert Edmund
197	Hall	George Alfred	18-Sep-13	13-Apr-16	Botolph Claydon	George
198	Thoburn	Dorothy Edith	18-Sep-13	21-Dec-15	Croydon	Ralph
199	Wynne	Ethel Doris	18-Sep-13	13-Apr-16	Edgbaston, Birmingham	George
200	Thomas	Gordon Edward	18-Sep-13	Unknown	Buckingham	William Henry
201	Phillips	Albert Frederick	18-Sep-13	30-Jul-18	Water Eaton & Buckingham	William
202	Walton	Gibson Henry	18-Sep-13	19-Apr-16	Buckingham	P.H.
203	Stevens	Norman Charles	18-Sep-13	20-Dec-16	Preston Bisset	John G.
204	Griffiths	John James Harry	18-Sep-13	Unknown	Buckingham	James
205	Cox	Harold	18-Sep-13	06-Apr-17	Steeple Claydon	Albert J.

	Surname	First name	Entry	Left	Previous Education	Guardian
206	Collingridge	John Thompson	18-Sep-13	17-Jul-17	Steeple Claydon	John
207	Pollard	Lewis Harry	18-Sep-13	20-Dec-17	Buckingham	Frank
208	Sellwood	John	18-Sep-13	27-Jul-16	Aylesbury	Maurice John
209	Harrison	Arnold George	5-Nov-13	20-Dec-13	London	William G.
210	Treadwell	Charles	20-Jan-14	19-Dec-14	Tingewick	Jeffrey
211	Crook	Thomas Arthur	20-Jan-14	26-Jul-18	Padbury	Arthur
212	Cecil	Julius Bernard	20-Jan-14	27-Jul-17	Buckingham	Cecil T. Schmitz
213	Stanton	Eric	20-Jan-14	07-Jul-14	Hampshire	George E.
214	Tomlinson	Jack Ernest	20-Jan-14	12-Apr-18	Buckingham	George P.
215	Stock	Gladys Dorothy	20-Jan-14	20-Dec-17	Buckingham	Henry
216	Cadd	Gertrude May	2-Mar-14	27-Jul-16	Hillesden	William J.
217	Rapley	Dorothy Aileen	30-Apr-14	20-Dec-17	Radlett, Herts	C.
218	Fuller	Rowland William Bevis	30-Apr-14	31-Jul-19	Buckingham	William
219	Tucker	Sidney Frederick Warner	30-Apr-14	10-Apr-19	Buckingham	F.W.
220	Kitchener	Lucy Grace	17-Sep-14	31-Jul-15	Steeple Claydon	S.J.
221	Plank	Millicent Nellie May	17-Sep-14	26-Jul-18	Winslow	S.H.
222	Green	Elsie Emily	17-Sep-14	Unknown	Winslow	Edward W.
223	Rich	Gladys Lucy	17-Sep-14	Unknown	Great Harwood	Alfred
224	Smart	May Doward	17-Sep-14	26-Jul-18	Brackley	James D.
225	Ayres	Elsie	17-Apr-14	27-Jul-16	Brackley	Jene R.

	Surname	First name	Entry	Left	Previous Education	Guardian
226	Sellwood	Annie	17-Sep-14	25-Jul-19	Buckingham	Maurice J.
227	Doe	Edith Amy	17-Sep-14	Unknown	Stony Stratford	Frederick
228	Bennett	Charles Frederick Thomas	17-Sep-14	31-Jul-15	Lillingstone Dayrell	Frank
229	Bond	Frank	17-Sep-14	29-Jul-20	Buckingham	Frank E.
230	Beckett	Gilbert James	17-Sep-14	Unknown	Nash	Gaius
231	Heady	Stanley John	17-Sep-14	27-Jul-17	Winslow	Henry J.
232	Harrison	Muriel Patty	17-Sep-14	22-Dec-20	Buckingham	Herbert R.
233	Holton	Mabel	17-Sep-14	20-Dec-17	Buckingham	John F.
234	Watling	Kathleen Nellie	17-Sep-14	10-Apr-19	Buckingham	Charles E.
235	Cox	Gladys Mabel	17-Sep-14	Unknown	Steeple Claydon	Albert J.
236	Salmon	Frances Marjorie	17-Sep-14	29-Jul-20	Buckingham	Perridge
237	Howlett	Frederick John	17-Sep-14	27-Jul-17	Buckingham	Frederick J.
238	Bell	Douglas	17-Sep-14	26-Jul-18	Buckingham	Mrs F.K.
239	Stanley	Fred Alder	17-Sep-14	10-Apr-19	Buckingham	William Isaac
240	Richards	Archie Clinton	17-Sep-14	13-Apr-16	Maids Moreton	Thomas
241	Collingridge	Percy Raymond	17-Sep-14	27-Jul-17	Steeple Claydon	John
242	Wootton	Henry David	17-Sep-14	21-Nov-15	Tingewick	Alfred
243	Clarke	Christopher George	17-Sep-14	24-Nov-20	Buckingham	George
244	Illing	Esme Gertude	17-Sep-14	31-Jul-15	Home	Edward
245	Parker	Eva Rose	3-Nov-14	27-Jul-17	Arncott, Oxford	John

	Surname	First name	Entry	Left	Previous Education	Guardian
246	Bunker	William Eric Benjamin	3-Nov-14	28-Jul-22	Chesham	William
247	Bowden	Pulba Gertrude Hope	19-Jan-15	31-Jul-15	Buckingham	Samuel H.
248	French	Mildred Pleasant	19-Jan-15	26-Jul-18	Buckingham	George W.
249	Painter	Edith	19-Jan-15	21-Dec-15	Buckingham	Frederick
250	Coles	Nancy Irene	19-Jan-15	27-Jul-17	Ruysselede, Belgium	Alexander
251	Culley	Edith Catherine	19-Jan-15	13-Apr-16	Maids Moreton	William
252	Judd	Margaret Evelyn	19-Jan-15	20-Dec-17	Brackley	William
253	Coles	Francis Stuart	19-Jan-15	20-Dec-16	Bruges	Alexander
254	De Haes	Marcel Marie Corneille	19-Jan-15	31-Jul-15	Antwerp	Victor
255	De Meulermeester	Maurice Louis Emile Marie	19-Jan-15	31-Jul-15	Antwerp	Guillaume
256	De Meulermeester	Marcel Alouis Clement Marie	19-Jan-15	31-Jul-15	Antwerp	Guillaume
257	Louillet	Robert Arthur Omer	19-Jan-15	31-Jul-15	Belgium	Joseph Des Champs
258	Lauwers	Ferdinande Laeonie Marie Mathilde	27-Jan-15	04-Aug-17	Ostende	Madame Mathilde
259	De Haes	Rene Janet Alexandre	19-Jan-15	13-Apr-15	Antwerp	Victor
260	Bossyns	Joseph Leon Maria	19-Jan-15	15-May-15	Antwerp	Leon
261	Hill	Vera Isabel	19-Jan-15	Unknown	Buckingham	Henry Byron
262	Van Couter	Camille Francois Laurent Jean Marie	19-Jan-15	21-Dec-15	Belgium	Josephine
263	Van Couter	Aime Victor Eugene Jean Marie	19-Jan-15	20-Dec-16	Belgium	Josephine
264	Bossyns	Xavier Francois	19-Jan-15	15-May-15	Antwerp	Leon

	Surname	First name	Entry	Left	Previous Education	Guardian
265	Bossyns	Charles Gerard Alphonse	19-Jan-15	15-May-15	Antwerp	Leon
266	Rider	Eleanor Harriet	1-Mar-15	Unknown	Tytherton, Chippenham	Arthur
267	Lake	Charles Ernest	4-May-15	27-Jul-17	Banbury	Eliza Marion
268	Taylor	Edgar William	4-May-15	27-Jul-16	Buckingham	George
269	Baker	Hatty Louise	4-May-15	20-Dec-16	Brackley	Edgar
270	Adams	Richard John	4-May-15	06-Apr-17	Lillingstone Dayrell	James
271	Jones	William George	4-May-15	06-Apr-17	Tingewick	William J.
272	Fulks	Robert Oscar	4-May-15	28-Jul-22	Winslow	Albert
273	Bonner	Joseph	4-May-15	20-Dec-16	Navenby, Lincs	Albert Evans
274	Aspeslagh	Germaine	4-May-15	04-Feb-16	Ostende	Richard
275	Ponjaerts	Rachel Stephanie	4-May-15	04-Feb-16	Ostende	Pierre
276	Aspeslagh	Gustaaf Richard	4-May-15	04-Feb-16	Ostende	Richard
277	Ponjaerts	Rudolph Pierre	4-May-15	04-Feb-16	Ostende	Pierre
278	Pringle	Vera	16-Sep-15	07-Apr-21	Buckingham	William S.
279	Van Couter	Blanche Leone Henri Marie	16-Sep-15	20-Dec-16	Belgium	Josephine
280	Stevens	John George	16-Sep-15	31-Mar-20	Preston Bisset	John George
281	Nobes	Rupert	16-Sep-15	Unknown	Buckingham	Richard
282	Everett	Violet Jesse	16-Sep-15	29-Jul-20	Maids Moreton	Richard
283	Sedgwick	Richard George Gardner	16-Sep-15	20-Dec-21	Syresham	Harry M.

	Surname	First name	Entry	Left	Previous Education	Guardian
284	Hemshall	Dorothy Eleanora	16-Sep-15	27-Jul-16	Buckingham	Hugh
285	Hill	Muriel Elaine	16-Sep-15	29-Jul-20	Buckingham	Henry Byron
286	Stanley	Dora Edna	16-Sep-15	29-Jul-21	Tingewick	William
287	Hammond	George Eton	16-Sep-15	26-Jul-18	Slough	George
288	Steer	Reginald John	16-Sep-15	29-Jul-21	Buckingham	John
289	Cheshire	Alexandra May	16-Sep-15	Unknown	North Marston	Henry W.
290	Knight	Mabel Elizabeth	16-Sep-15	27-Jul-17	Brackley	Harry F.
291	Haynes	Charles Edward	16-Sep-15	29-Jul-21	Marsh Gibbon	Jesse
292	Jenkins	Rose	16-Sep-15	27-Jul-17	Maidenhead	G. Hammond
293	Springer	Augustus Gerald Elwyn	1-Oct-15	06-Apr-17	London	Arthur A.
294	Cecil	Freda Elizabeth	1-Oct-15	22-Dec-20	Buckingham	Cecil Schmitz
295	Puffett	Hilda Mary	20-Jan-16	29-Jul-21	Winslow	Frederick W.
296	Bonham	Mary Hannah	20-Jan-16	29-Jul-20	Syresham	W.H.
297	Culley	Winifred Louisa	4-May-16	12-Apr-18	Maids Moreton	William
298	Phillips	George Francis	4-May-16	31-Mar-20	Buckingham	William B.
299	Smith	Stanley Robert	4-May-16	29-Jul-20	Ashendon	Mrs.C.H.
300	Sikes	Charles Wilfred	7-Feb-16	10-Apr-23	Home	John

GLOSSARY

This simple glossary may only be used in the context of this book. If more information is required the following books, which were used to compile this list, are recommended: 'The Oxford Dictionary of Local Family History' (Hey, 1997), 'Osborn's Concise Law Dictionary' (1994), 'The Batsford Companion to Local History' (Friar, 1991) and 'The Local Historian's Encyclopaedia (Richardson, 1993).

Alienate: the legal transfer of ownership.

Appurtenance: the rights and duties that are included with a property eg rights of common or way.

Archdeacon: the Bishop's deputy, who has a duty to maintain the fabric of the parish church and any other church property; and to ensure that everyone behaves as they should.

Bailiff : a person entrusted with the local administration of justice.

Benefice: an ecclesiastical position that paid an income to the local priest, vicar or rector.

Bishop: Governor of Diocese, and in addition to the authority of a priest, has the powers of confirming, instituting and ordaining.

Black Death : a pandemic of the bubonic plague. It has recently been estimated that some 50% of the population of England died of the Black Death between 1347-1351, and some 75 million people worldwide.

Burgess : A merchant or trader in a town who was a member of its governing body.

Capite: A tenant-in-chief who held land directly from the Crown.

Carucate: a term used in Scandinavian settlements for an area of land that elsewhere was called a hide or husbandland. The area was originally defined as the area that could be ploughed with one plough and a team of eight oxen at about the time of Domesday (1086) and was used for tax assessment. The actual area depended on soil quality, so stony ground was a larger area, but is generally thought to be 60-180 acres.

Chantry: The institution of a chantry began in the 12th century as a private chapel, often sited inside a church, where a priest or monk was employed to celebrate mass for the well-being of the souls of the departed founder. The founders were wealthy people, or craft and merchant guilds. In the late fourteenth and early fifteenth centuries the priest or monk often began schools in the chantries.

Cofeoffes: Trustees (see enfeoff).

Collegiate church: churches that received endowments from wealthy benefactors needed a community or 'college' of priests (up to about 12).

Consols : a form of safe investment in a Government bond.

Curate: until the 17th century this was the same as the parish incumbent. More recently it often means an assistant to the incumbent. A Perpetual Curate is where the incumbent had the rights to the Great Tithes (more lucrative than the Small or Vicaral Tithes).

Coroner : up to the 15th century, this was an official who investigated the death of anyone who was killed or died in suspicious circumstances, and administered inquests, treasure trove and deodands (confiscation of something that was implicated in the death of an adult).

Chancellor : Chancellor of England was the highest office in medieval England. The Chancellor of the Exchequer was the highest office in the finance ministry.

Endowment : a donation of money or property left to an ecclesiastical authority, that usually resulted in a regular income to that body.

Enfoeff: to leave money or property to trustees, usually so that the trustees will carry out the wishes of a wealthy person after their death. These trusts were often set up to circumvent customary inheritance practices.

First Fruits: a tax on a benefice of the first year's whole profits. Originally payable to the Pope, but then annexed to Henry VIII in 1534/35. Also called annates.

Glebe: land belonging to a parish priest that was farmed or leased out to provide an income.

Hanaper: the basket or hamper where writs were deposited in the Court of Chancery.

Incumbent: a rector, parson, minister or vicar who kept the parish registers

Lay Fee: lands held in the tenure of a lay (non-ecclesiastical) lord.

Mark: Before the British monetary system was decimalised in 1969, a penny was written 1d. The letter 'd' was the Latin for *denarius,* meaning a penny. There were 12d in a shilling, 20 shillings to the £1, and therefore 240p in a £1. The Mark was not actually a coin, but was the term used to express two-thirds of a £1, which was 160d or 13s 4d in 'old money' or 66.6p in 'new money'.

Medieval: the period from Domesday (1086) to the Reformation (1538).

Messuage: a dwelling house, its outbuildings and the land around it.

Mortmain: land granted to the church became exempt from taxes and customary dues, and therefore reduced the income of the local manorial lord. After 1279, there were penalties for transferring land into mortmain.

Obit: A mass celebrated on the anniversary of someone's death.

Perch: A unit of length; also called a rod or pole, usually 16½ feet or 5½ yards. (In todays measures, 1 perch would be approximately 5 metres). Forty perches was called a furlong.

Piscina: a stone washing basin with a drain, fitted into a wall near the altar, where the priest washed his hands during Mass, and the chalice after use. In most churches and chapels, the altar was usually located at the east end of the church (so that the congregation faced the Holy Land) and the piscina was usually located on the south wall.

Precentor: Director of singing and music.

Prebend: the stipend from the lands and tithes that derive from endowed land, manors or parish which was payable to a member of a cathedral. The recipient was called a Prebendary, which, in the case of the Prebend of Sutton-cum-Buckingham was usually an archdeacon until the Reformation.

Priest: Ordained Minister of the Catholic Church, derived from the Ecclesiastical Latin *presbyter*. A priest is able to offer sacraments and absolution. The term declined after the Reformation.

Recorder : Usually a barrister appointed to act as a Justice of the Peace and judge in a borough quarter sessions court.

Recusant: Before the Reformation, most people belonged to the Catholic faith, and the term was used to describe someone that refused to go to parish church services. After the Reformation, particularly during the reigns of Elizabeth I and James I, it was used to describe a Catholic that refused to attend Church of England services. Recusants, if prosecuted, had to pay huge fines for non-attendance from c1570 to 1791.

Rood: A unit of area; equivalent to 40 square perches, roughly a quarter of an acre, or 4840 square yards.

Scutage: The annual sum of money paid to excuse military service.

Surplice: vestments worn by a priest or vicar when celebrating divine service. Surplice fees were paid to the incumbent at marriages and burials.

Rector: Prior to the Reformation a rector was the incumbent who received all the Great tithes and other customary benefits. The rector could have been a monastery rather than an individual, and was responsible for the furnishing of the chancel and rectory, and for providing vestments and service books. After the Reformation, the rector could be a lay person (non-ecclesiastical) who had the authority to appoint a vicar with the approval of the bishop; but he still had to maintain the chancel and vicarage.

Tithe: the Great tithes were of corn and hay. The small tithes were livestock, wool, non-cereal crops and labour. A tithe was a tax of one-tenth taken for support of the clergy and church.

Vicar: Originally a deputy to the rector, who administered the parish, and who received the Small Tithes (see Curate and Rector). In the Church of England, the vicar was the incumbent of a parish where tithes formerly belonged to a chapter or religious house or layman.

INDEX